The Birds of New Jersey

The Birds of New Jersey

STATUS AND DISTRIBUTION

William J. Boyle, Jr.

Kevin T. Karlson, *photographic editor*

PRINCETON UNIVERSITY PRESS   PRINCETON AND OXFORD

Published by Princeton University Press, 41 William Street, Princeton,
New Jersey 08540
In the United Kingdom: Princeton University Press, 6 Oxford Street,
Woodstock, Oxfordshire OX20 1TW
press.princeton.edu
All Rights Reserved

Library of Congress Cataloging-in-Publication Data

Boyle, William J.
  The birds of New Jersey : status and distribution / William J. Boyle, Jr. ;
Kevin T. Karlson, photographic editor. — 1st ed.
      p. cm.
  Includes bibliographical references and index.
  ISBN 978-0-691-14409-2 (cloth : alk. paper) —
  ISBN 978-0-691-14410-8 (pbk : alk. paper)   1. Birds—New Jersey—
Identification.   2. Birds—New Jersey—Pictorial works.   3. Bird
watching—New Jersey   I. Title.
  QL684.N5B679 2011
  598.09749—dc22   2010035412

British Library Cataloging-in-Publication Data is available

This book has been composed in Sabon LT Std with Gill Sans Std
Family Display

Printed on acid-free paper.

Printed in China

10 9 8 7 6 5 4 3 2 1

TO LAURIE LARSON –
whose organizational skills and years of
devoted service to the birders of New Jersey
and the New Jersey Bird Records Committee
helped make this book possible

CONTENTS

ACKNOWLEDGMENTS

This book was inspired by the *Handbook of Texas Birds*, written by Mark Lockwood and Brush Freeman, and published in 2004 by the Texas Ornithological Society. When Robert Kirk of Princeton University Press approached me about writing a similar book on the birds of New Jersey, I readily agreed and have used the Texas book as a model on which to construct the present volume.

The Birds of New Jersey: Status and Distribution draws upon the work of many ornithologists and birders who have helped to document the bird life of New Jersey over the past two centuries. Most of our current knowledge of the state's birds is the result of observations reported in journals such as *Records of New Jersey Birds* (and its predecessors, *New Jersey Nature News* and *New Jersey Birds* [2003–2009]), *Cassinia*, and *North American Birds* (and its predecessors, *Audubon Field Notes* and *American Birds*). Since the reestablishment of the New Jersey Bird Records Committee (NJBRC) in 1990, we have come to rely on documentation supplied to the committee for evaluation of reports of unusual species. More recently, the online reporting service eBird has become an important tool for monitoring many aspects of bird population dynamics, such as arrival and departure dates, seasonal distribution and abundance. By contributing sighting reports to eBird, the committee, and the regional editors of the journals mentioned above, birders can help to maintain an accurate and up-to-date record of the status and distribution of New Jersey's birds. Other useful, but often unverified, sources of current bird sightings are the online listservs Jersey Birds and NJBirds, the latter of which includes transcriptions of the New Jersey Audubon Rare Bird Alert and the Cape May Birding Hotline.

In writing this book, I have relied heavily on *Birds of New Jersey*, published in 1999 by the New Jersey Audubon Society and compiled and written by Joan Walsh, Vince Elia, Richard Kane, and Tom Halliwell. Their book was originally intended to present just the Breeding Bird Atlas of New Jersey that was conducted from 1993 to 1997. It was expanded to include information on all birds known to have occurred in the state, with details on migrant and wintering species. Although some of the data in the book are somewhat out of date, it is still the best single source available. For the status of individual species in the state, I have used the assessment from *Birds of New Jersey*, modified by more recent reports and experience, where appropriate.

All or parts of the manuscript were reviewed by people knowledgeable about the bird life of New Jersey, some of them with experience going back more than three decades. I thank Hank Burk, Paul Guris, Tom Halliwell, Kevin Karlson, Michael O'Brien, Richard Veit, Chris Vogel, and Fred Weber for their comments and suggestions. Most of all, I would like to thank Paul Lehman, who read the first draft of the entire manuscript and made innumerable comments, corrections, and suggestions that have improved the book immensely, and my wife, Karen Thompson, who reviewed the manuscript with an eye for grammar and clarity. Other people who have provided help, directly or indirectly, are Tom Boyle, Susan Buffalino, Kathleen Clark, Don Freiday, Jennifer Hanson, Rob Hilton, Sandra Keller, Christina Kisiel, Laurie Larson, Sharyn Magee, and Rick Radis.

One feature of this book that sets it apart from other publications about the birds of New Jersey is the 200 color photographs that depict almost half of the species that have occurred in the state. For the photographs, I have been fortunate to have the editorship of Kevin Karlson, who has worked with me and Princeton University Press to assure the inclusion of many of the highest-quality pictures available. Kevin personally contributed more than half of all the photographs in the book, and he prepared all of them for publication. I thank the many other photographers who have graciously allowed me to use their work in this book: Bob Abrams, Bob Barber, Tom Boyle, Dick Burk, William S. Clark, Richard Crossley, Elaine Crunkleton, Michael Danzenbaker, Chris Davidson, Joe Delesantro, Gerry DeWaghe, Scott Elowitz, Mike Fahay, Shawneen Finnegan, Bob Fogg, Don Freiday, Jose Garcia, Jim Gilbert, Jerry Golub, Tom Halliwell, Jenny Harrington, Francis Hornick, Tom Johnson, Steve Kerr, Serge LaFrance, Paul Lehman, Karl Lukens, Jonathan MacCornack, Kevin McGowan, Bob Mitchell, Brian Moscatello, Michael O'Brien, William Pepper, Al Pochek, Keith Seager, Tom Southerland, Lloyd Spitalnik, Alex Tongas, Tonya Toole, Kevin Watson, Chris Williams, Jim Williams, and Angus Wilson.

From Princeton University Press, I thank Robert Kirk for

his encouragement and suggestions during the preparation of the manuscript and Dimitri Karetnikov for his guidance and recommendations in improving the quality of the maps.

Two people who deserve special mention are Rich Kane and Tom Halliwell. For many years, Rich maintained the New Jersey Photo File of rare birds, was the voice of the New Jersey Rare Bird Alert, was editor of *Records of New Jersey Birds*, and served on the NJBRC. Tom served on the NJBRC, was co-author of *New Jersey Birds*, and did much of the research into past records that led to the Historical Report of the NJBRC, known familiarly as the Halliwell Report.

Finally, I would like to thank the one person who, more than any other, has helped assure that the documentation of rare and unusual birds in New Jersey has been maintained and conserved. As transcriber of the New Jersey Audubon Rare Bird Alert for the Internet, long-time member and secretary of the NJBRC, and a co-author of the committee's Historical Report , Laurie Larson has for many years been the driving force in keeping the records of New Jersey's birds accurate and up to date. Although she has retired from active duty on the committee, her influence will be felt for many years to come.

INTRODUCTION

The purpose of this book is to provide an authoritative and up-to-date account of the status and distribution of New Jersey's birds at the end of the first decade of the twenty-first century. It can be considered an annotated list of all of the birds known or believed to have occurred in the state in modern times, including those that are now extinct. The official New Jersey State List is maintained by the New Jersey Bird Records Committee (NJBRC), but the committee relies on the efforts of many others who have contributed to the historical record and who help document the constantly changing face of the state's bird life.

Physical Geography and Natural Regions of New Jersey

The geologic processes that have formed New Jersey gave rise to four distinct landforms, or physiographic provinces. From the northwest to the southeast, these regions are called the Ridge and Valley, Highlands, Piedmont, and Coastal Plain Provinces (Dalton 2003). For the purpose of discussing bird distribution, I have followed Walsh et al. (1999) in separating some of the traditional provinces into smaller ones, where the regional ecology is different.

The Ridge and Valley Province, about 536 square miles or 7 percent of the state, includes the narrow northern Delaware River Valley, the Kittatinny Mountains, and the broad Kittatinny Valley. It lies entirely within Sussex and Warren counties. Ecologically, however, these areas are quite different and are separated into the Kittatinny Mountains (including the adjacent Delaware River Valley) and the Kittatinny Valley.

The Kittatinny Mountains range in elevation from 300 feet in the northern Delaware Valley to 1,803 feet at High Point and are dominated by the long ridge running from High Point in the northeast to Mount Tammany at the Delaware Water Gap in the southwest. This region has a distinctive northern flavor, supporting many bogs and coniferous woodlands, and the breeding birds include many northern species.

The Kittatinny Valley is characterized by the Walkill River in the north and the Paulinskill in the south, the two

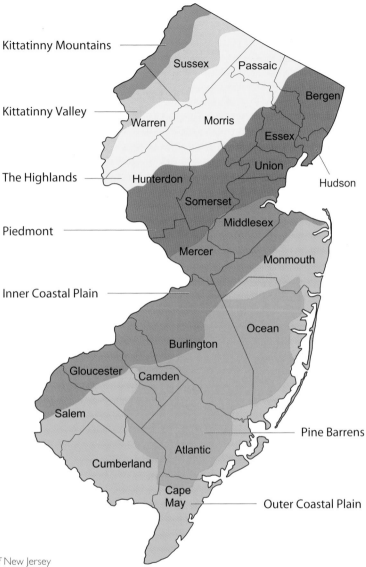

Figure 1. Natural Regions of New Jersey

rivers flowing in opposite directions. With elevations ranging from about 300 to 1,000 feet and containing a wide variety of habitats, this region has the highest diversity of breeding birds in the state.

The Highlands, occupying approximately 980 square miles or 12.5 percent of the state, exhibits a rugged topography consisting of a series of broad, discontinuous ridges separated by steep, narrow valleys. Elevations range from below 300 feet along the Delaware River to almost 1,500 feet at Hamburg, Wawayanda, and Bearfort mountains. The birds of the Highlands are similar to those of the Kittatinny Mountains.

The Piedmont, with approximately 1,600 square miles or 20 percent of the state, cuts a wide swath across some of the most heavily populated areas of New Jersey, from Bergen, Essex, and Hudson counties in the northeast to most of Hunterdon and Mercer counties in the southwest. Although elevations range from sea level to 914 feet, much of the province is a broad plateau sloping gradually from about 400 feet to sea level, but cut by a series of steep, linear ridges such as the Watchung Mountains and the Palisades.

The Coastal Plain adjoins the Piedmont along a boundary known as the Fall Line, which runs roughly from Carteret, Union County, to Trenton, and includes all of the state south and east of that line. It is by far the largest province, occupying approximately 4,667 square miles or 60 percent of the state. For bird distribution purposes, the Coastal Plain can be divided into two provinces, the Inner Coastal Plain and the Outer Coastal Plain. The Outer Coastal Plain includes the Pine Barrens, which are treated separately below.

The Inner Coastal Plain is separated from the Outer Coastal Plain by a series of low hills, which reach their highest point at Crawford Hill (391 feet above sea level) in northern Monmouth County. The division between these two regions continues southwest, reaching Delaware Bay near Salem, Salem County. Extensive agricultural, urban, and suburban development has diminished the available natural habitat, but the Inner Coastal Plain still has some excellent grasslands, hardwood swamps, and river marshes.

The Outer Coastal Plain takes in most of the state's tidal wetlands and barrier islands that provide breeding and feeding habitat for many of the state's resident and migrant water-associated species. In addition, this province includes the mostly deciduous, and often wet, woodlands of Monmouth, western Salem, and Cumberland counties, and parts of Cape May County. Except in Monmouth County, this province is far less developed than is the Inner Coastal Plain.

The Pine Barrens, although technically part of the Outer Coastal Plain, has a less diverse vegetation than the rest of the Coastal Plain and is dominated by dry, sandy soils supporting pitch pine and various scrubby oaks. Along streams and in wet, swampy areas, dense stands of Atlantic white cedar break the monotony of the pine forest. The Pine Barrens runs from extreme southern Monmouth to north Cape May counties and includes most of Ocean, Burlington, and Atlantic counties, plus parts of Camden and Gloucester counties.

History

Philadelphia was home to many of the well-known ornithologists of the nineteenth century, and it is from there that the first useful compendium of *The Birds of East Pennsylvania and New Jersey* originated in 1869 (Turnbull 1869). It treats 343 species, many of which are not recognized today, but it lacks thorough documentation. Nevertheless, it is interesting to read the names given many birds at that time and to wonder about some historical references. This was followed some decades later by *The Birds of Eastern Pennsylvania and New Jersey*, written by Witmer Stone and published by the Delaware Valley Ornithological Club in 1894. Stone's book lists 352 species and is much better documented than is Turnbull's.

The first book devoted solely to the birds of the state dates back to 1897, when the New Jersey Fish and Game Commission published *The Birds of New Jersey*, compiled by Charles A. Shriner, whose title was State Fish and Game Protector. This book has a much more expanded treatment of each species, but lacks any documentation.

By the time of the publication of Stone's *The Birds of New Jersey, Their Nests and Eggs*, written for the annual report of the New Jersey State Museum in 1908, the number of species had been whittled down to 340, including a few questionable ones. Stone's famous *Bird Studies at Old Cape May* includes reference to all of the species occurring in the state of which he was aware. The next publication to try to document all of the state's known species was David Fables Jr.'s *Annotated List of New Jersey's Birds*. This 1955 book listed 370 species, plus an additional 19 "hypothetical" species supported only by historical references or insufficient documentation. Of these, 5 were subsequently accepted by the NJBRC based on the historical evidence and all but 2 of the others have occurred since 1955.

Charles Leck, in his book *The Status and Distribution of New Jersey's Birds* (1984), listed 455 species, of which he considered 37 "hypothetical" for various reasons and 418 "well-confirmed." Of the 37 hypothetical species, all but 5 were subsequently removed from the State List by the NJ-BRC; 15 of them have been returned to the list based on records documented after 1983. In addition, 5 of the "well-confirmed" species were deleted from the list because of doubts about their natural origins. The "official" New Jersey State List, prepared by the newly reorganized Records Committee in 1991, listed 421 species, only 6 of which were not included in Leck's list of well-confirmed or hypothetical species. Both editions of *A Guide to Bird Finding in New Jersey* (Boyle 1986, 2002) included status and distribution information on species expected to occur within a five-year period, plus a list of extreme rarities seen at least once in the preceding twenty-five years.

Birds of New Jersey (1999) included the results of the 1993–1997 New Jersey Breeding Bird Atlas. In addition to breeding birds, the book contained an entry on all other species known to have occurred in the state, as accepted by the NJBRC through 1998. The State List then stood at 443, as some older records were accepted as a result of work by the Historical Project of the Records Committee, and an amazing 15 species were documented in the state for the first time in the years from 1991 to 1998. As of mid-2010, the official New Jersey State List includes 465 species, the additions being due to one split, one specimen discovery, one deletion, one species accepted based on wild provenance that was formerly considered of questionable provenance, one established introduction, and 19 records of species with no previously accepted reports. Inevitably, this rate of increase cannot continue, however, and in 2008 and 2009 there were, in fact, no new species added to the list.

The New Jersey Bird Records Committee (NJBRC)

The first group organized to gather and analyze data on the birds of New Jersey was the State List Committee of the Urner Ornithological Club, an organization based in Newark. Its efforts resulted in the publication in 1955 of the *Annotated List of New Jersey Birds* by David Fables Jr. A new committee was formed in 1958 to continue the work of the first, to present data collected through the end of 1958, and to serve the ongoing function of updating the status and distribution of the state's birds. The *First Supple-*

ment to the Annotated List was published in 1959 (Kunkle 1959), but no subsequent publications appeared.

In February 1976 the New Jersey Bird Records Committee was organized under the auspices of the New Jersey Audubon Society. It met a number of times over the next several years but soon became inactive, having failed to publish a state list or update the previous publications. The committee was reorganized in 1990 as an independent entity, and has been in continuous operation since then. In 1996 Chair Richard Crossley explained the goals of the committee in an article in *Records of New Jersey Birds,* and in 1998 the goals were summarized by Chair Paul Lehman in that same journal. They are:

- to solicit and maintain all data pertinent to records of rare birds reported in New Jersey;
- to establish standards of observation and reporting;
- to review reports of species and subspecies on the review list;
- to increase knowledge of the birds of New Jersey by publishing articles, data, and an official state list.

An annual report is published in *Records of New Jersey Birds* and an updated State List is published periodically. The Committee maintains a Web site, www.njbrc.net, where the most recent versions of the New Jersey State List, the Accepted Records List, and the New Jersey Review List can be found, along with other information useful to birders.

Criteria for Acceptance of Records of Review Species and New Species

When the New Jersey Audubon Society decided in 1995 to publish *Birds of New Jersey* as a major reference work beyond the scope of simply a breeding bird atlas, the NJBRC was asked to undertake the research to provide a basis for evaluating rare bird reports prior to 1990. The Committee established a Historical Project Subcommittee that spent hundreds of hours "combing the avian literature, contacting observers requesting documentation of specific bird repots, organizing the historical database, and evaluating the documentation received." The subcommittee established a set of criteria for assessing historical reports, recognizing that little or no documentation existed for many older records, that rare birds seen by dozens of observers were sometimes not documented, and that many photographs, specimens, and written notes had been lost over the years. Using these criteria, the Committee voted on which records would be "accepted" and which were "not accepted."

The Historical Report of the New Jersey Bird Records Committee, "Rare Bird Reports Through 1989" by Tom Halliwell, Rich Kane, Laurie Larson, and Paul Lehman, was published in *Records of New Jersey Birds* in 2000. Other members of the NJBRC who served on the subcommittee at various times were Pete Bacinski, Bill Boyle, P. A. Buckley, Shawneen Finnegan, and Greg Hanisek. The "accepted" records, which form the basis for inclusion on the Accepted Records List and the New Jersey State List, were chosen using the following standards:

- Accepted with documentation at contemporary standards. This normally means that there is accepted written documentation, photographs, videos, sketches, and/or sound recordings on file with the NJBRC.
- Accepted by the State List Committee of the Urner Club and published in Fables (1955) or Kunkle (1959). Unfortunately, the files from that committee have been lost, and many of the records accepted by the committee lack full documentation. Nevertheless, because these records were subject to a high level of scrutiny, the NJBRC is confident of their validity.
- Accepted via the Historical Standard. This standard was applied for certain rare bird reports that were almost certainly correct, but which lacked the documentation required by contemporary standards. Examples of such records included specimens that were reported but are now lost and otherwise unverified by photograph or description; photographed birds whose photos have been lost; birds once well documented in writing, to a regional editor or Christmas Bird Count compiler, for example, but whose descriptions have since been lost; birds seen by several competent observers, but for which no documentation is available.

Records that were not accepted fell into two main categories: those that lacked documentation of any kind and those that were supported by inconclusive documentation or possible misidentification. Many of the birds in the latter category were probably correctly identified, but the evidence is not good enough to support acceptance.

All records accepted since 1990 have met the first criterion cited above. The requirements are the same for any species on the Review List as well as any first state record. Records of birds that would be new to the State List do receive more intense scrutiny, however. Fortunately, almost all new species found since 1990 have been well photographed and/or seen by multiple observers.

Nomenclature

The species sequence and taxonomy used in the New Jersey State List and in this book follow the *Check-list of North American Birds*, seventh edition (AOU 1998), and all supplements through 2009. Supplements in recent years have included numerous changes to both common and scientific names, as well as rearrangement of taxonomic sequence and even relocation of some groups, e.g., tanagers, to a different family.

Species Accounts

The official State List of New Jersey birds, maintained and updated annually by the New Jersey Bird Records Committee, contains every species known to have occurred within the state in modern times. For each of these species, I have attempted to indicate the abundance and distribution for the different seasons and different regions of the state. For migrants, I have given the approximate migration periods and some reference to extreme dates, but I have not attempted to list specific early arrival and/or late departure dates for most species. Migration timing can vary widely from one end of the state to the other. Although the distance from High Point to Cape May is only 166 miles, the seasonal occurrence of some species may differ by weeks. For example, Yellow Warblers and American Redstarts are common breeders and migrants in northwestern New Jersey, but they are very scarce there after the beginning of September. In Cape May, however, these two species are regularly seen into early October, with a few seen as late as the end of that month.

Every current NJBRC Review List species is identified as such in the account header. For those species with five or fewer accepted records, each record is listed below the species account with date(s) of occurrence, location, the NJBRC record number (except for historical records), museum specimen number (if applicable and available), and NJPF (for New Jersey Photo File, where applicable). Some records, especially those prior to 1990, also include a literature reference to the sighting. Documentation and photos are currently stored with individual members of the committee, but will hopefully find a permanent home in the future. Inevitably, some of the data in a book such as this is out of date as soon as it appears, but the records of Review Species are complete through June 2010.

Maps

Each species account, except those for species that are extinct, is accompanied by a map that is intended to show the normal range for that species within New Jersey. Within that range, however, the species is ordinarily found only in "appropriate habitat," especially during the breeding season. For those species that are on the NJBRC Review List, the location of each accepted record is shown on the accompanying map as a red dot or, where there are multiple records for a location, a red dot with a number beside it. Figure 2 explains the colors and symbols used for depicting distribution. Dashed lines mean former, unknown, or irregular range.

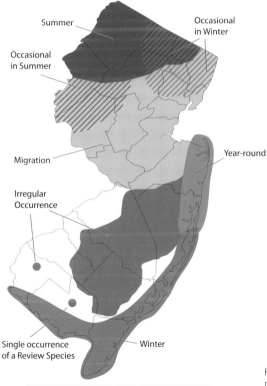

Summer

Occasional
in Winter

Occasional
in Summer

Migration

Year-round

Irregular
Occurrence

Single occurrence
of a Review Species

Winter

Figure 2. Color Key to
Distribution Maps

Status and Abundance Terminology

The status of each species is treated for each of the four seasons. For abundance, I have chosen to use a more expanded list than that chosen by the authors of *Birds of New Jersey,* including such categories as "abundant" and "accidental." Each of these terms is explained below.

Permanent resident: Occurs throughout the year within the range defined by the map and the text. Most of these species have stable breeding populations, but some are in flux. Some birds present in the summer versus the winter may not be the same individuals; in other words, some summer breeders may depart the region, to be replaced by breeders from farther north during the winter months.

Summer resident: Typically present from May through July, although many arrive earlier and most depart later. All of these species breed in New Jersey at the present time.

Summer visitor: Nonbreeding species present during the warmer months. These are typically pelagic species that nest in Europe (e.g., Cory's Shearwater), or especially the Southern Hemisphere (e.g., Wilson's Storm-Petrel), or are regular postbreeding visitors (e.g., Sandwich Tern).

Winter resident: Mainly migrants from farther north that spend the colder months in the state, but do not stay to breed.

Winter visitor: Migrants from other parts of the country that do not occur with sufficient regularity or in sufficient numbers at this season to be considered winter residents.

Migrant: Transient species that pass through in spring and/or fall. Some occur only in migration, whereas others may breed or winter in some parts of the state, but are found only as migrants in other parts.

Irregular: Species whose occurrence in the state is unpredictable. Some, like Dickcissel and Sedge Wren, occur annually as individuals or pairs, may rarely breed here, and may be found at almost any time of the year. Others, like White-winged Crossbill and Common Redpoll, tend to appear as individuals or small flocks in winter, but aren't expected every year.

Local: Typically found only in specific habitats or areas within a particular region. A few, like Upland Sandpiper, occur as breeders only at a handful of sites, whereas others, like Least Bittern, are widely distributed but have specialized habitat requirements.

Abundant: Present in such numbers that many individuals should be seen during a visit to the appropriate habitat on any given day at the proper season.

Common: Almost always present, easily encountered, and often numerous, in the proper habitat at the proper time of the year.

Fairly common: Usually present, and likely to be encountered but not necessarily numerous, in the proper habitat at the proper time of the year.

Uncommon: Usually present in limited numbers in the proper habitat, but one cannot be certain of finding an individual on any given day.

Scarce: Infrequently encountered and usually not present daily, even in the proper habitat at the proper time of the year.

Rare: On average, seen only a few times a year in a given area.

Very rare: Occurs regularly, but not expected every year.

Casual: Between six and fifteen records accepted by the NJBRC. Most can be expected to occur again within a five-year period.

Accidental: Five or fewer records accepted by the NJBRC. Many years may elapse between occurrences.

Abbreviations

AB	*American Birds*
ANSP	Academy of Natural Sciences, Philadelphia
AMNH	American Museum of Natural History, New York
AOU	American Ornithologists' Union
AR	Annual Report of the NJBRC
AFN	*Audubon Field Notes*, predecessor of *North American Birds*
BNB	Beach Nesting Birds
CBC	Christmas Bird Count
CWS	Colonial Waterbird Survey, NJ Division of Fish and Wildlife
ENSP	Endangered and Nongame Species Project, NJ Division of Fish and Wildlife
MMS	Minerals Management Service
MWWS	Mid-Winter Waterfowl Survey
NWR	National Wildlife Refuge
NJBRC	New Jersey Bird Records Committee
NJB	*New Jersey Birds*, successor to and predecessor of RNJB, 2003–2009

NJDFW	New Jersey Division of Fish and Wildlife
NJPF	New Jersey Photo File
pers. comm.	Personal communication
pers. obs.	Personal observation
RNJB	*Records of New Jersey Birds*
SP	State Park
UMMZ	University of Michigan Museum of Zoology
USNM	United States National Museum
WMA	Wildlife Management Area
*	Specimen

Glossary of Place Names

Avalon	Cape May County
Florence	Delaware River, Florence, Burlington County
Forsythe NWR	Brigantine Unit, Forsythe NWR, Galloway Township, Atlantic County
Hackensack Meadowlands	Wetlands, including parks and WMAs, along the Hackensack River, Bergen and Hudson counties
Higbee Beach	Higbee Beach WMA, Cape May
Hudson Canyon	Deepwater trench into the Continental Shelf, approximately 80–90 miles ESE of Barnegat Inlet
Island Beach	Island Beach SP, Ocean County
Mannington Marsh	Near Salem, Salem County
Oldman's Creek	Near Pedricktown, Gloucester and Burlington counties
Pedricktown	Gloucester County
Raccoon Creek	Near Bridgeport, Burlington County
Reeds Beach	Reeds Beach Road and Viewing Area, Middle Township, Cape May County
Round Valley	Round Valley Recreation Area and Reservoir, Hunterdon County
Sandy Hook	Sandy Hook Unit, Gateway National Recreation Area, Monmouth County
Spruce Run	Spruce Run Reservoir and SP, Clinton, Hunterdon County
Trenton Marsh	Hamilton-Trenton-Bordentown

	Marsh, Mercer and Burlington Counties
Tuckahoe WMA	Lester G. MacNamara WMA, Upper Township, Cape May County, and Estelle Manor, Egg Harbor Township, Corbin City, Atlantic County
Turkey Point	Turkey Point Road, Dividing Creek, Cumberland County
Wallkill River	Wallkill NWR, Sussex County

Pelagic Boundaries

For the purpose of documenting birds at sea off New Jersey, the NJBRC adopted "official" state boundaries at its November 2006 meeting. These were published (Guris 2007) and are shown approximately on the accompanying map out to the 200-nautical-mile economic exclusion zone. I have modified the southern (NJ–DE) boundary slightly to conform to that recognized by the U.S. government and published by the Minerals Management Service of the Department of the Interior (MMS 2008). The Bird Records Committees of New York and Delaware to the north and south use very different boundaries, and there is considerable overlap in these "official" state boundaries.

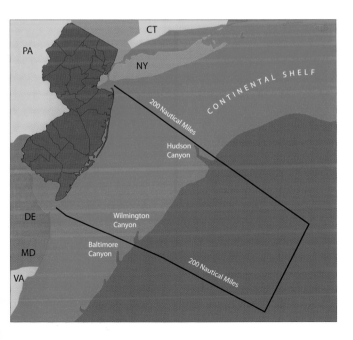

Figure 3. New Jersey's Pelagic Boundaries

Order Anseriformes

Family Anatidae: Swans, Geese, and Ducks

BLACK-BELLIED WHISTLING-DUCK
Dendrocygna autumnalis

Review Species

Accidental. There are just four records of this distinctive Neotropical duck, all since 2000, but we can expect more in the future. The first was at Forsythe NWR in 2000 (Moscatello and Ambrozy 2001), followed by a flock of nine in Cape May four years later, a flock of four there in 2009, and a flock of three, also in Cape May, in 2010. Interestingly, the first three records all occurred in a three-day span in late May. Formerly limited in the U.S. to southern Texas and southern Arizona, the species has experienced an explosive population growth and range expansion, with numerous extralimital sightings all over the eastern U.S. and an introduced, but growing, population in South Carolina.

27 MAY 2000, FORSYTHE NWR, ATLANTIC CO. (NJBRC 2001-006)
25 MAY 2004 (9), CAPE MAY, CAPE MAY CO. (NJBRC 2005-012)
26 MAY 2009 (4), CAPE MAY, CAPE MAY CO. (NJBRC 2010-043)
18+ JULY 2010 (3), CAPE MAY, CAPE MAY CO. (NJBRC 2011-038)

Black-bellied Whistling-Ducks have expanded their range substantially in recent decades and have shown a strong propensity to wander widely, especially in the Great Plains and eastern U.S. New Jersey's first record was at Forsythe NWR in 2000, and the third was a brief visit to Cape May, 26 May 2009, by the four birds pictured here. *Photograph by Bob Fogg.*

Review Species

Records since 1996

FULVOUS WHISTLING-DUCK *Dendrocygna bicolor*

The history of the occurrence of this species in New Jersey and the rest of the Northeast is mysterious. A flock of six Fulvous Whistling-Ducks that appeared at Forsythe NWR from 28 October into December 1961 was the first state record. From then through November 1985 there were at least twenty records in the state, including one flock of seventeen birds seen at Forsythe and later at Tuckahoe WMA in 1974. Reports included sightings from seven counties, including multiples from Bergen, Atlantic, and Cape May counties. Since 1985, there has been just one occurrence of four birds, noted below, and the duck was added to the Review List in 1996. During that time, there has been a decline in the southern Florida population, but not in the numbers along the western Gulf Coast.

1–6 AUG 2004 (4), FORSYTHE NWR, ATLANTIC CO. (NJBRC 2005-061, RNJB 30[4]:105)

From 1961 to 1985, there were at least twenty occurrences of Fulvous Whistling-Duck in the state, including a flock of seventeen birds in 1974. Since then, there has been just one record, a group of four birds that spent a week at Forsythe NWR in early August 2004. The individual shown here, one of a pair present at Lily Lake, Cape May Point, from 31 August to 9 October, 1974, was photographed on 16 September 1974. *Photograph by Keith Seager.*

GREATER WHITE-FRONTED GOOSE *Anser albifrons*

Rare spring and fall migrant; rare, but increasing, winter visitor, usually encountered in flocks of Canada Geese, but occasionally in small, homogenous, groups of up to eleven. Stone (1937) cites a nineteenth-century report, but the first modern record came from Barnegat Bay in 1926. Fables (1955) knew of only three others, all from that same area. Since 1975, the number of reports has increased substantially and there are now multiple sightings every year. Most of these birds are presumed to be vagrants from the West, but a few have been identified as belonging to the Greenland race; the difficulty of identification confuses the matter. Fall migrants are typically seen from mid-October to late November, but the species is more frequently encountered during the colder months. Spring reports are fewer, usually in late March into April. Because of the increased frequency of reports, this species was removed from the Review List in 1999.

SNOW GOOSE *Chen caerulescens*

Common to locally abundant spring and fall migrant; locally abundant winter resident. The first fall migrants show up in late September, with the bulk arriving in October. Tens of thousands gather at Forsythe NWR in November, and many thousands also concentrate at Merrill Creek Reservoir and adjacent Warren and Hunterdon County corn fields. Other thousands congregate along the Delaware Bayshore of Cumberland and Salem counties and commute daily to nearby farm fields. Depending on the severity of the winter, many of the migrants will remain throughout the season, departing for the north by the end of March. The "Blue Goose" color morph of Snow Goose represents a small (less than 5 percent) but increasing percentage of the birds that come to New Jersey.

ROSS'S GOOSE *Chen rossii*

Rare fall and spring migrant and winter resident throughout, usually in the company of Snow Geese. A relative newcomer to the state, New Jersey's first Ross's Geese, a pair, were found at Forsythe NWR in January 1972, where they stayed for months. Ten years would pass before the next one was discovered, also at Forsythe, but the species has been found there almost annually after that. In early 1995, a pair wintered with Snow Geese near Sharptown, Salem County, and that area has now become the site of annual visits by Ross's Geese. During the first decade of the twenty-first century, the species was detected in almost every county in the state. The geese arrive with the first large

flocks of Snow Geese in late October–early November and are often seen in March at staging areas, but they depart in early April. Because of the increased frequency of occurrence, the species was removed from the Review List in January 2002.

Snow Geese are common to sometimes abundant migrants and winter residents in New Jersey, but their smaller cousin, Ross's Goose, was first recorded here only in 1972. Since the 1980s, a few have been found annually at favored locations, such as Salem County and Forsythe NWR. This striking comparison shot was taken in December 2006. ID criteria for separating these similar species can be found in Appendix D. *Photograph by Kevin Karlson.*

BRANT *Branta bernicla*

The "Atlantic" Brant, subspecies *hrota*, is an abundant migrant and winter resident on the coast of New Jersey, where approximately half of the population of this subspecies spends the winter (MWWS). Flocks are sometimes seen along the ridges during migration, and odd individuals show up on inland bodies of water. Brant numbers declined dramatically during the early 1930s due to a blight suffered by eelgrass, their principal food (Stone 1937). Since then, because Brant switched to other food sources and eelgrass made a partial recovery, the geese have made a strong comeback (Reed et al. 1998). Fall migrants arrive in October–early November and many linger into early May. A few nonbreeders usually spend the summer in coastal bays. The western "Black" Brant, subspecies *nigricans*, is a very rare visitor to the state, and was added to the NJBRC Review List in 1996. There have been twenty accepted records since then.

The "Atlantic" Brant is a familiar sight in the coastal bays and estuaries of the state from October into early May. Approximately half of the population of this subspecies winters in New Jersey and is sometimes joined by a few individuals of the western "Black" Brant subspecies (right-hand photo). *Photographs by Kevin Karlson (left) and Michael O'Brien (right).*

BARNACLE GOOSE *Branta leucopsis*

Rare migrant and winter visitor in flocks of Canada Geese. Barnacle Goose was formerly placed in the "provenance uncertain" category because of its widespread presence in zoos and private collections. However, the dramatic increase in sightings in New Jersey and nearby states in recent years, combined with a substantial increase in the Greenland nesting population, cannot be attributed to escapes alone. In 2008 the NJBRC voted to add Barnacle Goose to the State List and to remove the "provenance uncertain" qualification from all accepted records from 2002 forward. From 2002 through 2009, there were fourteen records, but the species remains on the Review List and is recorded on average two to three times a year. Not every sighting is accepted, however, as there are still reports of excessively tame birds that may be escapes.

Review Species

Since 2002

CACKLING GOOSE *Branta hutchinsii*

The decision by the AOU in 2004 to split the small races of Canada Goose into a separate species, Cackling Goose, added a new bird to the State List. One race, "Richardson's" Goose, *B. h. hutchinsii*, nests in the central Canadian Arctic and is a rare, but probably regular, winter visitor to New Jersey. Most occurrences are of single individuals in flocks of Canada Geese, but family groups or small flocks are occasionally encountered. Cackling-type geese were added to the Review List in 1996, but removed in 2002 because of the large number of reports. Identification issues remain, however, and some reports of Cackling Geese in

New Jersey and other eastern seaboard states actually refer to smaller Canada Geese.

CANADA GOOSE *Branta canadensis*

Very common to abundant permanent resident throughout the state, with winter numbers augmented by migrants from the north. There is no evidence that Canada Geese nested in New Jersey prior to the 1930s (Stone 1937), but Fables (1955) suggested that some were summering two decades later. A deliberate effort to introduce nesting birds into the state by local and federal wildlife organizations during the 1960s succeeded beyond their wildest dreams. Today, the species is widely considered a nuisance and pest in public parks, at golf courses, and on corporate lawns.

MUTE SWAN *Cygnus olor*

Locally common permanent resident, with numbers augmented by migrants in winter. Mute Swans were brought to the United States from Europe during the late nineteenth century (Ciaranca et al. 1997) and had apparently escaped into the wild around New York City by 1910 (Bull 1964), reaching New Jersey by 1916 (Stone 1937). Today they nest in shallow lakes, ponds, and marshes, and can be found throughout the state, although they are uncommon in the Pine Barrens. They often gather in winter in loose flocks numbering in the dozens or hundreds at favored locations. Because of their habit of overgrazing aquatic vegetation and aggressively displacing native waterfowl, Mute Swans are often considered a nuisance species.

TUNDRA SWAN *Cygnus columbianus*

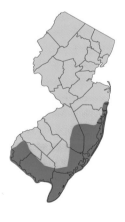

Locally fairly common fall migrant, uncommon winter resident and spring migrant, mainly along or near the coast. Shriner (1896) and Stone (1908) considered the Whistling Swan, as it was then known, to be a rare transient or winter visitor. During the twentieth century, they became much more common in New Jersey due, in part, to protection from the Migratory Bird Treaty of 1918 (Limpert and Earnst 1994). Tundra Swans are most easily seen in migration at Forsythe NWR and Mannington Marsh, but can usually be found, even in midwinter, well inland at old cranberry bogs such as Whitesbog and the Franklin Parker Preserve, both in Burlington County.

WOOD DUCK *Aix sponsa*

The strikingly plumaged Wood Duck is a common and widespread summer resident, nesting in cavities and nest boxes in wooded wetlands and ponds. The bulk of the population leaves the state from mid-October to mid-November, although some remain to winter in all but the northern counties. Spring migration is inconspicuous, but most are back on their breeding grounds by the end of March. Wood Ducks were nearly wiped out in the northeast by hunting in the late nineteenth and early twentieth century. Griscom (1923) considered them "extirpated, rare or local," but they have recovered strongly and by 1986 could again be considered "common . . . throughout the state" (Boyle 1986).

Wood Ducks were nearly extirpated from the Northeast by hunting during the nineteenth and early twentieth centuries, but have recovered strongly. They are now common and widespread breeding birds throughout the state and small numbers remain for the winter. The male Wood Duck is one of the most striking and handsome birds among all waterfowl. *Photograph by Kevin Karlson.*

GADWALL *Anas strepera*

Gadwall is a common migrant, both spring and fall, and a common and increasing winter resident. It is an uncommon and local summer resident, having first bred in the state in 1949. The first nesting records were along the coast, but the species has since expanded into the Hackensack Meadowlands, the Great Swamp, and, more recently, Hunterdon County. A few migrants appear in late summer, but most arrive from late October to early November. In winter, Gadwalls can be found in all regions but the Pine Barrens and the coldest parts of the state. March sees an influx of migrants from the south, but by the end of April only the breeders remain.

EURASIAN WIGEON *Anas penelope*

This Old World species is a rare but regular migrant and winter visitor to the state, mainly along the coast but occasionally at such inland locations as Spruce Run, the Hackensack Meadowlands, Trenton Marsh, and the Allendale Celery Farm. The majority of records, usually two to five individuals each winter, are from Forsythe NWR and the ponds along the north shore in Monmouth County, although a modern state-wide high count of seven birds was tallied at Cape May in December 2009. Fall birds may appear as early as late August (rarely July), arriving with migrant American Wigeons, and typically settle into a preferred area for the winter. Most depart during March, but one will occasionally linger into April and rarely into early May. Almost all records are of drakes, due to the difficulty of separating females from their American cousins.

Eurasian Wigeon is an annual visitor to New Jersey from fall to early spring, always in the company of American Wigeon. The male, on the right, is readily identified by its gray sides and rufous head and buffy forehead. Females and eclipse males are more difficult to identify due to their similarity to female American Wigeon. This female, on the left, shows warmer head tones, a grayer back, and lacks the black mark at the gape shown by her American cousin. *Photographs by Kevin Karlson (male) and Bob Fogg (female).*

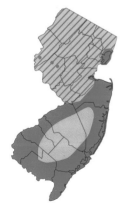

AMERICAN WIGEON *Anas americana*

The familiar American Wigeon is a common migrant and fairly common winter resident, especially along the coast and at Mannington Marsh. Early migrants arrive in late August, but peak southbound migration occurs in late October, and the majority of the migrants continue on to Virginia and the Carolinas. Many stay to winter, however, moving to the bays if the shore ponds are frozen. They are rejoined by the northbound migrants in March, and almost all have departed by the end of April.

American Wigeon is one of our most common wintering ducks, and flocks are a familiar sight on ponds, lakes, and estuaries from Sandy Hook to Cape May. The handsome drake wears his colorful plumage for most of the year, except for a few months in summer and early fall. *Photograph by Kevin Karlson.*

AMERICAN BLACK DUCK *Anas rubripes*

Common migrant and winter resident, fairly common summer resident in appropriate habitat throughout the state. Black Ducks were nearly extirpated by market hunting at the turn of the twentieth century, but recovered strongly with protection from the Migratory Bird Treaty of 1918 (Stone 1937). A subsequent decline during the 1960s and 1970s, again due to overhunting, was halted by a substantial reduction in harvest quotas beginning in 1983 (Longcore et al. 2000), and numbers have partly recovered. Hybridization with Mallards has been blamed by many for some of the long-term decline, but this view is not universally accepted (Morton 1998). Roughly half of the 200,000 or so Black Ducks on the Atlantic Flyway winter in New Jersey (MWWS 2001–2009).

MALLARD *Anas platyrhynchos*

Common and ubiquitous permanent resident. The commonest duck in North America is also the most common in New Jersey. This was not always so, as Stone (1937) considered them rare breeders and doubted the origins of breeding pairs, suggesting that they may have been escapes. Fables (1955) likewise described the nesting population as descendents of escaped or semiferal birds. Mallards surely benefited from stocking programs by federal and state wildlife authorities (Walsh et al. 1999), and have adapted to a myriad of habitats. The arrival of truly wild birds from the north

in fall is difficult to discern, but they augment the resident population to about 30,000 along the coast (MWWS 2001–2009), then return north in March and April.

BLUE-WINGED TEAL *Anas discors*

Common fall and fairly common spring migrant, rare and very local summer resident, very rare in winter. Blue-winged Teal have probably long been a relatively scarce breeder in New Jersey (Stone 1937, Fables 1955), although the Hackensack Meadowlands supported a sizable population in the early 1970s (Kane 1974). At present, they nest sporadically in places such as the Hackensack River marshes, Mannington Marsh, Forsythe NWR, and Cape May. Spring migration peaks in April, with most migrants continuing on to breeding grounds in eastern Canada. Southbound migrants pass through mainly in September and can total several thousand at Forsythe, but numbers vary from year to year, as the eastern breeding population shows much greater variation than the far larger mid-continent one. Only a few remain by December, when they are occasionally encountered on Christmas Counts, and even fewer (less than one on average) overwinter in the southern part of the state.

CINNAMON TEAL *Anas cyanoptera*

Review Species

Accidental. Surprisingly, there are only three accepted records of this western species in the state, although it breeds as far east as western Texas, eastern Colorado, Wyoming, and Montana. Another half-dozen reports were insufficiently documented to accept, and the species' status is further complicated by its prevalence in private waterfowl collections. The three birds listed below were present for two to three weeks and well documented. (*See photo page 139.*)

9 JUN–1 JUL 1974, FORSYTHE NWR, ATLANTIC CO. (AB 28[5]:886; NJNN 29[4]:188)

18 APR–8 MAY 1976, MANAHAWKIN WMA, OCEAN CO. (RNJB 2[8]:13; NJPF)

20 MAR–3 APR 2001, NORTHFIELD, ATLANTIC CO. (NJBRC 2002-013; NJPF)

NORTHERN SHOVELER *Anas clypeata*

Fairly common migrant throughout, fairly common winter resident, usually near the coast, very rare and local summer resident. This Holarctic duck is primarily a bird of the west and central regions in North America, but there are a few confirmed breeding records for New Jersey, including one from the Hackensack Meadowlands in 1994 (Walsh et al. 1999). Stone (1937) considered them to be rare visitors to Cape May, but numbers increased substantially during the twentieth century. Peak concentrations at any one place rarely exceed 200, but the first fall migrant Northern Shovelers appear in late August, and they can usually be found from September to April at the Meadowlands, Mannington Marsh, Forsythe NWR, and the North Shore ponds.

The large, spatulate bill of the Northern Shoveler, with its series of comblike lamellae along the sides as seen in this female, is ideally suited to straining small crustaceans. Northern Shovelers are a familiar sight from September to April, especially at ponds along the coast and at Forsythe NWR. *Photograph by Kevin Karlson.*

NORTHERN PINTAIL *Anas acuta*

Common spring and fall migrant, fairly common winter resident. The protracted fall migration of Northern Pintail begins in late August and continues into November. Concentrations at Forsythe at this season have reached 6,000+ in October 1995. Many hundreds stay to winter from Spruce Run and the Hackensack Meadowlands south to Mannington Marsh, Cape May, and Forsythe NWR. Pintails are one of the earliest nesting ducks in North America (Austin and Miller 1995) and wintering birds augmented by northbound migrants form staging concentrations from late February into early March. These can attain spectacular numbers, such as an estimated 50,000 at Oldman's and Raccoon creeks on 24 February 1990 and another 30,000 at nearby Pedricktown the same day (RNJB 16[2]:27). Such counts have not been repeated in recent years. There is one breeding record (Wander 1986), but Pintails are very rare in summer.

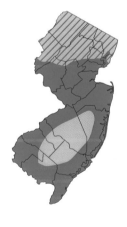

One of the most abundant waterfowl species in North American, Northern Pintail can be our most common dabbling duck during migration and in mild winters. Large concentrations sometimes gather in late winter at preferred sites, such as Mannington Marsh, Salem County, Pedricktown marshes, Salem and Gloucester counties, and Forsythe NWR. The elegant drake presents a distinctive profile with his long neck and tail. *Photograph by Kevin Karlson.*

GARGANEY *Anas querquedula*

Review Species

Accidental. Individual males of this striking species have been found in the state on two occasions, both times in early June (O'Brien and Tarlach 1998). Most of the occurrences of Garganey in eastern North America during the past forty years have been between April and early June (Spears et al. 1988). The second bird was first found in Barnegat Township, 2 June 2005; what was presumably the same bird was relocated at Forsythe NWR on 18 June and seen again on 30 June.

9–15 JUN 1997, FORSYTHE NWR, ATLANTIC CO. (NJBRC 1997-007; NJPF)
2–30 JUN 2005, BARNEGAT, OCEAN CO., AND FORSYTHE NWR, ATLANTIC CO. (NJBRC 2006-012; NJPF)

One of the smallest of the dabbling ducks, Garganey breeds across much of Eurasia and winters in Africa and Australasia. There are very few records for eastern North America and just two for New Jersey, both drakes that showed up in June. This individual was at Forsythe NWR in June 1997. *Photograph by Kevin Karlson.*

GREEN-WINGED TEAL *Anas crecca*

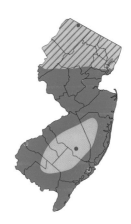

Very common fall and common spring migrant, fairly common winter resident, rare and local summer resident. The smallest of our dabbling ducks, Green-winged Teal extended their breeding range south and east during the twentieth century and first bred in New Jersey in 1960 (Bull 1964). They remain, however, one of our rarest breeding birds, nesting sporadically at a few locations, some of which are indicated on the map. Fall migration begins in late August and peaks in late October, often reaching spectacular concentrations at Forsythe NWR (25,000+, 22 October 1995; RNJB 22[1]:17). Most of the migrants continue on to the Carolinas, but about 10 percent of the Atlantic Flyway population remains to winter in the state (MWWS 2001–2009). Spring migration, peaking in late March, is more dispersed, as many of the teal feed in the marshes of Delaware Bay and River, but a few linger into May. The "Eurasian" Green-winged Teal (also called Common Teal), *A. c. crecca*, is a rare but regular visitor; only the males can be safely identified. Most records are from February to early April (one at Cape May to 12 May 1995), with just a few from late fall and early winter.

CANVASBACK *Aythya valisinaria*

This uniquely North American duck of the prairie parklands of mid-continent is a fairly common winter resident and an uncommon spring and fall migrant. Canvasbacks are late migrants, generally arriving in November, and are found mainly on rivers, bays, and estuaries during winter. Numbers wintering in the state have been highly variable over the past century, declining in the first third of the twentieth century, recovering to peak in the late 1970s, and then declining since the late 1980s (Walsh et al. 1999). CBC totals have ranged from a high of 30,229 in 1976 to a low of just 201 in 2008. The bulk of the East Coast population winters on Chesapeake Bay and departs for the north in March. There is one recent July record.

REDHEAD *Aythya americana*

Another exclusively North American duck, nesting primarily in the prairie pothole region, Redhead is a very uncommon migrant and winter resident, seldom found in groups numbering more than a half-dozen. Redhead was probably

never a common bird in New Jersey and, except for a brief peak in the late 1970s, the statewide CBC total has remained well below a hundred. The overall breeding population has fluctuated wildly in recent decades (Woodin and Michot 2002) and is currently near an all-time high (Zimpfer et al. 2009), but the vast majority (greater than 90 percent) winter along the Gulf of Mexico. Fall migrants usually arrive in early November and most depart in spring by the beginning of April. Redhead is accidental in summer.

RING-NECKED DUCK *Aythya collaris*

Common migrant and common winter resident on inland ponds, lakes, and reservoirs. Ring-necked Ducks became much more common in New Jersey during the twentieth century. Stone (1937) first encountered one in Cape May in 1935, and Fables (1955) considered them rare winter transients, while noting that their numbers were increasing. By 1986, Boyle called them common migrants and uncommon winter residents. This increase corresponded to the expansion of the species' breeding range east of the Great Lakes during the middle of the century (Hohman and Eberhart 1998). Fall migration peaks in early to mid-November and can produce some sizeable concentrations at preferred spots (e.g., 700 at Wolf Lake, Morris County, 14 November 1997). Most migrants continue on to the southeastern states, but many stay to winter as long as the fresh water is open. Recent statewide CBC totals have exceeded 2,000. Spring migration of returning birds and departing local winterers is mainly in March, but some remain into April and a few stragglers into May. Nonbreeders will rarely summer on inland waters.

In winter, Ring-necked Ducks can be found on almost any open body of freshwater in New Jersey that supports the emergent and submergent vegetation on which they feed. Both male and female exhibit the peaked head that give the species a pronounced angular profile. Although it is difficult to see, the drake does have a brownish ring on the neck, as seen in the photo. *Photograph by Kevin Karlson.*

TUFTED DUCK *Aythya fuligula*

Casual. There have been twenty accepted reports of wintering Tufted Ducks in the state between 1966 and 2003, most of which are believed to involve birds returning for more than one winter. As few as seven distinct records may be represented, with just one occurrence of multiple birds, three drakes at Monmouth Beach in 1994–1995, at least one of which returned for four more winters. The first New Jersey record was a drake found at Edgewater, Bergen County, in February 1966 that returned for two additional winters. Other returning birds have been at Bay Head, Ocean County (1971–1972); Weehawken, Hudson County (1989–1991); Point Pleasant, Ocean County (1999–2000); and Long Branch, Monmouth County (2002–2003). Tufted Ducks have always been found in the company of scaup.

Review Species

Tufted Duck is a Eurasian species that occurs annually in very small numbers on both coasts of North America, very rarely inland, and usually in association with scaup. There are now seven records for New Jersey, all involving birds that returned for more than one winter. Both male and female are distinguished by the "tuft" on the crown, but the drake, shown here, stands out from scaup with his white sides and contrasting black back. It was photographed at Lake Takanassee, Monmouth County, 24 February 2003. Photographs by Alex Tongas.

GREATER SCAUP *Aythya marila*

Common migrant and common to locally abundant winter resident. Greater Scaup begin arriving from northern Canada in early October, with peak numbers in early November (Walsh et al. 1999). Some continue south to the mid-Atlantic states, but many stay for the winter, when they gather on coastal bays and estuaries, sometimes in massive flocks. Mid-winter counts of 50,000 on Raritan Bay have been recorded on several occasions. They begin to depart in early March, and most are gone by mid-April. A few linger into mid-May, and very rarely nonbreeders may be found along the coast in summer.

LESSER SCAUP *Aythya affinis*

Fairly common migrant and uncommon winter resident. Like their Greater Scaup cousins, Lesser Scaup begin arriving in early October, with peak numbers in early November and are more likely to appear inland. Most continue south to the southeastern states, but some remain to winter, mainly on coastal ponds and bays, but also at inland lakes and reservoirs. Lesser Scaup are much less common in winter than Greater Scaup, except at these inland locations. The spring migration of northbound Lesser Scaup occurs from late March to early April and is more noticeable inland than along the coast (Walsh et al. 1999). A few linger into May, and nonbreeders are very rarely encountered in summer.

KING EIDER *Somateria spectabilis*

Rare migrant, rare and irregular winter visitor, primarily to the jetties at Barnegat Inlet, but can occur anywhere along the coast from Sandy Hook to Cape May, often in association with Common Eider and scoters. Most records are from November to March, but summering birds, usually immatures, are casually encountered. Prior to about 1980, this species was found more often than Common Eider, but today the reverse is true.

King Eider is much less likely to be seen along the New Jersey coast than its cousin, the Common Eider. Most King Eiders seen are females or young males, which can be difficult to identify. The left photo shows a female and young male King Eider in the foreground and a female Common Eider in the background. Note the very different head profiles. At right is a young male King Eider in flight. ID criteria for both species are discussed in Appendix D. *Photographs by Kevin Karlson.*

COMMON EIDER *Somateria mollissima*

Uncommon and irregular winter visitor, primarily to the jetties at Barnegat Inlet; uncommon migrant. Uncommon at Sandy Hook, Avalon, Stone Harbor, and Cape May, but

rare elsewhere along the coast, usually at jetties. Most frequently seen from November to March, but stragglers can occur outside this time frame, and summering birds are present on rare occasions. Prior to about 1980, Common Eider was less frequently encountered in New Jersey than its smaller relative, the King Eider. Today, it is by far the more common of the two.

Recent years have seen a substantial increase in the number of Common Eiders wintering along the New Jersey coast. As a result, adult males, such as this handsome drake, are more frequently encountered. *Photograph by Kevin Karlson.*

HARLEQUIN DUCK *Histrionicus histrionicus*

Rare spring and fall migrant, rare and irregular winter visitor, primarily at jetties along the coast from Sandy Hook to Cape May. Can reliably be found along the jetty at Barnegat Light, where a flock of twenty to forty has wintered every year for more than twenty years. The birds there are quite tame, often perching on the rocks and allowing close approach for photography or close-up study. Migrants are seen rarely along the coast from October to November and again from April to mid-May. (*See photo page 139.*)

LABRADOR DUCK *Camptorhynchus labradorius*

Extinct. There are no known extant specimens of Labrador Duck from the state, but several references, including the AOU Check-list, state that the species wintered south to New Jersey, probably to Chesapeake Bay. Giraud (1844), writing about Long Island(NY), noted that they were "rather rare" there and that "in New Jersey it is called the

Sand-shoal Duck." Unlabeled specimens in the Philadelphia Academy of Natural Sciences were supposedly taken in coastal New Jersey (Stone 1937, Fables 1955), and Audubon said that it was known to ascend the Delaware River as far as Philadelphia (Bent 1925). The last known specimen was taken on Long Island in 1875. Based on the published accounts, Labrador Duck was accepted on the State List by the NJBRC.

SURF SCOTER *Melanitta perspicillata*

Common spring and fall migrant, fairly common winter resident, very rare summer resident. The fall migration of Surf Scoters along the coast can be spectacular, with a maximum of 69,928 passing the Avalon Sea Watch on 26 October 2007. Seasonal totals there sometimes surpass 200,000. Far fewer winter along the coast, but good numbers can be found at that season at preferred feeding grounds where their favorite food of mollusks is available. CBC totals underestimate their presence, as many scoters stay a mile or more offshore. Spring migration is far less evident, but takes place from late March through April and is mainly overland at night. In some years, large flocks of Surf and Black Scoters gather a mile or so offshore in Delaware Bay at that time and can be seen, albeit distantly, from land. A few nonbreeding individuals or even small groups are found along the coast most summers.

Surf Scoter is our second most common sea duck, after Black Scoter, and is regularly seen close to shore in winter. The adult male, shown here, shows a bizarre pattern of black, white, and reddish-orange on the head and bill. *Photograph by Kevin Karlson.*

WHITE-WINGED SCOTER *Melanitta fusca*

Uncommon spring and fall migrant and uncommon winter resident. White-winged Scoters are by far the least common of the three scoters in migration, and numbers tallied at the Avalon Sea Watch are a tiny fraction of those of the other two, with a peak in mid- to late November. They are regularly seen in small numbers along the coast in winter and have even outnumbered one of the other scoters on statewide CBC totals on rare occasion, although not in recent years. In spring, White-winged Scoters depart early along the coast, but are the most likely scoter to be inland at that season, and the highest counts have occurred in May (e.g., ninety at Culvers Lake, 19 May 1994). Unlike the other two, lingering birds are seldom encountered in summer.

BLACK SCOTER *Melanitta nigra*

Common spring and fall migrant, common winter resident. Like Surf Scoters, Blacks begin to arrive in mid-September with a peak in mid- to late October, and the coastal flight can be spectacular. The one-day maximum at the Avalon Sea Watch, 74,998, occurred on the same day as the Surf Scoter maximum. Seasonal totals regularly exceed 100,000 and have reached 250,000. Black Scoters are regularly seen inland in small flocks at that season, mainly on large bodies of water. They are usually the most common scoter in winter, although numbers fluctuate widely from year to year. As with Surf Scoters, although tens of thousands of Blacks migrate past New Jersey in the fall, relatively few are noted northbound in spring, as migration is primarily overland at night. In some years, Black Scoters join with Surf Scoters in large offshore concentrations in Delaware Bay in late March and early April, and concentrations are also seen far out at sea. Small numbers of nonbreeders are found along the coast in summer.

LONG-TAILED DUCK *Clangula hyemalis*

Common wintering duck along the outer coast, less common in bays and sounds, and only occasionally seen along the Hudson and Delaware rivers. During migration, may show up on any sizeable inland body of water, especially in bad weather. Long-tailed Ducks begin to arrive in mid-

October, with peak migration in early December, and are present through March, with most departing by the end of April. Most of the Atlantic Flyway population winters off New England, and unusual conditions there can send more to New Jersey, as happened in 1981 when Nantucket Sound froze over. In March, large flocks may gather far offshore in preparation for migration. A few linger into May, and a summering bird is found on rare occasion. The delightful courtship call of the male Long-tailed Duck is one of the joys of late winter birding along the coast. (*See photo page 140.*)

BUFFLEHEAD *Bucephala albeola*

Common migrant and common winter resident throughout the state. Bufflehead is the most widely distributed diving duck in migration and in winter, and can be found on virtually any open body of water. Fall migrants begin to arrive in late October, with a peak in early November. From November to March they are common on ponds, lakes, and reservoirs unless driven to the coast by lack of open water. They are most common in the coastal bays and estuaries, but occur on the ocean as well. Spring migration is inconspicuous, but most Buffleheads are gone from the state by late April. Nonbreeding birds are rare in summer, but occur at inland locations as well as along the coast.

The smallest and most widely distributed of our diving ducks, the Bufflehead is a common sight on open bodies of fresh water, bays, estuaries, and even protected ocean waters from November to March. They are frequently seen in pairs, such as the one shown here, and are one of the few ducks that often keeps the same mate for several years. *Photograph by Kevin Karlson.*

COMMON GOLDENEYE *Bucephala clangula*

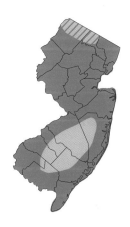

The cold-hardy Common Goldeneye is a fairly common migrant and winter resident, although it is much less common than its smaller cousin, the Bufflehead. Goldeneyes are late migrants, with large numbers stopping on inland lakes and reservoirs in November and early December. In winter, they are found mainly along the coast, especially Raritan Bay and Barnegat Bay, and are more common in the north than along the southern coast. Most of the Common Goldeneyes that winter along the Atlantic coast are found off New England, so conditions there can lead to greater or lesser numbers off New Jersey. Except for increased numbers on inland waters, the spring migration is inconspicuous. They are very rarely found in summer.

BARROW'S GOLDENEYE *Bucephala islandica*

Review Species

Casual winter visitor. There are nineteen accepted records of Barrow's Goldeneye in New Jersey, many believed to be birds returning for more than one winter. One of these was the famous drake that wintered on the Shark River estuary for fourteen consecutive years from 1970 to 1983. All but six of the records are from Monmouth County, especially the Raritan Bay side of Sandy Hook, where one or two Barrow's have joined the Common Goldeneye flock most years since 1995 through at least 2009. The only non-Atlantic coastal records are from Merrill Creek Reservoir, Foul Rift and Cinnaminson on the Delaware River, and East Point on Delaware Bay.

HOODED MERGANSER *Lophodytes cucullatus*

Common migrant and winter resident, rare and local summer resident. The first recorded breeding of Hooded Mergansers in New Jersey was in 1949, when a nest was parasitized by Wood Ducks, leading to a mixed brood of both species (Fables 1955). By 1984, Leck was able to cite seven nesting records, mainly from the northern tier of counties. During the Breeding Bird Atlas, many more breeding sites were found, primarily in the Kittatinny Valley and Highlands regions of Sussex, Passaic, and northern Morris counties, but the species is still rare as a nester. Hooded Mergansers are late fall migrants, peaking in late November, but they are widespread and common throughout the state. In winter, they can be found wherever there is open water, especially on coastal ponds and estuaries. The number of wintering individuals has increased several fold in the past two decades. Many Hooded Mergansers migrate early in spring, but some linger through April.

Rare and local as a breeding bird in the state, Hooded Merganser is common throughout most of New Jersey at other seasons. The female is a rather plain brown, but the striking male, shown here with crest displayed, is one of the most handsome of North American waterfowl. *Photograph by Kevin Karlson.*

COMMON MERGANSER *Mergus merganser*

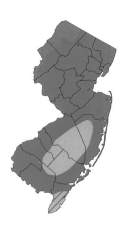

Common migrant and winter resident, very uncommon and local, but increasing, summer resident. The first confirmed breeding of this species in New Jersey was along the Delaware River in Sussex County in 1973 (Wolfarth 1973). Since then, they have expanded their range along the Delaware River as far as Mercer County, and added the Walkill River, Paulinskill, Musconetcong, and Big Flatbrook drainages, as well. Very late migrants in the fall, Common Mergansers gather in large flocks on inland lakes and reservoirs, especially Lake Tappan, Oradell Reservoirs, and the Canoe Brook Reservoirs in late November into December. The Hackensack-Ridgewood CBC, which includes Oradell Reservoir, counted a staggering 14,084 on 18 December 2004. In winter, they stay as far north as open water permits, and return to favored staging locations at the first sign of a thaw in late February or early March. Common Mergansers are rare in southernmost New Jersey, especially Cape May County.

RED-BREASTED MERGANSER *Mergus serrator*

Common migrant and winter resident, very rare summer resident. There have been only a handful of confirmed breeding records for this species in New Jersey. The first was on Barnegat Bay in 1937 and the most recent at Tuckerton in 1996. The regular presence of summering, non-breeding birds along the coast complicates confirmation of the very rare nesting occurrences. During fall migration from mid-October into December, Red-breasted Mergansers can be seen on inland waters throughout the state, but are most common along the coast. In winter, a few remain on large lakes and reservoirs, some of which are shown on the map, but the vast majority are found on the ocean or in large bays like Raritan and Barnegat. Spring migration, from late March into April, again brings modest numbers to inland lakes and reservoirs.

RUDDY DUCK *Oxyura jamaicensis*

Fairly common migrant and winter resident, rare and local summer resident. Ruddy Ducks were first found nesting in New Jersey in the Hackensack Meadowlands in 1958, and that is the only place where small numbers have been consistently found in summer, although pairs nested at Mannington Marsh and Petty's Island during the Atlas. Peak migration in fall is in mid-November, but most birds continue on to winter on Chesapeake Bay. Wintering Ruddy Ducks are widely distributed on inland lakes and reservoirs, the Hackensack Meadowlands, and shore ponds and estuaries. Spring migration is apparent on inland waters from mid-March to early April.

Order Galliformes

Family Odontophoridae: New World Quail

NORTHERN BOBWHITE *Colinus virginianus*

Uncommon and declining resident, mainly in the southernmost counties. The story of Northern Bobwhite in New Jersey is complicated by the repeated releases of non-native stock from the South to supplement the native ones for hunting purposes, a practice that started in the nineteenth

century and continued through the twentieth. Due to a combination of hunting pressure, releases, habitat alteration, and severe winters, the population has fluctuated widely over the years. Bobwhite were probably never common in the northern third of the state, but have now completely disappeared. They have also nearly vanished from the area shown by the dashed line on the map; there are probably few breeding birds there, and the released birds seldom survive the winter. Only in the southern counties does an apparently viable population exist, but this too is probably compromised by inbreeding with the introduced and less hardy southern subspecies

Family Phasianidae: Pheasants, Grouse, and Allies

RING-NECKED PHEASANT *Phasianus colchicus*

Uncommon, local, and apparently declining resident. Native to Asia, Ring-necked Pheasants were first successfully introduced into North America during the late nineteenth century (Giudice and Ratti 2001), with large-scale releases in New Jersey in 1897 (Stone 1908). They were fairly common throughout the state, although less so in the Pine Barrens and Outer Coastal Plain, through much of the twentieth century, but have decreased noticeably in recent years. The population is largely maintained through releases of captive-raised birds for sport hunting (Walsh et al. 1999).

RUFFED GROUSE *Bonassa umbellus*

Uncommon and local resident. Populations are known to be cyclical, but Ruffed Grouse were formerly fairly common in the northern third of the state and, even during the Atlas period, could be found in modest numbers throughout the Pine Barrens into Cumberland and Cape May counties. A decline that began in the 1980s has continued, so that today they are scarce and difficult to locate in the Kittatinny Mountains and the northern Highlands and are apparently extirpated everywhere else. The statewide total of Ruffed Grouse on CBCs, which peaked at seventy-two in 1982, has not exceeded one since 2003. It remains to be seen if this trend can be reversed.

The drumming of a male Ruffed Grouse was formerly one of the familiar sounds of spring throughout much of New Jersey's woodlands, especially in the northern third of the state. This low-pitched sound, made by a beating of the wings, has become very rare in recent decades as the grouse population has declined dramatically. Hopefully, this trend will be reversed in the future. *Photograph by Kevin Karlson.*

GREATER PRAIRIE-CHICKEN *Tympanuchus cupido*

Extinct. The nominate race of this species, *T. c. cupido*, was known as the Heath Hen and was once a common resident of the Pine Barrens of Burlington and Ocean counties (Stone 1908, Fables 1955). It ranged from Massachusetts to Virginia, but was extirpated from New Jersey by 1870 by excessive shooting. Stone (1937) provides an interesting account of the hunting practices that led to the species' demise. The last Heath Hen was recorded on Martha's Vineyard, MA, in 1932.

WILD TURKEY *Meleagris gallopavo*

Common resident throughout the state, even occurring locally in some heavily urbanized areas and on some of the barrier islands. As noted by Walsh et al. (1999), the history of Wild Turkeys in New Jersey is one of highs and lows. They were apparently abundant in colonial times (Stone 1937), but had been extirpated by 1840 (Fables 1955). Early attempts at reintroduction were unsuccessful, but in 1977 the NJDFW began a program of transplanting birds from wild stock of the native subspecies into the northwestern counties. This population gradually grew and spread, and, augmented by wild birds relocated within the state, has reached every corner of New Jersey.

Review Species

Records of Pacific Loon have increased in New Jersey since 1999, but it is still a much sought-after rarity, and many reports are of misidentified Common or Red-throated Loons. This photo, taken at Manasquan Inlet, Ocean County, in March 1992, shows the diagnostic neck pattern of a dark vertical stripe cleanly separating the white fore neck from the paler brown hind neck. The chinstrap or necklace is also a useful field mark, when present and visible, as is the lack of white around the eye. *Photograph by Kevin Karlson.*

Order Gaviiformes

Family: Gaviidae: Loons

RED-THROATED LOON *Gavia stellata*

Common spring and fall migrant, fairly common to common winter resident along the coast. The fall migration of Red-throated Loons along the coast can be spectacular, with 50,000 to 70,000 typically passing the Avalon Sea Watch from early November to early December. They are very uncommon inland at this season on large lakes and reservoirs and on the Delaware River, especially during foul weather, and rare in winter. Red-throated Loons winter on the ocean and large bays in numbers that vary from year to year. Hundreds annually gather on Delaware Bay in March in preparation for migration, but the number of migrants in spring is far below that in fall.

PACIFIC LOON *Gavia pacifica*

Casual visitor, mainly November to March. There are seventeen accepted records of Pacific Loon in New Jersey, the majority occurring between Sandy Hook and Manasquan Inlet. The first for the state was discovered at Round Valley Reservoir in 1978, and there are two other inland records, both from Warren County. A couple of birds have lingered into April, but one that spent three weeks of August 1986 at Tuckerton was unique. Since 1999, Pacific Loon has been recorded ten times, due either to increased birder awareness or an actual increase in vagrants.

COMMON LOON *Gavia immer*

Common migrant and fairly common winter resident, mainly along the coast. The main fall migration occurs from mid-October to mid-November, when Common Loons are often encountered on inland lakes and reservoirs, or seen moving along the coast. They winter mainly on the open ocean and coastal bays, with a few at scattered inland locations. Spring migration occurs primarily from early April to mid-May, when it is common to see them in full breeding plumage flying overhead anywhere in the state. A few nonbreeding birds are found along the coast in summer.

By the time migrant Common Loons begin arriving in the fall, they have already molted into their plain winter plumage. They retain this plumage into the spring, but by the time they are ready to depart for the north in April and early May, many have changed into the handsome summer dress shown here. *Photograph by Kevin Karlson.*

Order Podicipediformes

Family Podicipedidae: Grebes

PIED-BILLED GREBE *Podylimbus podiceps*

Fairly common winter resident, uncommon spring and common fall migrant, rare and local summer resident. Endangered Species as a breeding bird in New Jersey. The history of Pied-billed Grebe as a breeding bird in the state is poorly known, but by 1940 there were only twelve nesting localities in northern New Jersey (Bull 1984). Fables (1955) considered them locally common, and Kearny Marsh supported thirty family groups in 1983 (Walsh et al. 1999), but

was one of only two known breeding sites (NJDFW). However, Pied-billed Grebes nest in freshwater marshes associated with ponds, bogs, lakes, and slow-moving streams, and much of this habitat was steadily destroyed and degraded during the twentieth century. The steadily declining breeding population led to their being reclassified as Endangered in 1984. Fall migration peaks from October to November, with large concentrations on some inland lakes. In winter, the grebes can be found on unfrozen freshwater ponds, mainly in the southern two-thirds of the state. A few also winter in brackish and even salt estuaries and harbors. Spring migration from late March to mid-April is inconspicuous.

Pied-billed Grebes are found throughout New Jersey from fall to spring, but are more common in the southern part of the state in winter. They prefer fresh water, but can also be seen on brackish bays and estuaries. This adult, photographed in March 2007, is beginning the transition to breeding plumage. *Photograph by Kevin Karlson.*

HORNED GREBE *Podiceps auritus*

Fairly common spring and fall migrant, fairly common winter resident. Horned Grebes migrate mainly along the coast of New Jersey from late October into early December, but are regularly seen on large inland lakes and reservoirs, especially in stormy weather. Wintering birds are found mainly along the coast, especially in protected bays, but have declined substantially in numbers during the last few decades, as indicated by statewide CBC totals and birder observations. Spring migration occurs primarily from mid-March to mid-April, when molting Horned Grebes are often confused with Eared Grebes.

RED-NECKED GREBE *Podiceps grisegena*

Irregular migrant and winter resident. Occurs annually from October to April, usually fewer than twenty a year. Fall and spring migrants are more likely to be encountered on inland lakes and reservoirs than along the coast, while the reverse is true in midwinter. Occasionally, a major influx of Red-necked Grebes may occur, apparently related to freezing of the Great Lakes, as happened in mid-February 1994 when hundreds were found on the coast, mainly in Cape May County (RNJB 20[2]:60). Likewise, an easterly storm was responsible for the sixty-four or more found in northern New Jersey 5 April 1959 (Bull 1964).

EARED GREBE *Podiceps nigricollis*

Very rare, but increasing, visitor, mainly from December to March, but with records from September 1 into early June. The first Eared Grebe for the state was discovered at Shark River Inlet, 11 January 1948, and since then there have been almost a hundred additional reports and more than fifty accepted records, including twenty from 2000 to 2009 (Hanson 2010). With the exception of a report from Lake Malaga, 24 February 1990, and two recent lingering birds at Round Valley in 2006 and 2009, all records have been along the coast.

Review Species

Eared Grebe is an annual visitor in very small numbers from fall to early spring. In winter plumage, it is distinguished from Horned Grebe by head shape (peaked above the eye), slightly upturned bill with a dark tip, dark auriculars, and dusky neck. This individual was one of two that wintered near Atlantic City, November 2006 to February 2007. *Photograph by Karl Lukens.*

WESTERN GREBE *Aechmorphorus occidentalis*

Review Species

Casual visitor to the coast, mainly December to March, but there are two recent records for late spring. There have been twenty-one accepted occurrences of Western Grebe in New Jersey, all but one from the coast. The first was seen at Beach Haven, Ocean County, 8 January 1939 and there were only ten records prior to 1993, including the one inland sighting at Centennial Lake, Burlington County, 3–5 December 1968. There has been an increase in records in recent years, including repeat occurrences at South Amboy and Sandy Hook that probably represent returning birds.

Western Grebe is a species from western North America that has occurred as a vagrant many times in the East. There are now more than twenty records for New Jersey, some of them involving birds returning for multiple winters. The very similar Clark's Grebe, which has appeared a few times on the East Coast, shows white between the eye and the bill and a brighter, yellow-orange bill. This Western was at Sandy Hook, 29 February 2008. *Photograph by Tom Boyle.*

Order Procellariiformes

Family Diomedeidae: Albatrosses

YELLOW-NOSED ALBATROSS *Thalassarche chlororhynchos*

Review Species

Accidental. New Jersey's only Yellow-nosed Albatross was discovered flying along the Garden State Parkway just south of Cape May Court House to the astonishment of the finder. It disappeared, only to be relocated two days later along the Delaware Bayshore, where it was enjoyed by many. This individual apparently visited several other states both before and after its appearance in New Jersey (Finnegan 2001). (*See photo page 140.*)

21–23 MAY 2001, CAPE MAY COURT HOUSE AND DELAWARE
    BAYSHORE, CAPE MAY CO. (NJBRC 2001-001)

Family Procellariidae: Shearwaters and Petrels

NORTHERN FULMAR *Fulmarus glacialis*

Uncommon visitor far offshore, accidental from shore. Regularly seen in small and unpredictable numbers from October to June forty or more miles offshore, although occasionally much closer. There are five records from land, including two picked up alive in Bergen County (Bull 1964), one later released, and another captured at Beach Haven (Fables 1955).

DEC 1892, ORADELL, BERGEN CO. (AMNH 64081)
30 JAN 1949, BEACH HAVEN, OCEAN CO.
7 JAN 1956, RAMSEY, BERGEN CO.
22 SEP 1996, AVALON, CAPE MAY CO. (RNJB 23[1]:17)
12 FEB 1998, CAPE MAY PT., CAPE MAY CO. (RNJB 22[4]:48)

BLACK-CAPPED PETREL *Pterodroma hasitata*

Review Species

Accidental. Although this species probably occurs with some regularity far offshore in warm-water eddies of the Gulf Stream, there are only a handful of sight reports and two accepted records for the state, one of multiple birds seen from land immediately following a hurricane. The first record is of a bird photographed eighty-six miles east of Barnegat Light, at the mouth of the Hudson Canyon, which is actually closer to New York. Approximately eight Black-capped Petrels were observed from Sunset Beach, Cape May, flying south out of Delaware Bay following the passage of the remnants of Hurricane Bertha.

16 SEP 1991, 86 MILES E. OF BARNEGAT LIGHT, OCEAN CO. (RNJB 18[1]:17)
13 JUL 1996, CAPE MAY, CAPE MAY CO. (NJBRC 1996-128)

CORY'S SHEARWATER *Calonectris diomedea*

Fairly common visitor far offshore, rare from shore. Cory's Shearwaters are regularly seen in numbers from tens to several hundred on pelagic trips well offshore (20–100 miles) from late May to October. They are occasionally encountered much closer to land and are rare, but annual, at Cape May Point in July and August. The Avalon Sea Watch reported as many as thirty-one in July 1996, and they have also been seen from land at Island Beach SP in September.

Cory's Shearwater is a regular summer and early autumn visitor to the offshore waters twenty or more miles from the coast. It is also occasionally seen from land from Island Beach to Cape May. This bird, obviously in heavy molt, was photographed off New Jersey in September 2008. *Photograph by Bob Fogg.*

GREATER SHEARWATER *Puffinus gravis*

Common visitor far offshore, rare from shore. Greater Shearwaters migrate from their breeding grounds in the South Atlantic and are present off New Jersey from late May to November, usually twenty to a hundred miles from the coast. Highest concentrations occur on their northbound flight from late May to late June. They are sometimes found closer to shore, and are occasionally seen from Cape May Point in June and July, though not every year.

BULLER'S SHEARWATER *Puffinus bulleri*

Review Species

Accidental. The only recorded occurrence of this species in the North Atlantic Ocean was a bird seen on a pelagic trip off Barnegat Light in 1984. Fortunately it was well photographed, so the identity is not in question. Buller's Shearwater nests on islands off New Zealand and is a regular, though uncommon, migrant along the Pacific coast of North America.

28 OCT 1984, 31 MILES E.S.E. OF BARNEGAT LIGHT, OCEAN CO. (RNJB 11[1]:18; NJPF)

Buller's Shearwater, which breeds on islands off New Zealand, has occurred only once in the North Atlantic Ocean. This individual was observed on a pelagic trip out of Barnegat Light on 28 October 1984, some thirty-one miles offshore. *Photograph by Gerry DeWaghe.*

SOOTY SHEARWATER *Puffinus griseus*

Uncommon visitor offshore in May and June, rare at other seasons and rare from shore. Migrating Sooty Shearwaters arrive off the coast of New Jersey in May from their breeding grounds in the South Atlantic and reach peak numbers by early June. Rarely seen from shore, but reported almost annually from Cape May Point, May to July. As their migration continues clockwise around the North Atlantic, only stragglers and nonbreeding wanderers are seen at other times of the year. Sooty Shearwaters nesting in New Zealand undertake one of the longest known migrations of any bird, about 40,000 miles (Shaffer et al. 2006).

MANX SHEARWATER *Puffinus puffinus*

Uncommon visitor offshore, mainly May and October to December, very rare from shore. The first record of Manx Shearwater in New Jersey was at Hudson Canyon, 31 May 1975, but there are now records for every month but January. Unlike the other shearwaters, reports of Manx are fairly evenly distributed between near-shore waters (ten to fifteen miles) and the deeper canyons (seventy-five to ninety miles offshore). This may be a function of the frequency of

birder visits to these areas, however. Except for Audubon's Shearwater, Manx is the least likely of the five regularly occurring shearwaters to be seen from shore, averaging about one report every two years at Cape May Point.

AUDUBON'S SHEARWATER *Puffinus lherminieri*

Rare summer and fall visitor, July to September. The first New Jersey record of Audubon's Shearwater was one found dead at Cape May, 2 August 1926 (Stone and Pearson 1926), but it wasn't until the 1990s that regular offshore visits during the period of warmer ocean water temperatures in late summer and early autumn indicated that they are probably annual in late summer. The majority of the more than seventy-five reports are of one or two birds within forty miles of land, but the largest concentrations (225 in 1976, 25 in 2005) have been seventy-five to a hundred miles offshore. There are just a handful of land-based records from Cape May Point and one from Avalon.

Audubon's Shearwater is an uncommon, but regular, visitor to waters off New Jersey during late summer and early fall, especially in warm-water eddies that spin off the Gulf Stream. Most of the records are from far offshore, although the species has very rarely been seen within sight of land. *Photograph by Bob Fogg.*

Family Hydrobatidae: Storm-Petrels

WILSON'S STORM-PETREL *Oceanites oceanicus*

Common to abundant offshore visitor, primarily May to September, rare to uncommon from shore. A migrant from its breeding ground in Antarctica and the South Atlantic and one of the most abundant birds in the world, Wilson's Storm-Petrel arrives off New Jersey in May and remains common throughout the summer. This is the most likely pelagic species to be encountered, both near shore and far off-

shore. They are seen every summer at Cape May Point and from the Cape May–Lewes ferry, but are much less frequent farther north along the coast. The highest estimated state count was 50,000 to 75,000 from a pelagic trip to Hudson Canyon, 28 May 1983. They are rarely seen from land after Labor Day, but linger offshore to at least mid-September. Most sightings from shore are in June and July.

WHITE-FACED STORM-PETREL *Pelagodroma marina*

Review Species

Casual late summer/early autumn visitor, generally far off-shore. There have been six accepted records of White-faced Storm-Petrel in New Jersey, all but one from deep water at the edge of the continental shelf, about ninety miles from the coast. The first state record was a bird photographed twenty-two and a half miles southeast of Cape May, 26 August 1972 (AB 27[1]:17). Although it was initially re-ported as being in Delaware waters, the published coordi-nates place it several miles closer to New Jersey.

White-faced Storm-Petrel is a rare, highly sought-after visi-tor to the offshore waters of the state during the late sum-mer. It breeds on islands in both the Atlantic and Pacific oceans, but is highly pelagic for the rest of the year. This bird was photographed in offshore waters near the New Jersey/Delaware border on 15 September 2009. *Photograph by Ed Sigda.*

LEACH'S STORM-PETREL *Oceanodroma leucorhoa*

Review Species

Rare spring and very rare fall visitor far offshore, acciden-tal from shore. This deep-water species, which breeds on islands off New England and the Canadian Maritimes, has been recorded mostly on pelagic trips to deep waters in the Hudson Canyon area in late May or early June. Fables (1955) and Bull (1964) mention storm-driven birds brought to shore, and there is one recent example of one found dead on a street in Avalon, 25 September 1992 (Sibley 1997). A high count of twenty was noted on a pelagic trip, 27 May 1995, and a single bird was blown by Cape May during

Records since 2004

Hurricane Bertha, 13 July 1996. Since then, there have been only three reports (two in 2003, one in 2004) of this species on pelagic trips. Leach's Storm-Petrel was added to the Review List in 2004.

BAND-RUMPED STORM-PETREL *Oceanodroma castro*

Review Species

Accidental. There have been just four accepted records of this warm-water storm-petrel, three from Cape May, all storm related, and one late summer record from far off-shore. The first two sightings occurred immediately following the passage of the remnants of Hurricane Bertha in 1996 and included eleven individuals seen on 13 July. The most recent, in 2003, was associated with Hurricane Isabel.

13 JUL 1996, CAPE MAY, CAPE MAY CO. (NJBRC 1996-129)
14 JUL 1996, CAPE MAY, CAPE MAY CO. (NJBRC 1996-133)
15 AUG 1998, NEAR WILMINGTON CANYON (NJBRC 1998-104)
19 SEP 2003, CAPE MAY, CAPE MAY CO. (NJBRC 2004-053)

Order Pelicaniformes

Family Phaethontidae: Tropicbirds

WHITE-TAILED TROPICBIRD *Phaethon lepturus*

Review Species

Accidental. An adult White-tailed Tropicbird was seen by a group of birders as it flew in along the jetty at Barnegat Light, then turned and flew out the inlet, never to be seen again. This species nests in Bermuda and the Bahamas and is rare but annual on pelagic trips off Cape Hatteras, NC. There are no records for Maryland or Delaware, and no recent records for New York or Pennsylvania.

23 NOV 1985, BARNEGAT LIGHT, OCEAN CO. (NJBRC 12[1]:13)

RED-BILLED TROPICBIRD *Phaethon aethereus*

Review Species

Accidental. The only New Jersey occurrence was an imma-ture bird picked up by an unknown person and placed in a cardboard box on a lifeguard stand in Seaside, Ocean County, in May 1983. The partially oiled bird was taken to a rehab center, where it recovered and was eventually trans-ported to Puerto Rico, the nearest nesting site, for release into the wild. This species is a very rare but annual visitor to the waters off Cape Hatteras, NC. There are no records for Maryland or Delaware, and no recent records for New York.

23 OR 24 MAY 1983, SEASIDE, OCEAN CO. (RNJB 9[3]:63)

Family Sulidae: Boobies and Gannets

MASKED BOOBY *Sula dactylactra*

Accidental. The one accepted record is of an immature bird observed from shore as it flew by Island Beach SP, 24 August 2001 (Wenzelburger 2004). Although there is one record for New York, also in August, there are no others closer than North Carolina. There it is the most frequently encountered booby, with about three dozen records, mostly from the Gulf Stream, but also on shore.

24 AUG 2001, ISLAND BEACH SP, OCEAN CO. (NJBRC 2002-039)

BROWN BOOBY *Sula leucogaster*

Casual. There are eight accepted reports of Brown Booby, plus several undocumented sightings that may be correct. Most of the sightings have been from shore, including one that was present on the jetties at Cape May Point for two days in September 1989, having apparently been blown north by Hurricane Hugo. As seems to be the case for vagrants of this species, none of the other records appears to have been storm related. Most have been single birds, with the exception of two at Island Beach in October 1979 and two at Beach Haven in June 2001.

Brown Booby is an extremely rare visitor to New Jersey, with records from late May to December, and can be difficult to separate from subadult plumages of Northern Gannet at a distance. A helpful tip is that boobies plunge-dive into the water on an angle, while Gannet plunge-dives straight down. Most birds are not as cooperative as this juvenile, which was seen in flight and perched on a buoy ten miles east of Stone Harbor, Cape May County, on 14 September 2008. *Photograph by Mike Fritz.*

NORTHERN GANNET *Morus bassanus*

Common to locally abundant fall migrant, fairly common winter resident, common spring migrant often very close to shore. Gannets begin to arrive off New Jersey in mid-September, but the peak flights, which can be spectacular, occur during November to early December. Tens of thousands pass the Avalon Sea Watch, with a single-day high of 16,946 in 2009. Watching hundreds of birds in a feeding frenzy diving on a school of bait fish is a truly awesome experience. Winter numbers of Northern Gannets along the coast can vary markedly, depending on wind direction and availability of food. Adults are seen migrating north from late February into April, while flights consisting of mainly immature birds continue into mid-May, with stragglers remaining through the summer.

Northern Gannets are common migrants and winter visitors along the coast of New Jersey. Although they usually stay several hundred yards off shore, a school of bait fish may draw them closer, and the resulting feeding frenzy of birds diving from a hundred feet or more is a wonder to behold. This adult was photographed in January. *Photograph by Kevin Karlson.*

Family Pelicanidae: Pelicans

AMERICAN WHITE PELICAN *Pelicanus erythrorhynchus*

Rare visitor, occurring at any season, but mainly in late summer and fall. Most reports are along the coast, but there have been numerous inland sightings. Prior to the mid-1970s, there were just a handful of records of American White Pelican. Since then, however, the number of sightings has increased substantially, with a maximum of seven records in 1989 and at least one report in all but two years from 1990 to 2010. This increase may be a reflection of the eastward expansion of the breeding population in recent decades (Hayes 1984, Knopf and Evans 2004). Forsythe NWR has had the most records, and some of the visitors there have stayed as long as five to eight months. Some of the sightings involve multiple birds, with the biggest single group being a flock of eleven at Cape May, 29 November 2009.

BROWN PELICAN *Pelicanus occidentalis*

Uncommon to fairly common visitor to the shore north to Island Beach, rare from there to Sandy Hook, occurring mainly from May to October. Stone (1937) never saw Brown Pelicans in New Jersey, and Fables (1955) knew of only seven records. Four more were added prior to 1980 (Walsh et al. 1999), but since then they have been recorded every year, peaking in 1992. In 1992 and 1994, a small colony of pelicans built nests, but laid no eggs, at Barnegat Bay (Burger et al. 1993). There have been no known attempts at breeding since. Brown Pelicans can be found anywhere along the coast, but especially at Barnegat, Little Egg Harbor, and Hereford inlets. Although the biggest numbers occur from July to September, there are records for every month of the year and one inland record at Merrill Creek Reservoir, 27 November 2007.

Family Phalacrocoracidae: Cormorants

DOUBLE-CRESTED CORMORANT *Phalacrocorax auritus*

Common to abundant spring and fall migrant, common winter resident, fairly common and increasing summer resident. Double-crested Cormorants were heavily persecuted during the eighteenth and nineteenth centuries and were extirpated from New England, but the population began to recover in the early twentieth century (Hatch and Weseloh 1999). After a sharp downturn in mid-century, rapid expansion resumed. Increasing numbers during the summer from the mid-1970s led to the suspicion of breeding in New Jersey, which was finally confirmed in 1987 (Parsons et al. 1991). They are now fairly common nesters at reservoirs, along major rivers and bays and estuaries along the coast, joined by many nonbreeders. Fall migration brings an average of 200,000 past the Avalon Sea Watch from late August to early November, and ever increasing numbers winter at the same locations used by breeding birds. Spring migration peaks in late April or early May.

GREAT CORMORANT *Phalacrocorax carbo*

Uncommon migrant and winter resident. The occurrence of this species changed dramatically during the twentieth century. Stone (1937) was not aware of any record for Cape May County, but Fables (1955) wrote that although it was "formerly a rare and local winter visitant, this species seems to have increased in recent years." By the mid-1980s, Great Cormorants were uncommon but increasing (Boyle 1986), and easily found in winter at preferred sites, such as Sandy Hook, Jersey City, and Barnegat Inlet. About that time, they began to winter in small numbers along the Delaware River between Trenton and Philadelphia, and several dozen are there every year. Individuals have also shown up at many different inland lakes and reservoirs over the past two decades. Where Stone saw none, the Cape May CBC recorded sixty-seven Great Cormorants in 2008.

Family Anhingidae: Darters

ANHINGA *Anhinga anhinga*

Review Species

Casual vagrant from the South. The first record for New Jersey was a bird observed by many soaring over Cape May, 25 September 1971. There have been several dozen reports since then, but only fourteen accepted records due to insufficient documentation and the likelihood of confusion with soaring cormorants. Other than the record noted above and a specimen found dead at Whiting, Ocean County, in January 1989, all sightings have been between late April and early July. Cape May has had four and Sandy Hook two, but the other records are scattered around the state (see map).

Family Fregatidae: Frigatebirds

MAGNIFICENT FRIGATEBIRD *Fregata magnificens and Frigatebird species*

Very rare visitor from southern waters. There have been twenty-four accepted records of frigatebirds in New Jersey. Because of the difficulty of separating Great, Magnificent, and Lesser frigatebirds in the field, only four of these have been accepted as Magnificent, based on unequivocal photographs. It is very likely that all the records pertain to this species, but the NJBRC has taken a conservative approach because of the proven occurrence of the other two in the continental United States. Great Frigatebirds have been found as close as Oklahoma, with others recorded in California, while Lesser Frigatebirds have appeared in Maine, Michigan, Wyoming, and California. Except for a single occurrence in early April, the remaining records are evenly spread over the period from mid-May to early November.

Review Species

Frigatebirds are very rare visitors to New Jersey, and most cannot be identified to species with absolute certainty. This juvenile Magnificent Frigatebird is an exception because of its distinctive and diagnostic plumage features. It was photographed flying over Cape May Point on 18 May 2006. *Photograph by Karl Lukens.*

Order Ciconiiformes

Family Ardeidae: Bitterns and Herons

AMERICAN BITTERN *Botaurus lentiginosus*

Uncommon summer resident, uncommon spring and fall migrant, rare winter resident. American Bittern is considered a Threatened Species as a breeding bird in New Jersey. It is a difficult species to monitor, but has clearly declined substantially from former numbers in the state (Stone 1937, Bull 1964) and the country (Lowther et al. 2009). Bitterns require extensive freshwater wetlands for nesting, and the loss of this habitat is the primary cause of their decline. They are nocturnal migrants and scarce at any sea-

son, but more conspicuous in the fall along the coast, when they are often seen leaving marshes at dusk. The maximum count at Cape May Point is twenty-three on 17 October 1997 (Walsh et al. 1999). A few are found every winter on coastal CBCs.

LEAST BITTERN *Ixobrychus exilis*

Uncommon and local summer resident, seldom seen in migration, and very rare in winter. Like its cousin, the shy and secretive Least Bittern has disappeared from many areas as its freshwater marsh breeding habitat is destroyed (Fables 1955, Leck 1984), but it seems to have fared better than the larger American Bittern. Nocturnal migrants, Least Bitterns apparently depart by mid-October and arrive at their breeding sites in early May (Walsh et al. 1999). In some years, a few attempt to winter in southern New Jersey, but they are very rarely encountered on CBCs.

Our smallest heron, Least Bittern is usually a shy and secretive denizen of freshwater marshes in scattered locations around the state. Occasionally, however, one will perch in the open to give the birder or photographer a better look. Females, like the one shown here, and males have similar plumage, but the males' coloring, especially the black of the crown, mantle, back, and scapulars, is much darker. This adult female was photographed at the South Cape May Meadows in July 1996. *Photograph by Kevin Karlson.*

GREAT BLUE HERON *Ardea herodias*

Fairly common permanent resident throughout New Jersey, although most withdraw from the extreme northwestern counties in winter. Considered a Threatened Species as a breeding bird prior to 2000, Great Blue Herons have recovered strongly from a low point of just five active colonies in 1982 (Galli 1982). Many migrants from farther north are seen along the coast in fall, occasionally producing large concentrations, such as the 3,200 seen on 2 October 1994 flying past Cape May Point. They are much more common along the coast than inland in winter, and returning migrants peak in late March. The white color morph, known as "Great White" Heron, has occurred twice in New Jersey (see below) and is on the Review List.

9–23 SEP 2000, NUMMY ISLAND, CAPE MAY CO. (NJBRC 2001-077)
26 MAY–7 JUN 2001, BLAWENBURG, SOMERSET CO. (NJBRC 2002-004)

GREAT EGRET *Ardea alba*

Common but local summer resident, fairly common spring and fall migrant, scarce winter resident. Great Egrets were extirpated from New Jersey and almost from the country in the late nineteenth century, but they began to return once protected by legislation that ended most plume hunting (Griscom 1923). All nesting colonies are along the Atlantic coast or Delaware River, but foraging birds wander widely from colonies in Delaware and around New York City. A recent aerial survey of the coastal colonies found more than 1,500 birds, more than triple the 1985 total (Kisiel 2008). Postbreeding dispersal brings Great Egrets to every corner of the state in late summer and early fall. Most migrate south in October, but a few usually try to winter in the southern coastal salt marshes. Returning birds are seen from mid-March to April.

WESTERN REEF-HERON *Egretta gularis*

Review Species

Accidental. The only record for New Jersey is of a bird seen by just a single observer and, unfortunately, not photographed. However, it was reported just days before a Western Reef-Heron, almost certainly the same bird, appeared in Brooklyn, NY, only twenty miles distant, where it remained for most of July and August 2007. This coincidence, supported by an excellent written description, was sufficient for acceptance of the sighting as a first state record.

30 JUN 2007, SOUTH AMBOY, MIDDLESEX CO. (NJBRC 2008-033)

SNOWY EGRET *Egretta thula*

Common, but local and declining, summer resident, common spring and fall migrant, rare winter resident. Snowy Egrets were extirpated from New Jersey and much of the United States in the late nineteenth century due to plume hunting, but began to return in 1928 (Stone 1937) and nested in 1939 (Bull 1964). Numbers increased dramatically after that, reaching a peak of more than 3,000 birds in the late 1970s. Although the number of colonies has remained relatively stable at about 25, numbers of individuals have declined sharply in recent years, with only 500 found on the last aerial survey (Kisiel 2008). Like most herons, Snowy Egrets wander widely after the breeding season, then migrate south in October, returning from mid-March to April. Very few attempt to winter.

Snowy Egrets were extirpated from New Jersey due to plume hunting during the late nineteenth century, but recovered strongly during the mid-twentieth century, reaching peak numbers in the 1970s. They can be seen from spring through fall, mainly in the coastal marshes from Ocean County to Cape May County. Their numbers have dropped sharply in the past few decades. *Photograph by Kevin Karlson.*

LITTLE BLUE HERON *Egretta caerulea*

Uncommon, very local, and declining summer resident, uncommon spring and fall migrant, very rare winter resident.

Little Blue Heron was very uncommon in the state during the first half of the twentieth century, but began to increase thereafter. Aerial colonial waterbird surveys in 1978 found 206 individuals in fifteen colonies, increasing to 223 birds in nineteen colonies in 1995, and the population was thought to be stable or increasing (Walsh et al. 1999). Birders noted a steady decline in the new century, however, and the recent survey located only about 45 birds in twelve colonies (Kisiel 2008). Migration is mainly in September/October and March/April, and one or two will attempt to winter most years, but like many other half-hardy herons, shorebirds, and marsh sparrows, they are more regular in December and early January than later in the season when the marshes often freeze over.

TRICOLORED HERON *Egretta tricolor*

Scarce, very local and declining, summer resident, rare spring and fall migrant, very rare winter resident. Tricolored Heron is a relatively recent addition to the breeding birds of New Jersey, first nesting at Stone Harbor in 1948 (Bull 1964). The increase that followed coincided with the rapid expansion of the species' breeding range on the East Coast from the 1940s to 1970s (Kaufman 1996, Frederick 1997). Aerial surveys indicated a stable or increasing population through 1995, with about 200 individuals, but more recently have shown a dramatic decline to only about a dozen birds in five colonies in 2008 (Kisiel 2008). Some Tricolored Herons go undetected by aerial surveys because of the dark plumage, and one colony had 20 birds in 2009, but this species is clearly of serious concern. A few are found along the south coast in most winters.

Tricolored Herons first appeared as breeding birds in New Jersey during the middle of the twentieth century and increased to a total of about 200 birds by 1995. Since then, however, their numbers have declined dramatically, and we can only hope that we do not lose this very attractive addition to our avifauna. *Photograph by Kevin Karlson.*

REDDISH EGRET *Egretta rufescens*

Accidental. An immature dark morph was discovered at Forsythe NWR on the morning of 24 August 1998. Fortunately, the news quickly spread, and numerous observers were able to see and photograph this rarity (Burgiel et al. 1999). It was supposedly seen on two subsequent days, but no documentation was provided. Although this species has occurred annually in North Carolina for the past few decades, there is only one record for New York, one for Rhode Island, and two for Delaware. All accepted records for the East Coast north of Florida refer to dark morphs.

24 AUG 1998, FORSYTHE NWR, ATLANTIC CO. (NJBRC 1998-040; NJPF)

Reddish Egret is a fairly common resident of Florida and the Gulf Coast, but has very rarely occurred in the Northeast. New Jersey's only record is this individual that was present at Forsythe NWR, 24 August 1998. *Photographs by Kevin Karlson.*

CATTLE EGRET *Bubulcus ibis*

Scarce and very local summer resident, rare spring and fall migrant. The story of Cattle Egret in New Jersey has been one of boom and bust. First reported in the state in 1952 and found nesting in 1958 (Fables 1955), it was, by the late 1970s and early 1980s, a common breeding bird in coastal heronries and an abundant visitor to Salem County from the heronry at Pea Patch Island, Delaware. Beginning in the late 1980s, the breeding population plummeted and, despite a slight uptick in 2001, has almost completely disappeared (Kisiel 2008), as is the case in neighboring states (Telfair 2006). Small flocks from Delaware, where several hundred pairs still nest, continue to occur in Salem County, and individuals or groups are seen in the Cape May area and at Forsythe, mainly in late summer. Occurrence at other places is sporadic and unpredictable. There are no recent winter records.

GREEN HERON *Butorides virescens*

Fairly common and widespread summer resident, fairly common spring and fall migrant, accidental in early winter. Unlike our other herons and egrets, Green Herons are usually solitary nesters in woodlands near water throughout the state. They begin to arrive in mid-April, and, despite their shy and secretive nature, the "skeow" flight call is a familiar reminder of their presence. The southbound migration begins in late August, and by mid-October most have departed New Jersey. They are rarely found on a CBC, and there are just a few midwinter records.

BLACK-CROWNED NIGHT-HERON *Nycticorax nycticorax*

Common fall and fairly common spring migrant, fairly common, but local, summer resident, uncommon winter resident. Threatened Species as a breeder in New Jersey. Black-crowned Night-Herons declined as a breeding species in the state during the twentieth century due to persecution and habitat loss, especially at inland and northern colonies (Griscom 1923, Fables 1955). Colonial Waterbird Surveys have shown a pronounced decline of coastal nesters since 1977 (Walsh et al. 1999), although numbers appear to have stabilized in recent years at about 20 percent of the 1970s population (Kisiel 2008). They are primarily nocturnal in migration, arrive at breeding colonies from late March into April, and wander widely after the nesting season. Many depart in early October, when groups are often seen at sunset. They are regularly found at favored roosts along the coast in winter.

YELLOW-CROWNED NIGHT-HERON
Nyctanassa violacea

Scarce and local summer resident, scarce spring and fall migrant, accidental in winter. Threatened Species in New Jersey. Yellow-crowned Night-Herons, usually only a few pairs but rarely as many as twenty, nest primarily in colonies with other herons and egrets along the coast of Atlantic and Cape May counties. Occasionally, an individual pair will nest alone in a suburban setting well away from the coast, and birds from colonies around New York City forage in the Hackensack Meadowlands. They are difficult to census, but surely number fewer than a hundred pairs in the state. Migration is inconspicuous, as they arrive at nesting colonies in late March and April and depart by the end of October. One is seen on a CBC about every ten years, but there are no recent midwinter records.

WHITE IBIS *Eudocimus albus*

Review Species

Records since 1996

Rare visitor, mainly as a postbreeding wanderer from the southern states. There have been more than a hundred reports of White Ibis in New Jersey, all but two since 1950, and missing only five years since 1975. The biggest influx occurred in 1977, when more than fifty birds were found in nine different counties from Warren and Bergen to Cape May. Almost all the visitors are immature birds, but there have been about twelve adults, including two in 2009. Reports dropped off to about one or two per year in the 1990s, and the species was added to the Review List in 1996.

White Ibis is an almost annual visitor to New Jersey from the southeastern states, mainly in summer and early fall. The majority of the birds that show up are juveniles, but there have been about a dozen adults, such as this one photographed at Cape May on the somewhat early date of 28 June 2009. *Photograph by Karl Lukens.*

GLOSSY IBIS *Plegadis falcinellus*

Fairly common spring and fall migrant, fairly common but local summer resident, very rare in winter. The first nest of Glossy Ibis in New Jersey was found in 1955 (Kunkle et al. 1959), but they spread rapidly after that and by 1978 were the most common colonial waterbird in the state (Walsh et al. 1999). Numbers declined dramatically in the next two decades, however, although they appear to have stabilized in the twenty-first century at 350 to 400 birds, about 10 percent of the 1978 population (Kisiel 2008). Spring migration peaks in mid-April, and, although they disperse along the coast and inland, Glossy Ibis are early fall migrants and are scarce after mid-September. They were formerly rare in winter, but there have been no recent records after December.

WHITE-FACED IBIS *Plegadis chihi*

Rare, but increasing, visitor to the southern part of the state. New Jersey's first White-faced Ibis was discovered at Forsythe NWR, 17 April 1977 (Galli and Penkala 1978), then four more were found in the 1980s. Since 1990, however, there have been more than thirty accepted records, plus numerous undocumented sightings, many of which are probably correct. Almost all reports are from April to August, although one bird spent a week at Cape May in early November 2004. There is one recent record of a bird thought by many to be a hybrid with Glossy Ibis, a cross that has been discussed recently (Arterburn and Grzybowski 2003).

Review Species

White-faced Ibis is a relative newcomer to the state's avifauna, first appearing in 1977. It has occurred annually since 2001, and is most often picked out from the very similar Glossy Ibis in spring and early summer when the white facial border, cherry red eye, and pink facial skin and legs are most noticeable. This bird was present with several others for a month and a half near Cape May Court House and photographed here on 30 May 2006. *Photograph by Karl Lukens.*

ROSEATE SPOONBILL *Platalea ajaja*

Accidental. The first New Jersey record, an immature bird, was noted by a single observer on August 24, 1992, along the Arthur Kill in Linden. Unbeknownst to him, the same bird had been discovered at Goethals Bridge Pond, just two

miles away, and in New York State four days earlier, where it was seen by many observers. The second record, an adult, spent most of the summer and early fall at Forsythe NWR, and was enjoyed by hundreds. In summer 2009, Roseate Spoonbills, including New Jersey's third, a subadult that stayed at Forsythe for more than three months, appeared at several places in the Northeast. (*See photo page 141.*)

24 AUG 1992, LINDEN, UNION CO. (NJBRC 1993-020)
12 JUL–6 OCT 2007, FORSYTHE NWR, ATLANTIC CO. (NJBRC 2008-025; NJPF)
18 JUL–26 OCT 2009, FORSYTHE NWR, ATLANTIC CO. (NJBRC 2010-054; NJPF)

Family Ciconiidae: Storks

WOOD STORK *Mycteria americana*

Casual. There have been twelve accepted records of Wood Stork in New Jersey, the first dating from 10 August 1922 at Cape May, followed the next year by a group of four there (Stone 1937). There followed a twenty-eight-year gap until the next one at Stone Harbor and another twenty-six years for the next at Cape May. Four of the records are from midsummer, the rest are from the fall. Although there were five records from 1999 to 2001, there have been none since. As expected, all of the birds identified as to age have been subadults.

Wood Stork is a casual vagrant to New Jersey from the southeastern U.S. It has occurred only twelve times, always in summer or fall, and always as juveniles or subadults. This immature bird was present for ten days at Cape May, 11–20 November 1994. *Photograph by Karl Lukens.*

Order Falconiformes

Family Cathartidae: Vultures

BLACK VULTURE *Coragyps atratus*

Common resident throughout the state except in the heart of the Pine Barrens, where it is uncommon. Black Vulture is a relative newcomer to New Jersey, the first known nest dating from Tewksbury, Hunterdon County in 1981 (Hanisek 1981). Fables (1955) knew of only eight reports of the species, but they were reported more frequently in the 1960s and then annually from 1972 in ever-increasing numbers. From their foothold in Hunterdon County, Black Vultures rapidly colonized the entire state over the next twenty years. Some appear to migrate past the Hawk Watches in the fall, but most remain year-round. Statewide CBC totals increased from the first two in 1980 to 1,480 in 2006.

TURKEY VULTURE *Cathartes aura*

Common resident throughout. At the beginning of the twentieth century, Turkey Vultures were common in southern New Jersey, but considered rare in the north (Stone 1908). Numbers increased, however, as Griscom (1923) wrote that they were common in the north, but absent as breeders in the eastern part of the state. Today they are widely distributed, although still uncommon nesters in the highly developed northeastern counties. There is a noticeable migration of Turkey Vultures through the state in the fall, but wintering numbers have increased dramatically since the early 1970s, as shown by statewide CBC totals of 142 in 1973 and 4,460 in 2006. Because of the large wintering population, spring migration is inconspicuous.

Family Accipitridae: Osprey, Eagles, Kites, and Hawks

OSPREY *Pandion haliaetus*

Common fall and fairly common spring migrant, fairly common but local summer resident, very rare in winter. Threatened Species in New Jersey. Historically, ospreys were common nesting birds in the state, although shore development had its impact even in the late nineteenth cen-

tury (Stone 1908). By the 1970s, habitat loss, persecution, and pesticide residues had combined to reduce the breeding population from an estimated 500 pairs prior to 1950, to just 68 pairs in 1975 (Frier 1982). A program initiated in 1979 by the ENSP to provide nesting platforms and replace the eggs in unproductive nests with those from healthy populations resulted in a gradual increase in both numbers of pairs and productivity per nest. As of 2009, there were 485 nesting pairs in New Jersey, concentrated along the Atlantic coast and Delaware Bayshore, but spreading steadily northward (Clark 2009). Ospreys are common migrants, both inland and even more so along the coast, from September to October, where the season average at Cape May has increased from about 1,200 in the 1970s to around 2,500 in the 2000s. Some linger into the early winter, with an average of 2 to 3 on CBCs, and there are a very few records of successful overwintering. Returning Ospreys arrive in mid-March, and migration peaks in mid-April. (*See photo page 141.*)

SWALLOW-TAILED KITE *Elanoides forficatus*

Review Species

Rare spring visitor, accidental in fall. There have been about eighty accepted records of Swallow-tailed Kite in New Jersey and numerous other undocumented reports that were probably correct. The first state record occurred in 1857 (Stone 1908), and there were five others in the late nineteenth century. No others were reported until 1940, and by 1972 the total stood at twelve. Since then, this striking species has occurred almost annually, with as many as three or four sightings in some years and a record eight in

Swallow-tailed Kite, surely the most elegant of raptors, is an almost annual visitor to New Jersey from the southeastern U.S. There have been more than eighty occurrences of this species, mainly since the early 1970s. This individual was photographed at Cape May, 22 June 2005. *Photograph by Richard Crossley.*

spring 2010. All records have been of single birds except for two at Morristown in 1887, three together at Cape May, 11 May 2009, and two more there 8 April 2010. Most reports are from April to June, but there is one from late August, five in September, and one in early October.

WHITE-TAILED KITE *Elanus leucurus*

Accidental. The only state record is of a bird found by two lucky observers and photographed, both perched and hunting over a field, at Hidden Valley Ranch, West Cape May, 4 June 1998. Unfortunately, the bird did not linger. The only other records of this species for the East Coast north of North Carolina are from New York (1983), Massachusetts (1910), and Virginia (1988, 1998). All of these reports are from late April to early June (Pochek and Halliwell 2000.

Review Species

4 JUN 1998, WEST CAPE MAY, CAPE MAY CO. (NJBRC 1998-029; NJPF)

One of the least expected rarities of the past few decades was this White-tailed Kite that made a brief appearance at Cape May, 4 June 1998. There have been only four other reports of this species along the Eastern Seaboard north of North Carolina. *Photograph by Al Pochek.*

MISSISSIPPI KITE *Ictinia mississippiensis*

Scarce spring and early summer visitor, rare in late summer, and very rare in fall. Small numbers of Mississippi Kites, mainly immature, are annual visitors to Cape May in spring, but they have also been recorded in many other places throughout the state. Early arrival dates are in late April, but most birds are present from mid-May into early June. There are occasional reports from midsummer into September, and even one for late October. The highest concentration is twelve kites together in Cape May, 19 May 2007, but groups of seven and eight have been seen several times (RNJB). Isolated pairs of Mississippi Kites have nested recently in New Hampshire and Connecticut, but there is still no breeding record for New Jersey.

BALD EAGLE *Haliaeetus leucocephalus*

Uncommon, but increasing, permanent resident, winter numbers augmented by migrant visitors. Scarce spring and uncommon fall migrant. Endangered Species in New Jersey. The recovery of the Bald Eagle is a phenomenal tribute to the efforts of the Endangered and Nongame Species Project. Because of persecution and habitat destruction, they were already declining at the turn of the twentieth

The Bald Eagle, like the Osprey, has made a dramatic recovery from the dreary outlook of the 1970s. From just one nest in the early 1980s, the population grew to 85 territorial pairs in 2009, with many more individuals during the winter (282 birds in the January 2009 New Jersey ENSP official count). Today it is no longer unusual to see a Bald Eagle during a casual day of birding, but the sight is still spectacular. *Photograph by Kevin Karlson.*

century (Stone 1908), and by 1957 there were just 15 nests, all in the southern counties (Bull 1964). Egg-shell thinning due to pesticide residues brought the eagle to the brink of extinction in the lower forty-eight states, and by 1970 there was just one nest in New Jersey; it produced no young for many years. Beginning in 1982, ENSP began a program of incubating eggs and, in 1983, introducing eagles from viable populations (hacking). Thanks to its efforts and the ban on DDT, the Bald Eagle population began to grow. By 1997 there were 14 active nests in the state and in 2009 an amazing 69 active nests and 85 territorial pairs, mostly in the south, but including at least one in eighteen of the twenty-one counties (Smith and Clark 2009). Wintering birds continue to increase as well, with a record 282 found on the January 2009 survey.

NORTHERN HARRIER *Circus cyaneus*

Common fall and fairly common spring migrant, fairly common winter resident, scarce and local summer resident. Endangered Species in New Jersey as breeding bird. Northern Harriers were apparently much more common breeding birds in the state in the early 1900s (Stone 1937) than they are today, when there are probably only a few dozen pairs (Walsh et al. 1999). Most nesting occurs in the salt marshes of Delaware Bay and the Atlantic coast., with a few at scattered inland locations. The prolonged fall migration brings hundreds past the Hawk Watches, especially along the coast, and the winter population, while concentrated mainly along the coast, is well represented inland, as well. Spring migration peaks in early April, but is relatively inconspicuous.

Northern Harrier seems to be on almost everybody's short list of favorite raptors. Although the species is now scarce as a breeding bird, it is still locally fairly common in migration and winter, especially in the coastal marshes and along Delaware Bay. The striking adult male "Gray Ghost" is much less commonly seen than the female and immature. *Photographs by Kevin Karlson.*

SHARP-SHINNED HAWK *Accipiter striatus*

Common fall and fairly common spring migrant, fairly common winter resident, scarce and local summer resident. Although Sharp-shinned Hawks may be found breeding in many parts of the state, as indicated by the map, most nesting is confined to the northwestern counties, where they are present in small numbers at scattered locations. The protracted fall migration usually peaks in early October, with the greatest numbers along the coast, where greater than 85 percent are hatching-year birds (Sibley 1997). Hawk Watch data from Cape May shows a sharp decline starting in the late 1980s, and numbers in recent years have been less than half the long-term average of about 27,000 birds per season (NJB). Part of this decline has been attributed to an increase in birds wintering farther north than their historical wintering grounds in the southeastern U.S. This trend is evident in the CBC data from the northeastern U.S., including New Jersey, and Canada (Bildstein and Meyer 2000, CBC). The spring migration is mainly coastal, and peaks in late April.

COOPER'S HAWK *Accipiter cooperii*

Common spring and common fall migrant, fairly common winter resident, fairly common and increasing summer resident. Cooper's Hawks have always been the most common nesting accipiters in the state, but the past century has been one of ups and downs. Griscom (1923) described them as relatively common breeders in northern New Jersey, but by 1976 they were considered "sadly diminished" (Hanisek 1976) and placed on the state's Threatened Species list. Since that time, they have shown a remarkable recovery and can now be found nesting in almost every corner of the state, from suburban backyards to the forests of the Pine Barrens and northern counties. They are common migrants, especially in the fall along the coast, but have also increased as wintering birds, as reflected by CBC totals. (*See photo page 142.*)

NORTHERN GOSHAWK *Accipiter gentilis*

Scarce and local summer resident, rare to scarce migrant and winter resident in irregular and unpredictable numbers. The first known nest of Northern Goshawk in New

Jersey was discovered in Passaic County in 1964 (Speiser and Bosakowski 1984). After that, the nesting range slowly expanded, to other parts of the Highlands and to the Kittatinny Mountains. During the Atlas, two nests were found in the Pine Barrens, but the species remains a very uncommon breeding bird. The fall migration is mainly in November and highly variable from year to year. Goshawks are rarely encountered in winter and virtually undetected in spring migration.

RED-SHOULDERED HAWK *Buteo lineatus*

Uncommon resident throughout, uncommon migrant in spring, fairly common in fall. Endangered Species in New Jersey as a breeding bird, Threatened Species nonbreeding. Red-shouldered Hawks are widely distributed in small numbers during the nesting season, but are much more common in the northern tier of counties than in the south (Walsh et al. 1999). In the U.S., this species apparently suffered a major decline during the mid- to late 1900s, probably due to habitat destruction, but it has partially recovered and populations appear stable (Dykstra et al. 2008). Fall migration peaks in early November, whereas the less noticeable spring migration peaks in mid-March.

One of our most colorful raptors, Red-shouldered Hawk is an Endangered Species as a breeding bird in New Jersey and a Threatened Species overall. Habitat destruction seems the most plausible explanation for its decline in recent decades. Most Red-shouldered Hawks winter south of New Jersey, but good numbers of adults, such as the one shown here, are seen in fall migration. *Photograph by Kevin Karlson.*

BROAD-WINGED HAWK *Buteo platypterus*

Common fall and uncommon spring migrant, uncommon summer resident, accidental in winter. Broad-winged Hawks nest in dense woodlands and are most common in the northwestern counties and in the Pine Barrens, relatively scarce in the Piedmont and Inner Coastal Plain. They are early migrants, with the bulk of the inland flight occurring in mid-September and sometimes reaching spectacular numbers, such as 18,500 at Scott's Mountain, 14 September 1983; 17,420 at Montclair, 16 September 1988; and 17,491 at Chimney Rock, 20 September 1996. Along the coast, some birds linger into November, and Broad-wings have been recorded on a few CBCs, though most such reports are likely misidentifications. There is one documented record of an overwintering bird. Spring migration is fairly late and is concentrated in mid-April, but it continues into early or mid-June, involving mostly one-year-old birds.

SWAINSON'S HAWK *Buteo swainsoni*

Review Species

Rare fall migrant, accidental at other seasons. There have been more than a hundred reports of Swainson's Hawk in New Jersey since the first state record at Oradell, Bergen County, 22 October 1947 (Bull 1964), the vast majority of them involving immatures at Cape May in September to November. Curiously, Stone (1908, 1937) makes no mention of this species. It was added to the NJBRC Review List in 1996, and the map shows records since 1994. These include one each from May, late June, and late July, the latter an adult photographed in Ocean County in 2008.

Records since 1994

Swainson's Hawk is a rare vagrant to New Jersey from western and central North America, occurring almost annually in fall. Almost all are juveniles seen at Cape May, where they occasionally linger for a few days. This juvenile was an exception by spending three weeks there in November 2009. *Photograph by Karl Lukens.*

RED-TAILED HAWK *Buteo jamaicensis*

Common and widespread resident, common migrant along the coast and mountain ridges, winter numbers augmented by migrants from the north. Red-tailed Hawks have increased substantially in modern times. Stone (1937) reported a nest in Salem County in the 1930s as "the only known nesting record anywhere in southern New Jersey," and Leck (1984) described them as scarce breeding birds. Today they can be found nesting throughout the state, even in urban areas. The prolonged fall migration peaks in early November, whereas the much smaller spring migration is mainly mid-March to mid-April. Statewide CBC totals grew threefold during the 1970s and 1980s, reflecting the increased presence of wintering birds. Two of the western subspecies, *B. j. krideri* and the dark morph *B. j. calurus*, have been reported a few times (Sibley 1997).

Red-tailed Hawk is the most common and conspicuous raptor in New Jersey and is known to almost everyone, even non-birders. Resident birds are joined during the colder months by wintering birds from farther north. The characteristic red tail is not acquired until the bird is two to three years old. *Photograph by Lloyd Spitalnik.*

ROUGH-LEGGED HAWK *Buteo lagopus*

Scarce to uncommon winter resident, scarce fall migrant, rare in spring. Rough-legged Hawks are late migrants, passing the Hawk Watches in small and irregular numbers, mainly in November. Wintering numbers vary considerably, presumably in response to prey availability to the north and west (Bechard and Swem 2002), but CBC totals since 1990 have averaged less than half of the average for the period from 1970 to 1989. In winter, Rough-legged Hawks can be found in open farmland in the north, but more commonly in coastal marshes and the Hackensack Meadowlands.

GOLDEN EAGLE *Aquila chrysaetos*

Scarce fall migrant and rare winter resident and spring migrant. The first migrant Golden Eagles appear along the inland ridges in mid-October, with the peak flight in early to mid-November. The Kittatinny Mountains get the most birds, with an average of about sixty a season at Raccoon Ridge, including one-day maximums of seventeen on several occasions, but they are reliable at the other watches as well. On the coast, Cape May averages thirteen a year, with a peak of thirty-eight in 1996. Very few are encountered in winter, usually along the Delaware Bayshore and in coastal marshes near Forsythe NWR; the statewide CBC average is only three. The rare spring migrants are seen in March and early April.

EURASIAN KESTREL *Falco tinnunculus*

Review Species

Accidental. There have been six reports of this Eurasian falcon in New Jersey, but only one was sufficiently well documented to be accepted. That was a bird captured, photographed, and banded on 23 September 1972 (Clark 1974). The only other records for eastern North America are from Massachusetts in 1887 and 2002, the latter remaining on Cape Cod for more than two weeks; New Brunswick in 1988; and Florida in 2003.

23 SEP 1972. CAPE MAY, CAPE MAY CO. (AB 27[1]:37; NJPF)

Eurasian Kestrel is a widespread falcon of the Eastern Hemisphere that has appeared just five times in eastern North America. The second occurrence, and New Jersey's only record, was a bird banded and photographed at Cape May, 23 September 1972. *Photograph by William S. Clark.*

AMERICAN KESTREL *Falco sparverius*

Fairly common spring and fall migrant, uncommon winter resident, scarce summer resident. Earlier writers considered American Kestrels to be common to abundant residents throughout the state (Griscom 1923, Stone 1937, Leck 1984), but the species has suffered a steep decline both as a nester and as a migrant in the past few decades for reasons that are not clear. The fall migration totals for Montclair and Cape May have dropped by 50 percent for the 2000s compared to the 1980s, and an even sharper decrease has been seen at Sandy Hook in the spring. Statewide CBC totals declined during that same period from an average of 642 per year to just 130. Neighboring New York (Nye 2008) and Pennsylvania (Fazio and Wiltraut 2009) have likewise experienced serious declines in the numbers of both breeders and migrants.

American Kestrel has declined severely in New Jersey in recent decades as a breeding bird, migrant, and wintering species. Reasons for this decline are not clear, but a similar precipitous decline has been noted at all Eastern hawk watches. The male, shown here, is distinguished from the female by silvery-gray wings and fore crown and solid rusty tail with a black subterminal band and white tip. *Photograph by Kevin Karlson.*

MERLIN *Falco columbarius*

Common fall and uncommon spring migrant, scarce, but increasing, winter resident. Merlins are mainly coastal migrants, appearing from late August to November, with a peak in late September to early October. Numbers in-

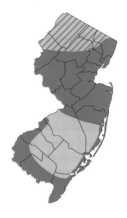

creased substantially at Cape May during the 1980s, with a seasonal high of 2,785 in 1985 and an average of about 1,600 per season since then. Winter records have also increased dramatically, as reflected in CBC totals averaging two to three coast reports in the early 1970s to more than 40 in the late 2000s from many parts of the state. Spring migration is also mainly coastal and peaks in mid- to late April. Merlins have been expanding their breeding range south in New England and upstate New York (Warkentin et al. 2005, McGowan 2008) and may someday breed in New Jersey.

GYRFALCON *Falco rusticolus*

Review Species

Very rare visitor, mainly November to March. There have been eighteen accepted records, primarily from the Kittatinny Mountains and the coast from Forsythe NWR to Cape May. Most of the occurrences have been for one day only, but several have stayed for months, including two at Forsythe in 1972.

There have been fewer than twenty records of Gyrfalcon in New Jersey and only a few have been of the white morph. This individual spent the winter at a golf course in Linwood, Atlantic County, from November 1982 to April 1983. *Photograph by Michael Danzenbaker.*

PEREGRINE FALCON *Falco peregrinus*

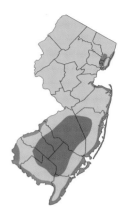

Common fall and scarce spring migrant, uncommon winter resident, scarce and local summer resident. Endangered Species in New Jersey. Peregrine Falcons historically nested in the northern part of the state on cliffs such as the Palisades of the Hudson River, but were extirpated by about 1960. The resident subspecies, *anatum*, plus migrant *anatum* and Arctic *tundrius* were severely impacted by pesticide residues and nearly disappeared from eastern North America (White et al. 2002). With the ban on DDT, populations began a strong recovery, as reflected in the fall migration totals at Cape May from an average of just over a hundred in the late 1970s to over a thousand per season in the 2000s. The successful reintroduction of Peregrine as a breeding species in New Jersey used a hybrid subspecies and placed nests on towers in salt marshes, where the species had never nested historically. Today, the state's fifteen or so pairs nest on large bridges and tall buildings, as well as in the artificial towers. Winter numbers have also increased in recent decades, from a statewide CBC average of about four in the 1970s to about fifty in the 2000s. Peregrine Falcons are seldom noted during spring migration.

Peregrine Falcon is noticeably more common today in New Jersey than it was as recently as 1980. The ban on DDT and a reintroduction program have increased both the resident and migrant populations of this dynamic species. This adult was photographed at Cape May in September 2006. *Photograph by Kevin Karlson.*

Order Gruiformes

Family Rallidae: Rails, Gallinules, and Coots

YELLOW RAIL *Coturnicops noveboracensis*

Review Species

Records since 1900

Very rare spring and fall migrant. There have been almost forty accepted records of Yellow Rail in New Jersey, including twenty-one specimens, but many encounters are not reported to the Records Committee. The majority of the records are from late September to late October, but there are two recent December sightings. There are only two old specimens from the spring, but heightened birder activity has indicated that Yellow Rails may visit regularly in migration along the Delaware Bayshore in April and early May and may be detected by their calling at this season.

The majority of the nearly forty records of Yellow Rail in New Jersey are specimens of birds found dead. This individual was found alive in Beechwood, Ocean County, on 5 October 1989, taken to a rehabilitation facility, and subsequently released. *Photograph by Bob Mitchell.*

BLACK RAIL *Laterallus jamaicensis*

Rare and local summer resident; migrant and winter status poorly known. Threatened Species in New Jersey. Black Rails nest mainly in brackish and saltwater marshes in southern New Jersey, although there is one recent record from a freshwater marsh in Sussex County. Their shy and secretive nature makes them very difficult to locate, but they are clearly far less common today than they were in the early twentieth century. Stone (1937) and Fables (1955) mention two individuals who each located dozens of nests of Black Rail in Ocean, Atlantic, and Cape May counties. Kerlinger and Sutton (1989) heard territorial birds at a few spots along the Atlantic coast, as did the Atlas, but the majority of breeding sites located during the Atlas were on the Delaware Bayshore in Cumberland and Cape May counties. Migration is apparently from mid-March to early May in spring and mid-September to mid-October in fall (Eddleman et al. 1994). There are two reports of Black Rails on CBCs during the past decade, but winter status is essentially unknown. (*See photo page 142.*)

CORN CRAKE *Crex crex*

Review Species

Accidental. The three New Jersey records of this Eurasian rail are all represented by specimens housed in the Academy of Natural Sciences in Philadelphia and date from 1854, 1856, and 1905. This species declined in numbers dramatically during the twentieth century due to changes in farming practices in Europe and is unlikely to occur again in the state. The last U.S. record was a specimen taken on Long Island, NY, in 1963, but a Corn Crake was found dead at St. Pierre on St. Pierre and Miquelon, in the Atlantic south of the province of Newfoundland and Labrador, in 1989. More recent are a well-photographed bird in Nova Scotia in 1997 and a multiple-observer sight record in Newfoundland in 2002.

FALL 1854, SALEM, SALEM CO. (*ANSP) JAN 1856, BRIDGETON,
    CUMBERLAND CO. (*ANSP)
11 NOV 1905, DENNISVILLE, CAPE MAY CO. (*ANSP)

Amazingly, there are three records of Corn Crake (a small rail native to Eurasia), from southern New Jersey. The last of these was shot at Dennisville, Cape May County, 11 November 1905, and the specimen resides in the Academy of Natural Sciences in Philadelphia. *Photograph of specimen by Tom Halliwell.*

CLAPPER RAIL *Rallus longirostris*

Common summer resident, uncommon winter resident, migration rarely observed. Although shooting, egg collecting, and draining of wetlands have reduced the population from colonial times (Stone 1908, 1937), Clapper Rail is still a common denizen of the salt marshes of New Jersey, from the Delaware Bayshore of Salem County to the tidal Hackensack Meadowlands in the north. It is the easiest of our rails to see, as they often forage in the open at places like Forsythe NWR and Turkey Point. Many Clapper Rails apparently migrate south in fall and return in spring, but the species is still regularly encountered in the southern counties in winter.

KING RAIL *Rallus elegans*

Scarce and local summer resident, rare at other seasons. Nests in freshwater marshes and, occasionally, brackish marshes in the southern part of the state, where the similarity of its call to that of Clapper Rail makes positive identification difficult. In addition, these two rails have been known to hybridize where their ranges overlap. King Rail is one of New Jersey's rarest breeding birds, and only the Great Swamp, Walkill River, and Cedar Swamp Creek, Cape May County, areas consistently support nesting populations. Its migration is poorly known and it is very rare in winter; there have been no CBC reports since 1999.

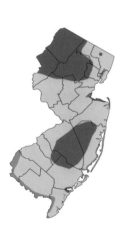

VIRGINIA RAIL *Rallus limicola*

Fairly common but local summer resident, scarce winter resident, occasionally encountered in migration. Like many wetland species, Virginia Rails have declined substantially during the past century, even in areas where suitable habitat is available (Walsh et al. 1999). They prefer freshwater marshes, but can be fairly common in brackish marshes, where they coexist with Clapper Rails. Because of their secretive nature, they are usually detected only by voice, and little is known about their migration. They arrive at breeding sites in April, and most apparently depart between mid-October and mid-November. Two to three dozen are found on CBCs, mainly along the coast, but a few are present at inland marshes that haven't frozen over. It is likely that most of those inland and many along the coast do not make it through the winter

Virginia Rail is an uncommon to fairly common summer resident of fresh and brackish marshes throughout the state. It is usually hard to see as it scurries through thick vegetation, but occasionally one wanders into open view. *Photograph by Lloyd Spitalnik.*

SORA *Porzana carolina*

Uncommon spring and fall migrant, scarce and local summer resident, accidental in winter. Sora is the most abundant and widely distributed rail in North America (Melvin and Gibbs 1996), but it has declined steadily in New Jersey as a breeding bird during the past century (Walsh et al. 1999). Soras nest in freshwater marshes in the Piedmont of Morris County, the Highlands, and Walkill River basin. Unlike our other rails, they are most frequently encountered in migration, especially along the coast and bay shores from August to October and April to May, when they seem to be less shy than at other times. They are seen rarely in early winter, averaging about one every two years on CBCs, but there is only one recent midwinter record (February 2006).

PURPLE GALLINULE *Porphyrula martinica*

Review Species

There have been more than sixty accepted records of this very rare, but almost annual, vagrant from the south. Prior to 1985, the majority of reports were from April to June, but since then about two-thirds have come from the autumn, mainly September and November (Walsh et al. 1999, Hanson 2010). Although there have been a half-dozen records of summering Purple Gallinules in appropriate habitat, there has been no evidence of nesting. A few pairs formerly nested at a site in northern Delaware but disappeared during the 1980s. Most records are from the immediate coast, especially Cape May County, but some birds have appeared far inland in Sussex, Hunterdon, Morris, Bergen, and Passaic counties. There are even three pelagic records of birds that came aboard boats.

Purple Gallinule is a colorful rail common in the southeastern United States. Although it appears to be a weak flyer, it is a long-distance migrant and well known for a widespread pattern of vagrancy well outside the breeding range. It has occurred more than sixty times in New Jersey at all seasons. This yearling was present for over a month in the parking lot of the Wetlands Institute in Stone Harbor in April and May 2004. *Photograph by Richard Crossley.*

COMMON MOORHEN *Gallinula chloropus*

Uncommon and local summer resident, uncommon spring and fall migrant, very rare in winter. Common Moorhens were first discovered nesting in New Jersey at Trenton in 1904 (Stone 1908), but spread to many parts of the state during the early to mid-twentieth century. From the 1960s to 1980s, they were common in Trenton Marsh, Great Swamp NWR, and Hackensack Meadowlands, with several hundred pairs at the latter site. They continue at these sites and others, but the populations are subject to dramatic swings in response to conditions in the freshwater and brackish marshes that they prefer. Southbound migration is mainly in September, and returning birds arrive in late April. Common Moorhens formerly wintered in small numbers at some of the breeding locations, but there have been only two CBC reports since 1996 and just one record after early January.

AMERICAN COOT *Fulica americana*

Very common fall and common spring migrant, common winter resident at ponds and estuaries along the coast and at some inland lakes and reservoirs, scarce and very local summer resident. The first fully documented nesting record of American Coot in New Jersey was at the Newark Marshes in 1907 (Griscom 1923), and Fables (1955) considered the species locally common from Trenton Marsh northward. A population explosion in the 1950s and 1960s produced 300 nesting pairs in 1962 (Bull 1964) and similar numbers persisted into the 1980s (RNJB 9[4]:82). By the time of the Atlas, however, statewide breeding numbers had been reduced to a remnant few pairs, a situation that continues today. Large flocks of fall migrants arrive from mid-October to late November, and many stay to winter. Spring migrants peak in March as soon as open water is available.

Family Gruidae: Cranes

SANDHILL CRANE *Grus canadensis*

Rare spring and fall migrant, rare winter resident. Rare permanent resident in Salem and Cumberland Counties, where a small, but growing, flock (sixteen birds in 2009), descended in part from a hybrid mating of an escaped Common Crane and a wild Sandhill Crane, has been present since the late 1990s (Boyle and Larson 2009). The flock appears to include some pure Sandhill Cranes as well as obvious hybrids. At least one pair of uncertain provenance has nested recently in the vicinity of New Egypt, Ocean County. Stone (1937) cites a record of three Sandhill Cranes at Beesley's Point, Cape May County, in 1857, but he knew of none in his lifetime, and Fables (1955) did not include the species in his list of New Jersey birds. The first modern record was one at Tuckerton, 12 May 1957, followed by two at Cape May Point, 1–6 October 1958. Starting in 1969, reports became more frequent at all seasons, but especially in the fall, and since 1984 the species has been recorded annually, often as many as ten sightings per year from all parts of the state.

Since the mid-1980s, Sandhill Cranes have occurred annually in small numbers in many places throughout the state, and a small flock of uncertain origin is permanently resident in Cumberland County. Most migrant birds are seen in the fall, but some remain for the winter, such as this bird photographed at Cape May, 23 December 2009. *Photograph by Bob Fogg.*

Order Charadriiformes

Family Charadriidae: Plovers

NORTHERN LAPWING *Vanellus vanellus*

Accidental. There have been just two records of this Eurasian plover in New Jersey, both in the south. The first was discovered in a wet field north of Fortescue on 8 March 1953, one week before what was presumably the same bird was found just across the river in Delaware (Arnett 1953). The second was seen by many following its appearance at Goshen on New Year's Day 1997. This species has occurred twice more in Delaware and twice in New York, all during the 1990s.

8 MAR 1953, 20–30 MILES N. OF FORTESCUE, CUMBERLAND CO. (NJBRC 1993-014, AR 1993)
1–4 JAN 1997, GOSHEN, CAPE MAY CO. (NJBRC 1997-013; NJPF)

Northern Lapwing, a plover native to Eurasia, is a very rare vagrant to eastern North America. It has occurred twice in New Jersey, most recently in Goshen, Cape May County, where this individual spent the first four days of 1997. Although this photograph taken on 1 January 1997 is rather distant, the key field marks are evident. *Photograph by Kevin Karlson.*

BLACK-BELLIED PLOVER *Pluvialis squatarola*

One of our most familiar shorebirds, Black-bellied Plovers are very common fall and common spring migrants, and fairly common winter residents along the coast. The protracted fall migration begins with the arrival of the first adults in mid-July, followed by the juveniles in late August, and continues into November. A few appear at inland sod farms and reservoir edges, but the main migration is coastal. They first began wintering in New Jersey in the mid-1900s, but are now regular at that season along the coast. Spring migration, when many are in their spectacular breeding plumage, runs from late April into early June, especially notable on the Delaware Bayshore. A few non-breeders, usually in basic plumage, summer along the coast.

One of our most familiar shorebirds, the Black-bellied Plover spends most of the year in its drab nonbreeding plumage. By mid-May, however, most migrant and wintering birds have molted into their handsome breeding plumage. Returning adults in July are often still in this striking attire, but by August they have begun to fade. *Photograph by Kevin Karlson.*

AMERICAN GOLDEN-PLOVER *Pluvialis dominica*

Uncommon fall and rare spring migrant. Adult American Golden-Plovers, some still in their beautiful breeding plumage, begin to arrive in mid-August, with the majority occurring inland at sod farms and reservoir margins and lesser numbers at preferred coastal sites such as Sandy Hook and Forsythe NWR. Peak flight of adults is in early September, followed by the arrival of juveniles at midmonth, with their peak flight usually in late September. Some migration continues through mid-November. Formerly rare spring transients, American Golden-Plovers increased in numbers during the late twentieth century, but have recently declined to rarity status again.

PACIFIC GOLDEN-PLOVER *Pluvialis fulva*

Accidental. New Jersey's only Pacific Golden-Plover, an adult molting out of breeding plumage, was discovered on 4 September 2001 at the Johnson Sod Farm, a regular site for American Golden-Plover and short-grass–loving sandpipers (Crossley 2002). It remained for almost two weeks,

Review Species

often allowing direct comparison with its close relative. The only previously published record for the eastern U.S. was one collected in Maine in 1911. Subsequently, there has been one in Massachusetts (April–May 2002), one in New York (September 2003), and one in Newfoundland (June–July 2007). A controversial plover in Delaware in July 1989 was originally identified as European Golden-Plover, but later accepted on the State List as Pacific Golden-Plover. (*See photo page 143.*)

4–16 SEP 2001, DEERFIELD, CUMBERLAND AND SALEM COS. (NJBRC 2002-044)

LESSER SAND-PLOVER *Charadrius mongolicus*

Review Species

Accidental. A breeding-plumaged Lesser Sand-Plover (formerly called Mongolian Plover) was discovered at North Wildwood on the morning of 13 July 1990. It disappeared at high tide, then returned that evening on the low tide, but was gone the next morning (Holt 1997). This was the first record for the Atlantic coast and there has been just one, in Rhode Island, since. A disputed sand-plover in interior Virginia in 2009 may prove to be this species.

13 JUL 1990, NORTH WILDWOOD, CAPE MAY CO. (RNJB 16[4]:70)

New Jersey's only record of Lesser Sand-Plover was this breeding-plumaged adult at North Wildwood, Cape May County, on 13 July 1990. It did not allow close approach for better photographs and was gone the next day, much to the chagrin of dozens who went to look for it. *Photograph by Keith Seager.*

WILSON'S PLOVER *Charadrius wilsonia*

Very rare. Wilson's Plovers nested in New Jersey until the 1840s (Stone 1937), then returned as breeders in 1935 (Bull 1964) and nested irregularly in Ocean and Atlantic

Counties for several decades (Fables 1955). The last known breeding attempt was at Holgate in 1963. Since then, there have been sixteen accepted records (Walsh et al. 1999, Hanson 2010), all but one in spring. Except for one each at Sandy Hook and Bivalve, all sightings have come from the shores of Cape May County north to Holgate.

Review Species

Records since 1963

Wilson's Plover last nested in the state in 1963 and has since become a very rare visitor to coastal New Jersey, with records from Cumberland County to Sandy Hook. There was a slight increase in sightings from 1999 to 2007, when nine different birds were documented. This female spent almost three week at Sandy Hook, where this photo was taken on 10 May 2005. *Photograph by Mike Fahay.*

SEMIPALMATED PLOVER *Charadrius semipalmatus*

Common spring and fall migrant, rare winter resident. As with many of our shorebirds, the fall migration of Semipalmated Plovers is quite drawn out. The first adults arrive from the north in early July and the first juveniles in mid-August. Peak numbers occur from late August to mid-September, but migration continues through November. The birds are most common along or near the coast, from the Hackensack Meadowlands to the Delaware Bayshore, but they also occur in small numbers at inland lakes, reservoirs, and even flooded fields and sod farms. A very few winter along the coast from Forsythe NWR to Cape May. The spring migration begins in late April and continues into early June, although a few nonbreeding birds linger through the summer.

PIPING PLOVER *Charadrius melodus*

Uncommon and local summer resident, uncommon spring and fall migrant, accidental in winter. Endangered Species in New Jersey. Piping Plovers nest on open sandy beaches above the high tide line, where development, human traffic, and predators have combined to threaten their continued existence. They are early migrants in spring, often arriving at their breeding locations in early March. At present, about 120 pairs nest in scattered small groups and colonies along the New Jersey coast, with Sandy Hook hosting the largest population. In late summer, small flocks of local birds augmented by migrants gather at favored sites, such as Stone Harbor, but few are seen after mid-September. Piping Plovers are very rare in early December, and CBC records average about one per decade. They are accidental in midwinter. (*See photo page 143.*)

KILLDEER *Charadrius vociferus*

Common and widespread summer resident, spring and fall migrant, fairly common in winter, especially in the southern half of the state. Killdeer are apparently much more common as breeding birds now than they were in the early twentieth century (Griscom 1923, Fables 1955), having adapted to a wide variety of habitats. Fall migration is protracted, but concentrations are seen on sod farms from August to October. Winter numbers, as reflected by CBC totals, are highly variable and probably depend on the degree of snow cover. Spring migration peaks in late March.

Family Haematopodidae: Oystercatchers

AMERICAN OYSTERCATCHER *Haematopus palliatus*

Fairly common, but local, summer and winter resident, fairly common spring and fall migrant. American Oystercatchers were extirpated from New Jersey by 1896 (Griscom1923), but returned at the middle of the last century (Bull 1964). Since that time, they have colonized most of the coast from Ocean County south, as well as portions of the Delaware and Raritan bayshores. Their willingness to utilize marshes, as well as beaches, has contributed to their success. Large migrant flocks gather along the coast in September and October, but many don't leave. Oyster-catchers were rare in winter prior to 1980, but CBC numbers showed a dramatic increase during the next two decades and now average 400 to 500, mainly in Cape May and Atlantic counties. Spring migration is primarily in March.

American Oystercatchers were extirpated from New Jersey during the nineteenth century, but began to return in the mid-twentieth. Today, they can be found nesting along much of the coast, and have even taken to wintering in the bays of Atlantic and Cape May counties, where over 300 individuals have been recorded on some of the recent Cape May CBCs. Numbers drop during mid-winter, but quickly rebound in early spring. This adult feeding two chicks was photographed at Stone Harbor in June 1999. *Photograph by Kevin Karlson.*

Family Recurvirostridae: Stilts and Avocets

BLACK-NECKED STILT *Himantopus mexicanus*

Very rare spring and summer visitor, casual fall visitor. Black-necked Stilts were probably fairly common breeding birds in southern New Jersey in the early 1800s, but the only nesting record in the twentieth century was an unsuccessful attempt at Goshen, Cape May County, in 1993. The vast majority of records are from May and June, perhaps representing overshoots from breeding grounds in Maryland and Delaware. The birds occur annually in ones and twos, primarily from Cumberland to Atlantic counties. Some recent occurrences from the Hackensack Meadowlands in late summer to November fall outside the normal pattern, prompting questions about where those late fall birds originated.

Black-necked Stilts nest as close to New Jersey as southern Delaware and were probably regular breeding birds here in the early nineteenth century, but have not succeeded in re-establishing themselves in the state. They occur annually in very small numbers, mainly in the southernmost counties. This beautiful flight shot shows a female, distinguished from the male by the brownish versus jet black tones on the back. *Photograph by Kevin Karlson.*

AMERICAN AVOCET *Recurvirostra americana*

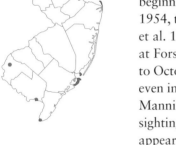

Rare fall and very rare spring migrant, accidental in winter. American Avocets nested in New Jersey in the early 1800s, but were soon extirpated (Stone 1937). There were only five records in the first half of the twentieth century, but beginning with a large influx of forty birds at Fortescue in 1954, the species has been reported annually in fall (Walsh et al. 1999). Most occurrences are of groups of two to ten at Forsythe NWR (especially) or Cape May from late July to October, but some have lingered through November and even into mid-December. There is one January record from Mannington Marsh, a bird that stayed into April. Spring sightings are very unusual, but a flock of fourteen avocets appeared at Forsythe 29–31 May 1992.

Family Scolopacidae: Sandpipers, Phalaropes, and Allies

SPOTTED SANDPIPER *Actitus macularias*

Common spring and fall migrant, uncommon summer resident, very rare in early winter. Spotted Sandpipers are apparently less common breeders in New Jersey now than they were a century ago (Walsh et al. 1999), primarily due to loss of the freshwater wetlands they require for nesting. This is especially true in the southern part of the state. Spring migration runs from late April into early June, but fall migration is early, peaking in late July to early August. Spotted Sandpipers are rare after September, and, although there are occasional CBC records, they are not found in midwinter.

SOLITARY SANDPIPER *Tringa solitaria*

Fairly common fall and uncommon spring migrant through-out. The first Solitary Sandpipers arrive from their tropical wintering grounds in late April. Peak migration is in early May, and by the third week of the month the birds are mostly gone. Southbound migrants can appear as early as late June, but the main flight is from mid-July to early September, with a few stragglers lingering into October. At all seasons, they are much more common inland than along the coast. There is one CBC report from mid-December, but there are no true wintering records.

SPOTTED REDSHANK *Tringa erythropus*

Accidental. There are three accepted records of this Eur-asian shorebird for the state, although there are several ear-lier reports that were not accepted by the Historical Review Committee. All records have come from Forsythe NWR, where the first was found 18 September 1978 (Fahay 1979), and what was most probably the same bird appeared the following year. The last occurrence was one present for only two days at the refuge in 1993. Spotted Redshank has been found twice on Long Island, NY, twice in Massachusetts, and once each in Connecticut and Rhode Island.

Review Species

14–28 SEP 1978, FORSYTHE NWR, ATLANTIC CO. (RNJB 5[1]:11; NJPF)
28 SEP–8 OCT 1979, FORSYTHE NWR, ATLANTIC CO. (RNJB 6[1]:11; NJPF)
22–23 OCT 1993, FORSYTHE NWR, ATLANTIC CO. (RNJB 20[1]:28; NJPF)

Spotted Redshank is a Eurasian shorebird that is a casual vagrant to North America. It has occurred about a dozen times in the Northeast, including three times in New Jersey. All three sightings have come from Forsythe NWR, in 1978, 1979, and—the bird shown here—22–23 October 1993. *Photograph by Brian Moscatello.*

GREATER YELLOWLEGS *Tringa melanoleuca*

Common spring and fall migrant, uncommon winter resident. One of our most familiar shorebirds, southbound Greater Yellowlegs pass through from mid-July (rarely earlier) into early November, with peak numbers at Forsythe NWR and other favored spots occurring in early to mid-October. Variable numbers winter along the coast, depending on the severity of the season, but spring migrants appear as early as mid-March. Peak numbers occur in April, then decline throughout May. Although much more common along the coast than inland, Greater Yellowlegs can be found at wetlands, lakes, and reservoirs around the state during migration, especially in spring. A few are seen during June and early July, but it's difficult to distinguish summering birds from early migrants.

Greater Yellowlegs is a common and familiar shorebird that can be found at favored sites throughout much of the year, especially during migration. The heavily marked breeding plumage shown here is seen primarily in late April and May and again in July and August. The closely related Lesser Yellowlegs is smaller, has a shorter, thinner, finer-tipped bill and less extensive barring on the flanks in breeding plumage. *Photograph by Kevin Karlson.*

WILLET *Tringa semipalmata*

Common summer resident, common spring and fall migrant, scarce but increasing winter resident. Historically, Willets were abundant breeding birds in New Jersey but were extirpated from the Atlantic coast by 1889 (Fables 1955), although some may have persisted along the Delaware Bayshore (Stone 1937). They began to return in the mid-1900s, increased dramatically during the next decades, and are now common during the nesting season in salt marshes from Middlesex County to Salem County, missing only from portions of Monmouth County There are two subspecies, and the Willets that breed in New Jersey, *T. s. semipalmatus*, arrive in mid-April and soon begin nesting. Adults begin to migrate in late June, and most of the East Coast population has passed through by early August. Small numbers of juveniles are found through August, and a few have been seen late as mid-September. Western Willets, *T. s. inornatus*, begin to arrive in small numbers by mid-July, and most individuals encountered after mid-August are *inornatus*. A few Western Willets began to winter at Brigantine Island and Hereford Inlet in the 1990s, and a total of thirty to fifty are now regular winter residents at these sites; there are also a few June records of basic-plumaged nonbreeding Western Willets. Willets are accidental away from the coast.

LESSER YELLOWLEGS *Tringa flavipes*

Common fall and fairly common spring migrant, rare to scarce winter resident. Lesser Yellowlegs, like their larger cousins, are early spring migrants, but are less common than Greater Yellowlegs. Migrants are seen from mid-March to mid-May, with a peak in mid-April. They are scarce, but regular, inland, and are apparently more common on the coast than formerly, as Stone (1937) had only three spring records. Southbound adults arrive as early as late June, and migration peaks in late July or early August, with juveniles an increasing percentage of the flocks. They are more often encountered inland at this season than in the spring. Numbers dwindle during September and October, but a few dozen are typically found on CBCs in December. They become very scarce thereafter.

UPLAND SANDPIPER *Bartramia longicauda*

Scarce to uncommon fall and rare spring migrant, rare and local summer resident. Endangered Species in New Jersey. Upland Sandpipers were once fairly common migrants and breeding birds in New Jersey, but a combination of unrestricted hunting and habitat loss drastically reduced the population during the 1800s and early 1900s (Stone 1908, Griscom 1923). Because their preferred habitat of grasslands and open fields is ephemeral in the state,

they have frequently abandoned nesting areas from one year to the next. Today, they nest only at two sites, an airport and a military base, and are rarely encountered in spring migration. In the southbound migration, small numbers appear at sod farms, mainly in Salem and Cumberland counties, from mid-July to late August, and rarely at other scattered locations, where many birds are simply calling fly-overs.

ESKIMO CURLEW *Numenius borealis*

Presumably extinct. Eskimo Curlews were once common migrants up the Mississippi Valley in spring and offshore along the Atlantic coast in fall. They were apparently rare, but regular, on the New Jersey coast in September and October. Giraud (1844) states that "In New Jersey, New York, Massachusetts, and Rhode Island, this species is seen every season [i. e., fall] . . . It arrives among us in the latter part of August and remains until the first of November." The only specimen record for the state was taken at Manasquan in the summer of 1880 and is in the Denver Museum of Natural History (Iverson and Kane 1975).

WHIMBREL *Numenius phaeopus*

Common spring and fairly common fall migrant, accidental in winter. Whimbrels pass through New Jersey in spring in a compressed migration from mid-April to mid-May, with decreasing numbers through the end of the month. They are exclusively coastal, and prefer the salt marshes to open beaches. Some preferred sites, where hundreds may sometimes be seen, include Shell Bay Landing, Cape May County, Linwood, Atlantic County, and Forsythe NWR. The first southbound migrants, probably failed breeders, appear as early as late June, and numbers peak in late July then diminish through August, as these long-distance migrants head for their wintering grounds in South America. A few are seen in September, but CBC records average about one per decade, and there is a single midwinter record from Nummy Island. A Eurasian subspecies, *N. p. ssp.*, has been recorded about fourteen times (red dots on the map), discounting probable returning individuals, and is on the NJBRC Review List.

LONG-BILLED CURLEW *Numenius americanus*

Accidental. Long-billed Curlews were common migrants in the coastal marshes of New Jersey, both spring and fall, during the first half of the nineteenth century, but declined rapidly due to hunting, and were rare by the 1870s (Stone 1937). Three birds shot in Cape May County from 1880 to 1898 were the last confirmed records in the state until one was seen at Cape May, 9 October 1987. There have been three additional records, including a bird present from 30 September 2002 to 24 April 2003 at several spots in Atlantic and Cape May counties, finally settling in at Wildwood. It returned again the following fall and spent two months at nearby Stone Harbor. More unexpected was a migrant present well inland at Whiting, Ocean County, in October 2003.

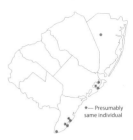

Review Species

Records since 1900

*— Presumably same individual

9 OCT 1987, CAPE MAY, CAPE MAY CO. (RNJB 14[1]:16)
1 SEP 2001, FORSYTHE NWR, ATLANTIC CO. (NJBRC 2002-081)
30 SEP 2002–24 APR 2003, BRIGANTINE, ATLANTIC CO., AND
  AVALON AND NORTH WILDWOOD, CAPE MAY CO. (NJBRC
  2003-058; NJPF)
11 OCT–14 DEC 2003, STONE HARBOR, CAPE MAY CO. (NJBRC
  2004-068)
24–26 OCT 2003, WHITING, OCEAN CO. (NJBRC 2004-067; NJPF)

Long-billed Curlew was once a common migrant along coastal New Jersey, but indiscriminate hunting in the 1800s drastically reduced numbers. There were no records after 1889 until one was seen at Cape May in 1987. From 2001 to 2003, three birds were found, including the one shown here, which was present for seven months from late September 2002 to April 2003 (photo taken 29 March 2003) and returned again the follow autumn for a shorter stay. *Photograph by Al Pochek.*

Review Species

BLACK-TAILED GODWIT *Limosa limosa*

Accidental. Remarkably, New Jersey's only Black-tailed Godwit spent the entire summer at Brigantine (now Forsythe) NWR in 1971. It was in full breeding plumage when it arrived in May and had molted to winter plumage by the time of its departure. At the time, it was only the third occurrence of the species in North America. A rare Bar-tailed Godwit was present during part of that summer, as were Marbled and Hudsonian Godwits. Some observers had the unique experience of seeing all four of the world's godwits on the same day.

22 MAY–13 SEP 1971, FORSYTHE NWR, ATLANTIC CO. (AB 25[4]:717; AB 25[5]:841)

HUDSONIAN GODWIT *Limosa haemastica*

Scarce fall migrant, very rare in spring, accidental inland. In the fall, most Hudsonian Godwits migrate far offshore on their way to southern South America, but a few are found each year along the New Jersey coast, especially at Forsythe NWR. Flocks typically number less than ten, but thirty or more have been seen after storms with strong easterly winds. Most occur between mid-August and mid-September, but occasional stragglers remain through October and even into November. In spring, Hudsonian Godwits migrate through the Great Plains and are very rare to casual on the East Coast. From 1975 to 1999, there were ten spring reports in New Jersey, but there have been none since.

Review Species

BAR-TAILED GODWIT *Limosa lapponica*

Accidental. There have been six accepted records of Bar-tailed Godwit in New Jersey, including one remarkable individual that appeared at Longport, Atlantic County, during late April into May in seven of the eleven years from 1972 to 1982. A bird that summered at Forsythe NWR in 1971 joined the other three Godwit species to mark the only known occurrence of all of the world's godwits at one place at the same time. The most recent visitor, the first in twenty-five years, was also at Forsythe NWR, 13–18 May 2010.

Bar-tailed Godwit is primarily a Eurasian shorebird that also nests in western Alaska. There are six records for New Jersey, including the bird shown here, which appeared in spring at the Longport sod banks in Atlantic County for seven of the eleven years from 1972 to 1982. This photo was taken on its last visit, 22 May 1982. *Photograph by Serge LaFrance.*

MARBLED GODWIT *Limosa fedoa*

Scarce fall and rare spring migrant, rare winter resident. Fall migrant Marbled Godwits, usually in ones or twos, show up in late July and August, especially at Forsythe NWR, but in recent years larger assemblages have gathered at select spots along the coast from September to November. Forsythe, Brigantine Island, and Hereford Inlet are preferred sites, and as many as two dozen have wintered at the latter two in the last two decades. Wintering birds depart early, and Marbled Godwits are rare in spring, with most records from late April to mid-May. Except for occasional sightings in the Hackensack Meadowlands, they are essentially unknown away from the immediate coast. Records of this species have increased greatly in New Jersey and other East Coast states since the 1980s, and it is now far more often seen than Hudsonian Godwit, a reversal of the status prior to 1980.

Marbled Godwit is a tall, handsome shorebird that breeds in the prairie grasslands of the western United States and southern Canada. It is a scarce migrant in New Jersey, mainly in fall, but has increased markedly in occurrence since the 1980s. In recent years, small flocks have wintered most years at Brigantine Island, Atlantic County, and Hereford Inlet, Cape May County. *Photograph by Kevin Karlson.*

RUDDY TURNSTONE *Arenaria interpres*

Common spring and fall migrant, fairly common winter resident. The main spring migration of Ruddy Turnstones, from mid-May to early June, is tied to the abundance of horseshoe crab eggs along the Delaware Bayshore in late spring. Tens of thousands of turnstones mingle with Sanderlings, Red Knots, and Semipalmated Sandpipers in an awesome feeding frenzy that has, unfortunately, diminished in recent years. Summering nonbreeders, rare but annual in very small numbers, are joined by the first fall migrants in early July. Migration peaks in August, with numbers gradually dwindling through November to the modest winter population. Ruddy Turnstones are very rare migrants away from the coast.

RED KNOT *Calidris canutus*

Locally common spring and uncommon fall migrant, uncommon winter resident. Threatened Species in New Jersey. Spring migrant Red Knots, even more than Ruddy Turnstones and Sanderlings, are critically dependent on the horseshoe crab eggs of Delaware Bay, as virtually the entire eastern population (*C. c. rufa*) of the species stops there

Almost the entire population of the eastern subspecies (*C. c. rufa*) of Red Knot pauses on its northward migration in late spring to feed on horseshoe crab eggs in Delaware Bay. This has left them vulnerable to the overharvesting of the crabs, and the spectacular concentrations of former years have not been seen in the past two decades; the over 80 percent decline in numbers has been documented by an international research team. Efforts are underway to help this attractive species recover its former numbers. *Photograph by Kevin Karlson.*

between late April and early June (Sibley 1997, Harrington 2001) on the way to Arctic breeding grounds. Due, at least in part, to the overharvesting of the crabs and subsequent decline in their population, the number of Red Knots feeding in Delaware Bay has dropped by as much as 80 percent during the past two decades. In addition to the Bayshore, knots are seen along the outer coast during May and again on their return in late July and August. Variable numbers remain on the beaches and mudflats of Atlantic and Cape May counties throughout the winter, with a peak of 998 on the 2001 Cape May CBC.

SANDERLING *Calidris alba*

Abundant spring and fall migrant, common winter resident. Sanderlings are common on New Jersey beaches throughout the year, except for a couple of weeks in mid- to late June when only small numbers of lingering non-breeders are present. Large concentrations gather on the Delaware Bayshore in late spring to feed with Ruddy Turnstones and Red Knots on horseshoe crab eggs, but at other seasons they are primarily found on the outer beaches. Southbound migrants appear in early July, but peak migration is difficult to discern, as Sanderlings are always common on the beaches, although much less so in winter than in migration. They are rare inland, with most occurrences involving migrants in August and September.

SEMIPALMATED SANDPIPER *Calidris pusilla*

Abundant spring and fall migrant. Semipalmated Sandpipers are the most common shorebirds seen in New Jersey during fall migration. The first adults arrive in early July, with peak numbers seen into early August. Juveniles follow in mid-August and outnumber adults by September, when many thousands of Semipalmated Sandpipers gather at Forsythe NWR and other favored stopovers, mainly along the coast, although they can be fairly common inland as well. A few spring migrants appear in late April, but the bulk of the flight occurs from mid-May to early June, when many thousands gather to feed on horseshoe crab eggs on the Delaware Bayshore. Semipalmated Sandpipers are much less common inland in spring than in the fall. A few nonbreeders linger into late June, but are soon outnumbered by returning migrants.

WESTERN SANDPIPER *Calidris mauri*

Common fall migrant, scarce winter resident, casual spring migrant. The first migrant adult Western Sandpipers arrive in early to mid-July followed a month later by the first juveniles. Peak numbers occur in late August and early September, when both age groups are present, and may reach several thousand at preferred sites, such as Forsythe NWR. They are scarce but regular inland, and much more common in southern New Jersey than in the north. Many linger through the fall, and variable numbers are found in winter, although most move farther south in severe weather. Records from March and April are probably birds that wintered in the state or nearby, but true spring migrants are casual in May. A few nonbreeders have been seen in June at Stone Harbor Point several times since 2000.

Western Sandpiper is a fairly common fall migrant along the New Jersey coast, with the first adults arriving from the western Arctic breeding grounds in July, followed by juveniles a month later. Juveniles, such as the bird pictured here, are told from young Semipalmated Sandpipers by the orange tones to the scapulars a longer, slightly drooped bill (females), a larger, puffier head and more chest-heavy weight distribution. *Photograph by Kevin Karlson.*

RED-NECKED STINT *Calidris ruficollis*

Review Species

Accidental. There have been just three accepted records of this primarily Asian species, all from the southern part of the state and all of adults in late summer. The difficulty of detecting this species among the thousands of peeps that migrate through sites such as Forsythe NWR, where the first was found (Nixon and Lesser 2000), makes it likely that they occur more often than is known. In addition, the problem of separating juveniles or nonbreeding adults from the more common species further compounds the uncertainty of determining the frequency of occurrence. (*See photo page 144.*)

15–17 AUG 1999, FORSYTHE NWR, ATLANTIC CO. (NJBRC 1999-023; NJPF)
21 JUL 2003, WILDWOOD CREST, CAPE MAY CO. (NJBRC 2004-083)
30 AUG 2008, WILDWOOD CREST, CAPE MAY CO. (NJBRC 2009-051)

LITTLE STINT *Calidris minuta*

Accidental. The three occurrences of this Eurasian species have all been adults in breeding plumage in July. Even more so than the preceding species, the difficulty of picking out an individual among flocks of the common peeps makes finding a Little Stint a particular challenge. The problem is further compounded by the superficial similarity of bright juvenile Least Sandpipers, which are often misidentified as this species in late July and August.

22–24 JUL 1985, FORSYTHE NWR, ATLANTIC CO. (NJBRC AR 1991)
11–18 JUL 1999, CAPE MAY, CAPE MAY CO. (NJBRC 1999-024)
9–10 JUL 2003, STONE HARBOR, CAPE MAY CO. (NJBRC 2004-032)

Little Stint is a Eurasian sandpiper closely related to Red-necked Stint. Identification of stints is very tricky, and bright juvenile Least Sandpipers are often confused with this species. There have been three confirmed records in New Jersey—all involving adults—including this individual present at Stone Harbor, 9–10 July 2003, and photographed on the second day. In the right hand photo, note the longer primary extension and rusty back of the Little Stint compared to the salt-and-pepper Semipalmated Sandpiper, not in full breeding plumage, to its right. *Photographs by Scott Elowitz.*

LEAST SANDPIPER *Calidris minutilla*

Common spring and fall migrant, very rare winter resident. Like many of our other shorebirds, the first southbound adult Least Sandpipers arrive in early July and numbers peak in early August, when the adults are joined by juveniles. They become less common after mid-September, but a few remain into December. Least Sandpipers prefer drier or grassy areas compared to the other peeps and are fairly common inland on sod farms and reservoir edges. A few are recorded each year on CBCs, but they are very rare in midwinter. Spring migration runs from early April to early June, with a peak in early to mid-May. The occasional birds seen in late June may be nonbreeders or early returning migrants.

WHITE-RUMPED SANDPIPER *Calidris fuscicollis*

Fairly common fall and uncommon spring migrant. The largest of our regularly occurring peep, White-rumped Sandpipers arrive later in fall migration than the more common ones, with the first adults arriving in late July or early August and juveniles not until September. Numbers are highest after northeasterly winds and rain, and they are often found inland after such storms. Numbers dwindle into November, and, other than a few early CBC reports, there are no winter records. White-rumped Sandpipers tend to be less common in spring, appearing, often mixed with Semipalmated Sandpipers, along the Delaware Bay-shore and at Forsythe NWR, rarely inland, from mid-May to early June.

The largest of our regularly occurring peep, White-rumped Sandpiper is an un-common migrant in late spring, when it is wearing the fresh breeding plumage shown by this bird photo-graphed in early June at Stone Harbor Point. Early re-turning birds in late July or August show some of this plumage, but soon molt into their winter dress. *Photograph by Kevin Karlson.*

BAIRD'S SANDPIPER *Calidris bairdii*

Scarce fall migrant. Juvenile Baird's Sandpipers are scarce, but regular, fall migrants to New Jersey. They appear at sod farms, on grassy edges of reservoirs and impoundments, especially Forsythe NWR, but rarely on beaches. Most re-cords are between mid-August and mid-September, but stragglers are sometimes found in October. There is one well-documented mid-December occurrence on the Cape May CBC, but there are no winter records. Adults are very rare, as they migrate primarily through the Great Plains and Mountain West both spring and fall.

PECTORAL SANDPIPER *Calidris melanotos*

Common fall and fairly common spring migrant. Pectoral Sandpipers are common inland, preferring wet fields, sod farms, and the grassy edges of reservoirs and impoundments. Southbound Pectorals show an even more pronounced difference in the movement of adults and juveniles than other shorebirds. Adults begin arriving in late July and peak in mid- to late August. Most have departed before the juveniles appear between mid-September and mid-October. Pectoral Sandpipers migrate early in spring, with several recent records for late March at Cape May, where Stone (1937) never recorded one in spring. Numbers vary considerably from year to year, but peak in early to mid-April at inland locations such as Pedricktown Marsh. They are scarce after early May.

SHARP-TAILED SANDPIPER *Calidris acuminata*

Accidental. There have been two accepted records of this Asian vagrant in New Jersey, both of juveniles in the fall. The first was discovered at Stone Harbor in 2002, a year in which several Sharp-tailed Sandpipers appeared in the Northeast (Fialkovich and Hess 2003); unfortunately, the bird remained for only an hour. The second was a more cooperative bird that lingered at a Cumberland County sod farm for three days in September 2003.

Review Species

8 OCT 2002, STONE HARBOR, CAPE MAY CO. (NJBRC 2003-057; NJPF)
3–5 SEP 2003, JOHNSON SOD FARM, CUMBERLAND CO. (NJBRC 2004-073; NJPF)

There are just two records of Sharp-tailed Sandpiper in New Jersey, both of juvenile birds in fall. A vagrant from Asia, it closely resembles Pectoral Sandpiper. This bird on the left was present for just one hour at Stone Harbor, 8 October 2002, while the one on the right was at a Cumberland County sod farm, 3–5 September 2003. *Photographs by Kevin Karlson (left) and Karl Lukens (right).*

PURPLE SANDPIPER *Calidris maritima*

Fairly common winter resident. The first fall Purple Sand-pipers arrive from their high Arctic breeding ground in mid-October, rarely earlier, and become fairly common in November. They winter on jetties along the coast from Sandy Hook to Cape May, occasionally visiting the lower Hudson River in the north and Reed's Beach in the south. Interestingly, because of their preference for rocky shore-lines, Purple Sandpipers did not winter in New Jersey prior to the construction of rock jetties in the early 1920s (Stone 1937, Walsh et al. 1999), but the statewide CBC average is now about 400. They linger in spring into mid-May, occasionally later, before departing for the Far North. There are no recent reports of summering nonbreeders.

DUNLIN *Calidris alpina*

Abundant fall migrant and winter resident, common spring migrant. A few Dunlin, probably nonbreeders or failed breeders, are seen along the coast in summer, especially at Stone Harbor, but the main fall migration begins in mid-September and peaks in late October to early November. They are regularly seen inland at this season, much more so than in spring. Many thousands winter at beaches and tidal mudflats near the coast, and statewide CBCs average 15,000 to 20,000. Spring migration peaks in early May, as the Dunlin are molting into breeding plumage, and large concentrations can be seen at mudflats and impoundments at Forsythe NWR, Heislerville WMA, and similar locations.

Review Species

Records since 1996

CURLEW SANDPIPER *Calidris ferruginea*

Rare vagrant from Eurasia. Curlew Sandpipers have been reported in small numbers in New Jersey every year but three since 1950, but the frequency of reports declined in the 1990s, and the species was added to the Review List in 1996. Since then there have been twenty-one accepted re-cords, some involving two to three birds, and several un-documented reports. Almost all records are of adults in full or partial breeding plumage in May or July into August. Historically, the vast majority of reports has been from Forsythe NWR, but recently Heislerville WMA has been a favored spot in spring. The only inland record is also the one confirmed juvenile, a bird present at Columbus, Burlington County, 8 September 1996. (*See photo page 144.*)

STILT SANDPIPER *Calidris himantopus*

Fairly common and local fall and rare spring migrant, primarily along the coast from southern Ocean County to eastern Cumberland County. Also regular at Sandy Hook and the Hackensack Meadowlands. Very rare inland except at Spruce Run Reservoir in early autumn. In the fall, adult numbers peak in late July to early August, followed by mainly juveniles in late August to early September. Stragglers occur into October and, very rarely, early to mid-November. A few individuals are found each spring, mainly late April into May, most often along the Delaware Bayshore of Cumberland County. There is a 30 March 1993 record from Oldman's Creek and a 31 March 2010 record from Sandy Hook.

BUFF-BREASTED SANDPIPER *Tryngites subruficollis*

Scarce to uncommon fall migrant. Almost all of the Buff-breasted Sandpipers seen in New Jersey are juveniles, as most adults migrate through the Great Plains both spring and fall. The main passage is from mid-August to mid-September, when they are seen on sod farms and the grassy edges of reservoirs and impoundments, rarely on upper beaches. Occasionally, unusual weather patterns can produce a fallout of high numbers, such as eighty-nine at Forsythe NWR on 8 September 1995 and sixty-six at Cape May on 2 September 1981 (Walsh et al. 1999). Stragglers are sometimes encountered into early October. (*See photo page 145.*)

RUFF *Philomachus pugnax*

Rare spring and fall migrant. Ruffs are rare visitors from Eurasia. Stone (1937) reported a single specimen from the nineteenth century, and Fables (1955) knew of just five sight records from 1932 to 1952, but a few have been reported annually since the late 1950s. Most spring records have come from Salem and Gloucester counties, especially Pedricktown, where Ruffs began appearing regularly in 1978, peaking at twelve birds in April 1985, but declining since then to about one a year. Many were males in their spectacular breeding plumage. Fall sightings are mainly along the Atlantic coast from mid-July into September, rarely into October. Only a few of the fall records involve juveniles.

Ruff is a Eurasian shorebird that occurs as a rare vagrant in North America, especially along the East and West Coasts. It exhibits the most pronounced sexual dimorphism, both in size and appearance, of any shorebird. The male may appear in a wide variety of colors and patterns, but the female, or Reeve, is also distinctive in fresh breeding plumage. This heavily marked female was photographed at Reeds Beach, Cape May County, 19 May 2005. *Photograph by Kevin Karlson.*

SHORT-BILLED DOWITCHER *Limnodromus griseus*

Very common fall and common spring migrant, very rare winter resident. Adult Short-billed Dowitchers are the first fall migrant shorebirds to arrive in large numbers, beginning in late June and peaking in mid- to late July. Juveniles follow during August, and numbers of both age groups diminish during September. Two subspecies occur, with *L. g. griseus* being the more common, while the more colorful *L. g. hendersoni* represent 10 to 20 percent (Sibley 1997) and occur mainly as southbound migrants in July and August. A few Short-billed Dowitchers linger into early winter, but are very rare in midwinter. Spring migrants, almost exclusively *L. g. griseus*, arrive in mid-April and peak in early May. The species is rare inland, especially in spring. Small numbers of nonbreeders summer at selected sites, such as Stone Harbor.

LONG-BILLED DOWITCHER *Limnodromus scolopaceus*

Uncommon fall and casual spring migrant, very rare winter resident. Long-billed Dowitchers nest only in extreme

northwestern North America and eastern Russia, and arrive in New Jersey a month later than their Short-billed cousins. The first adults appear in late July followed by the juveniles in September, and the largest numbers of the species are encountered from late September to mid-October, especially at Forsythe NWR. Although this is the "inland" species of dowitcher over most of the country, they are seldom seen away from the coast in New Jersey. A few Long-billed Dowitchers are seen on CBCs every year, and a dowitcher found in January to March is more likely to be this species, although both occur. They are casual during spring migration in late April to early May and not found every year.

WILSON'S SNIPE *Gallinago delicata*

Fairly common spring and fall migrant, scarce winter resident, very rare and local summer resident. There have been very few confirmed nesting records of Wilson's Snipe in New Jersey, but courting birds in mid- to late May at Walkill River and Great Swamp suggest breeding at these locations. They are widespread migrants from late July to early November, usually in small groups, and some remain into the winter, especially in the southern counties. Statewide CBC totals average about seventy-five, but have declined in recent years. Wilson's Snipe are early migrants throughout the state in spring, mainly mid-March to early May, and are often seen in concentrations of dozens to a hundred or more at favored stopovers such as Mannington Marsh and Pedricktown.

EURASIAN WOODCOCK *Scolopax rusticola*

Review Species

Accidental. There are two records of this vagrant from Eurasia: one collected in Monmouth County in 1859 and the second a bird seen by numerous observers at Goshen in 1956. This species was reported during the 1800s twice in eastern Canada, twice in Pennsylvania, and once each in Alabama and Virginia. The only other twentieth-century record is from Ohio in 1937.

6 DEC 1959, SHREWSBURY, MONMOUTH CO.
2–9 JAN 1956, GOSHEN, CAPE MAY CO. (NJBRC AR1996)

AMERICAN WOODCOCK *Scolopax minor*

Fairly common migrant and summer resident, uncommon in winter. American Woodcocks nest throughout the state, but require fields adjacent to woodlands and are more common in the northern tier of counties. Migration is difficult to detect because of their secretive nature, but concentrations are found at Cape May in November. In winter, they are found in small numbers, especially in the southern counties, but are vulnerable to hard freezes, ice storms, and heavy snowfalls, which limit their ability to probe the ground for food. Statewide CBCs average about a hundred. In spring, American Woodcocks are back on their breeding grounds by late February or early March.

The American Woodcock is a bizarre-looking shorebird of wet woodlands, with eyes set far back on the head to provide rearward binocular vision and a long bill specialized for feeding on earthworms. This individual has clearly been successful in its search for food during a cold snap in Cape May in February 2005. *Photograph by Kevin Karlson.*

WILSON'S PHALAROPE *Phalaropus tricolor*

Scarce fall and very rare spring migrant. Most Wilson's Phalaropes migrate through the Great Plains, both spring and fall, and few make it to the East Coast. Southbound adult females have been seen already in mid-June and adult males a few weeks later, but most New Jersey records are of juveniles from mid-August through September, occasionally in October. The vast majority of fall reports are from Forsythe NWR. Spring records, mid-May to early June, have come from a variety of places, but Wilson's Phalaropes are very rare at that season and not recorded every year.

RED-NECKED PHALAROPE *Phalaropus lobatus*

Rare to scarce fall and rare spring migrant onshore, much more numerous offshore. Red-necked Phalaropes are pelagic during migration and winter, but are recorded annually onshore in fall, mainly in August and September. Most records are from Forsythe NWR, but they are occasionally found inland at this season. In spring, they have been recorded from 1 May to 6 June onshore, usually in singles or pairs, but sometimes in flocks of up to a dozen in association with large coastal storms. The infrequent pelagic trips in late May regularly encounter small flocks well offshore.

RED PHALAROPE *Phalaropus fulicarius*

Very rare spring and fall migrant onshore, uncommon to common but irregular offshore spring and fall, rare and irregular offshore in winter, mainly December. Red Phalaropes are highly pelagic and spend most of their lives far out at sea, except during the short breeding season. Fall records from land are mostly from September and October, whereas spring sightings occur from early April into early June. Although this is not a Review Species due to its frequency at sea, the map highlights land-based reports since 1996. Offshore, Red Phalaropes are sometimes seen in midwinter, but the largest concentrations occur in late fall and spring, the state record being an estimated 17,000 about fifty miles east of Atlantic City, 18 April 1980 (Walsh et al. 1999, RNJB 6[3]:46).

Records since 1996

Away from its breeding grounds on the high Arctic tundra, Red Phalarope is highly pelagic and rarely seen on land. This juvenile bird was at Cape May, 15 September 1999. *Photograph by Kevin Karlson.*

Family Laridae: Gulls, Terns, and Skimmers

LAUGHING GULL *Leucophaeus atricilla*

Abundant but local breeding bird, very rare winter visitor. Laughing Gulls nest in large colonies in the salt marsh along the Atlantic coast of Cape May, Atlantic, and southern Ocean counties, but roam widely in search of food in migration as well as during the breeding season. Once nearly extirpated from New Jersey by hunting, they recovered strongly, although aerial surveys showed a decline from roughly 54,000 adult Laughing Gulls in 1979 to 39,000 in 1995. Numbers diminish along the coast in October and November, with only a few remaining to be tallied on CBCs in mid- to late December. Likewise, a few can sometimes be found on the Delaware River at Florence until late November. They are rarely encountered in January or February, but returning birds are seen in early March and are common by the end of the month. Large numbers gather on the Delaware Bayshore in late spring to feed on horseshoe crab eggs in competition with shorebirds.

Laughing Gull is our most common nesting gull, although it was nearly extirpated from the state by hunting during the nineteenth century. Adults arrive in early spring already wearing their handsome breeding plumage, as shown by the bird on the right. By late summer, the adults have started to lose their red bill and black hood, but the begging youngsters don't seem to mind. *Photographs by Kevin Karlson.*

FRANKLIN'S GULL *Leucophaeus pipixcan*

Very rare. Franklin's Gulls migrate through the middle of North America both spring and fall and are very rare vagrants to the East Coast. The first New Jersey record came from North Arlington in February 1975 (Kane and Roche 1975), but there have been many reports and more than twenty accepted records since then. Most records are from September to November, but they have been reported in every month but March, most often in Cape May County. In addition to the sightings indicated on the map, there have been a similar number of undocumented, but likely correct, reports. All records have been of single birds, except for a group of three at Cape May in 2005 and an unprecedented storm-driven invasion of fifty-plus birds from Avalon to Cape May, 14–15 November 1998.

Review Species

Franklin's Gull is a very rare vagrant that has occurred almost annually in New Jersey over the past few decades. Individuals can show up at any time of the year, but are most frequent in autumn, when they migrate from mid-continent to South America. Perhaps surprising for a vagrant, adults are more frequently seen than young birds, but this first-cycle Franklin's Gull spent the winter of 1994–1995, seen here on 30 January 1995, at a McDonald's fast food restaurant in Atlantic City. *Photograph by Shawneen Finnegan.*

LITTLE GULL *Hydrocoloeus minutus*

Rare to scarce spring and fall migrant, rare winter visitor. Little Gulls are more frequent in spring than in fall, and are usually found as individuals or small groups in larger flocks of Bonaparte Gulls from late February to early May, mainly at Cape May, Sandy Hook, and Spruce Run. During the 1960s and 1970s, they were regular, with a maximum of seventeen, at South Amboy and Jersey City, but they are seldom seen in those places today. Nonbreeders have lingered through the summer, but fall migrants don't appear until November and early December. Little Gulls were formerly more common in winter, especially in the lower Hudson River, and were recorded annually on CBCs during the 1970s and early 1980s, but have been found in only seven years since 1986.

Little Gull is a rare migrant and winter visitor to the state, but is now much less numerous than it was during the 1960s and 1970s. It is most often seen with flocks of Bonaparte's Gulls, especially in late winter and early spring, as was the bird on the right, which was photographed at Cape May on 19 February 2009. The immature bird on the left was present at Cape May, 21 September 2005. *Photographs by Richard Crossley (left) and Bob Fogg (right).*

BLACK-HEADED GULL *Chroicocephalus ridibundus*

Rare migrant and winter resident. This abundant Eurasian species also nests in small numbers in Newfoundland and winters south along the Atlantic coast. Black-headed Gull was first discovered in New Jersey on the shore of Raritan Bay on 21 November 1948. By the mid-1950s they were recorded annually, and the numbers climbed to a peak in the mid-1970s but have declined sharply since then. Most records are from November to March, with occasional migrants seen in March and April and again in October. State-wide CBC totals reached twenty-six in 1975, but Black-headed Gulls have been found on only four CBCs since 1995. Caven Cove in Jersey City was the best place to find one, but they are rarely encountered there anymore. More recently, one or two have been regular at Cape May in late winter.

BONAPARTE'S GULL *Chroicocephalus philadelphia*

Locally common spring and fall migrant, uncommon winter resident, rare in summer. A few Bonaparte's Gulls, usually immatures, are found around the state in summer and the first fall migrants show up in late August, but the main push of southbound birds occurs from late October into early December. Migration is mainly along the coast, but the birds are regular inland on large lakes and reservoirs. Bonaparte's Gulls are much less common in winter now than they were in the mid-1970s, when CBC totals averaged about 10,000. In recent years, only 1,000 to 3,000 have been counted, and most of these move on after the New Year. Spring migrants are seen as early as late February, but the peak flight is in mid-April, when they are more common inland than in the fall.

BLACK-TAILED GULL *Larus crassirostris*

Accidental. The occurrence of this native of the northern Pacific coast of Asia has been confirmed twice in New Jersey, but the exact number of birds is uncertain. An adult was discovered at Cape May on 3 December 1998, and it, or a different one according to some observers, was seen there seven days later, but not in between. One month later, an adult Black-tailed Gull was found at Point Pleasant, almost a hundred miles to the north. It showed features similar to those of the first Cape May bird, but whether it was the same individual will never be known (Sullivan 2002).

Review Species

3–10 DEC 1998, CAPE MAY, CAPE MAY CO. (NJBRC 1998-080)
10–11 JAN 1999, POINT PLEASANT, OCEAN CO. (NJBRC 1998-101; NJPF)

Black-tailed Gull is native to the northern Pacific Coast of Asia, but has now been seen in most Atlantic Coast states. New Jersey's two records occurred just one month and a hundred miles apart and may represent just one bird. This adult was present at Manasquan Inlet, Ocean County, 10–11 January 1999 and is shown here on the second day. *Photograph by Chris Williams.*

RING-BILLED GULL *Larus delawarensis*

Abundant winter resident, common migrant, uncommon to scarce in summer. Subadult and nonbreeding Ring-billed Gulls are present all summer, but they are not known to

nest in New Jersey. The first returning migrants may appear in late July, but the peak flights occur in late October and early November. These gulls winter commonly throughout the state, are abundant on inland lakes and reservoirs, and are especially partial to fast-food restaurant parking lots. Their numbers have increased substantially in recent decades, with an average of 50,000 tallied on CBCs from 2000 to 2009. Spring migration peaks from late March to early April.

CALIFORNIA GULL *Larus californicus*

Review Species

Accidental. There are just three records of this vagrant from western North America, but it may occur more frequently than evidence suggests due to its similarity to Ring-billed and Herring gulls. The first two were accepted on the basis of detailed written descriptions of birds seen on the New Jersey side of the Delaware River opposite the huge Tullytown, PA, dump that attracts many thousands of gulls in winter. The most recent record was a near adult photographed on the beach at Cape May on the surprising date of 28 June 2007; there are summer records for nearby states.

12 MAR 1997, FLORENCE, BURLINGTON CO. (NJBRC 1997-016)
10 NOV 2001, FLORENCE, BURLINGTON CO. (NJBRC 2002-046)
28 JUN 2007, CAPE MAY, CAPE MAY CO. (NJBRC 2008-011; NJPF)

HERRING GULL *Larus argentatus*

Abundant winter resident, common migrant, and common but local summer resident. First recorded nesting in New Jersey in 1946 (Fables 1955), Herring Gulls have become common breeding birds along the coast from Ocean to Cape May counties, with one colony on the Arthur Kill, Union-Middlesex counties. About 4,000 individuals were counted in colonies on a recent aerial survey (CWS 2007), although this is a decline from the peak of almost 10,000 in 2001, but many subadults summer, as well. Fall migration is difficult to discern, but the population swells to an average of more than 60,000 on CBCs, with many more clearly uncounted. Spring migration also goes largely unnoticed as the numbers gradually dwindle in March and April.

THAYER'S GULL *Larus thayeri*

Review Species

Accidental. There have been eleven accepted records of this difficult-to-identify species in New Jersey, all but four from Florence, Burlington County, on the Delaware River opposite the huge Tullytown, PA, dump. The first documented record was at Thompson's Beach, Cumberland County, in 1997 (Bardon and Lehman 1998). Unfortunately, the similarity of Thayer's Gull to Kumlien's Gull, the eastern North American race of Iceland Gull, makes positive identification of the species a serious challenge. Only a few of the records have been documented by compelling photographs, but detailed descriptions of the others have been deemed convincing.

Thayer's Gull is a difficult-to-identify species that appears intermediate in plumage between Iceland and Herring Gulls, but is actually easiest to identify during its first year. This first-cycle bird, the first of the eleven accepted records for New Jersey, was present for four days at Thompson's Beach, Cumberland County, and is pictured here on the last day, 27 May 1997. *Photograph by Paul Lehman.*

ICELAND GULL *Larus glaucoides*

Scarce migrant and winter resident. Most Iceland Gulls seen in New Jersey are immatures, especially first-winter birds, and they are usually found among concentrations of other large gulls at landfills, large lakes and reservoirs, and along the Atlantic coast at ponds and on the beaches and jetties. They are seldom seen before late November and are most common in February and March, with some lingering into April, May, and even early June. Florence, on the Delaware River, has had the highest numbers in recent decades, sometimes a dozen or more, and the Sussex County landfill has been a reliable spot for the species. Overall, however, the numbers of Iceland Gulls wintering in the state appear to have declined from the peaks in the 1970s.

LESSER BLACK-BACKED GULL *Larus fuscus*

Uncommon to scarce winter resident, except at Florence, Round Valley, and Spruce Run, where it is sometimes common. Uncommon migrant, and scarce summer resident. The status of Lesser Black-backed Gull has changed dramatically in New Jersey since the mid-1980s. Up to that time, it was considered a relative rarity, seen predominantly on the North Shore ponds. With the discovery of the huge concentrations of gulls at Florence, opposite the Tullytown, PA, landfill, birders began seeing more and more of this species, including all age groups. Adjacent Bucks County, PA, has become the Lesser Black–backed capital of North America. In recent years, large groups of up to fifty or more have been regular at Round Valley and Spruce Run, and a day's birding along the coast will usually turn up a few. They are now regular in small numbers during summer as well, especially in Cape May, where more than a dozen could be found together in July and August 2008. Interestingly, the first North American sight record of this species was at Long Beach Island, 9 September 1934.

Lesser Black-backed Gull, a Eurasian species, was considered a rarity in New Jersey as recently as the mid-1980s. Since that time, it has become sufficiently regular that one expects to see a few on a winter birding trip, and a few nonbreeders may appear in summer. The two birds pictured here are an adult on the right, just losing its winter hood, and a third-cycle individual on the left. Both were photographed in New Jersey. *Photographs by Kevin Karlson.*

GLAUCOUS GULL *Larus hyperboreus*

Scarce winter resident, rare migrant, and very rare to casual summer visitor. The less common of the two "white-winged" gulls in New Jersey, Glaucous Gulls are usually found among concentrations of other large gulls at landfills and reservoirs and along the Atlantic coast. Almost all the birds of this species found here are immatures, usually first-winter, and adults are extremely rare. Florence and the Sussex County landfill are the two most reliable places for Glaucous Gulls at the present time. Although CBC totals are not the most reliable indicator of gull abundance, the numbers of this species have declined substantially from the totals in the 1970s and early 1980s, when the landfills in the Hackensack Meadowlands were active and regularly attracted large flocks of gulls.

GREAT BLACK-BACKED GULL *Larus marinus*

Very common winter resident, common spring and fall migrant, common but local summer resident. Historically, Great Black-backed Gulls were uncommon winter residents in New Jersey, but numbers increased rapidly during the middle of the twentieth century, and the first nesting occurred in 1966. Great Black-backs are now fairly common breeders in colonies from northern Ocean to southern Cape May counties. Migration is difficult to detect, but by late summer large concentrations of all age groups gather at roosts along the coast, and winter populations are augmented by visitors from the north. Ten to twenty thousand are typically found on CBCs. Great Black-backs are much less common inland than along the coast, but they can be encountered almost anywhere in the state. Large numbers gather on the Delaware Bayshore in late spring to feed on horseshoe crab eggs in competition with shorebirds.

SABINE'S GULL *Xema sabina*

Rare fall and very rare spring migrant. There have been eighteen accepted records of Sabine's Gull in New Jersey, the first as recently as 1979, although there were two earlier, undocumented reports that may have been correct. Somewhat surprisingly, there have been more records of adults and second-year birds than of juveniles. Most re-

Review Species

ports are from late August to mid-November, but there are four from spring, one from summer, and one from early December. Inland records are from Overpeck Park, Bergen, County; Warren Township, Somerset County; and Merrill Creek Reservoir.

Sabine's Gull is a highly pelagic species that breeds in the Arctic and migrates far offshore, as a rule. However, most of New Jersey's nearly twenty records have been of adults seen along the coast, plus three inland sightings. This handsome adult on the left spent three weeks at Sandy Hook in May 2002, while the bird on the right, in transition plumage next to a Laughing Gull, was at Stone Harbor, 9 May 2001. *Photographs by Steve Kerr (left) and Kevin Karlson (right).*

BLACK-LEGGED KITTIWAKE *Rissa tridactyla*

Scarce and irregular migrant and winter visitor on shore, common but irregular winter visitor offshore. Black-legged Kittiwakes are mainly pelagic in New Jersey and infrequently seen from shore. The Avalon Sea Watch usually records a few in late November, and the pelagic birding trips that occasionally go out from November to March encounter numbers from a few dozen to hundreds, though numbers may vary substantially from year to year. Very small numbers are seen from shore during most winters, and rarely weather conditions will bring concentrations to shore. This last happened in December 1997, when the Lakehurst CBC tallied a hundred kittiwakes. Black-legged Kittiwakes were much more frequently seen from shore during the 1970s and early 1980s, when offshore fishing fleets attracted thousands of them.

ROSS'S GULL *Rhodostethia rosea*

Accidental. New Jersey's only Ross's Gull was photographed from a fishing boat just five miles off Manasquan Inlet. This rare phantom of the Arctic was unknown from the East Coast prior to the famous appearance in Newburyport, MA, in early 1975. Since then it has occurred in

Maryland, Delaware, Pennsylvania, New York, and Connecticut, in addition to New Jersey.

27 NOV 1993, 5 MILES E. OF MANASQUAN INLET, OCEAN CO. (NJBRC 1995-027; NJPF)

Unknown in the eastern United States prior to 1975, the rare and beautiful Ross's Gull has now been seen in seven states in the Northeast. New Jersey's only record is this individual seen by two lucky observers from a boat five miles east of Manasquan Inlet, Ocean County, 27 November 1993. *Photograph by Steve Kerr.*

IVORY GULL *Pagophila eburnea*

Accidental. There have been eight reports, but just five accepted records of Ivory Gull in the state. New Jersey's first was found dead at Island Beach in February 1940, and the second visited Manasquan Inlet for a week in winter 1955. The Lake Como and Liberty SP sightings, just six days apart, probably represent a single bird, but the photos are not definitive (Freiday 1986). After a break of twenty-three years, the immature at Cape May in 2009 entertained hundreds during its two-week stay. (*See photo page 145.*)

3 FEB 1940, ISLAND BEACH SP, OCEAN CO. (*ANSP)
30 JAN–5 FEB 1955, MANASQUAN INLET, OCEAN CO. (AFN 9[3]:244)
10 FEB 1986, LAKE COMO, MONMOUTH CO. (RNJB 12[2]:33; NJPF)
16 FEB 1986, LIBERTY SP, HUDSON CO. (RNJB 12[2]:28; NJPF)
27 NOV–11 DEC 2009, CAPE MAY, CAPE MAY CO. (NJBRC 2010-085; NJPF)

BROWN NODDY *Anous stolidus*

Accidental. Our only record of Brown Noddy is a bird that passed by the Cape May Point Hawk Watch in the wake of a tropical storm in early September 1979. This species occurred twice in Massachusetts during the 1950s but is otherwise unknown north of Virginia.

8 SEP 1979, CAPE MAY PT., CAPE MAY CO. (RNJB 6[1]:12)

SOOTY TERN *Onychoprion fuscatus*

Very rare vagrant following hurricanes or strong tropical storms. There have been forty accepted records of Sooty Tern in New Jersey, some of them representing multiple individuals. All but two occurred from July to September, and all were associated with storms coming up the Atlantic coast from the Caribbean. Several hurricanes have contributed to multiple sightings up and down the coast, as well as the few inland records. Hurricane Donna in September 1960 accounted for seven reports, with a maximum of thirty-five birds in one flock, while Hurricane David in September 1979 added nine reports, from Bergen County to Cape May.

All of the records of Sooty Tern in New Jersey have been associated with late summer tropical storms coming up the Atlantic Coast. Exhausted birds sometimes come to land to recover before heading out to sea and disappearing. This adult was brought north to Cape May by Hurricane Fran, 7 September 1996, but succumbed to exhaustion and died a short time after it was photographed. *Photograph by Kevin Karlson.*

BRIDLED TERN *Onychoprion anaethetus*

Very rare onshore following hurricanes or strong tropical storms, very rare offshore in late summer. There have been eighteen accepted records of Bridled Tern in New Jersey, including some with multiple (up to eleven) individuals. All but two occurred in August or September, and all records from shore are known or believed to be storm related. The off-shore records are probably associated with warm water eddies that break off from the Gulf Stream in August and September. Additional studies may reveal Bridled Tern to be more regular at that season.

LEAST TERN *Sternula antillarum*

Fairly common but local summer resident, uncommon spring and fall migrant. Endangered Species in New Jersey. Like so many other coastal waterbirds, Least Terns were nearly extirpated from New Jersey in the late 1800s by the millinery trade. They recovered somewhat in the new century, but their preference for nesting on sandy beaches has increasingly put them in conflict with development and human recreational activity. More recently, losses due to flooding and predation have intensified the threats to the species. They have nested at sand mines, but the major colonies are confined to the beaches. Overall, the breeding population has declined from an estimated 1,750 adults in 1979 (Galli and Kane 1981) and 1,938 adults in 2002 (BNB 2002) to about 1,200 in 2008. Least Tern migration is inconspicuous, as the birds arrive at their nesting areas in early May and depart abruptly in late August or early September. Only a few, mainly juveniles, linger into mid-September.

LARGE-BILLED TERN *Phaetusa simplex*

Review Species

Accidental. New Jersey's only record of this vagrant from the rivers of South America was discovered at Kearny Marsh, Hudson County, 30 May 1988, although it may have been present for several days prior to that (Kane et al. 1989). This was the first fully documented record for North America, although two previous sight reports in Illinois (1949) and Ohio (1954) have been accepted by the corresponding state records committees.

30 MAY 1988, KEARNY, HUDSON CO. (RNJB 14[3]:55; NJPF)

One of the least likely vagrants ever recorded in New Jersey was this Large-billed Tern. The third accepted record for North America and the first to be fully documented, it was present for several days at Kearny Marsh, Hudson County, before being correctly identified and photographed on 30 May 1988. *Photograph by Jerry Golub.*

GULL-BILLED TERN *Gelochelidon nilotica*

Uncommon and local summer resident, scarce migrant away from the breeding sites. Gull-billed Terns arrive at their nesting locations in Ocean, Atlantic, and Cape May counties in late April or early May. Only a few nest north of New Jersey on Long Island, NY, so migrants are seldom seen north of Long Beach Island. Although the species apparently bred in the state in the 1800s, there were very few nesting records in the twentieth century until the 1970s. The population grew from just 13 adults at scattered sites in 1979 to 140 birds in eight colonies in 2001. Since the early 1980s, flocks of up to three dozen birds have appeared well inland at cranberry bogs in Burlington County, first at Whitesbog and more recently near Chatsworth in July and August. Most Gull-billed Terns depart by the end of August, although a few hang around Forsythe into September.

CASPIAN TERN *Hydroprogne caspia*

Fairly common fall and uncommon spring migrant, rare and local summer resident. The first southbound Caspian Terns appear in August, and this is the best time to see them at inland sites such as Spruce Run. The bulk of the migration occurs in September and October, primarily along the coast, and November sightings are very rare. The terns are much less common in spring than in fall, with the main passage from mid-April to mid-May. Salem County, especially Mannington Marsh and Salem Cove, formerly attracted the largest concentrations of Caspian Terns both spring and fall, but these sites no longer seem so attractive to the terns. They were first found nesting in the state at Barnegat Bay, Ocean County, in 1984 (Burger et al. 1985), and small numbers have nested most years since then, mainly at Forsythe NWR.

BLACK TERN *Chlidonias niger*

Uncommon fall and rare spring migrant. Black Terns are far less common today than they were in the first half of the twentieth century, apparently due to destruction of wetlands on their breeding grounds and along their migration routes (Heath et al. 2009). This decline has been reflected in the number of migrants passing through New Jersey, though fall numbers seem to have increased in the past few years. Southbound birds may show up as early as late June, but the peak migration is usually between mid-August and early September. Most migrants are along the coast or off-shore, but inland sites such as Spruce Run and Mannington Marsh also attract good numbers. Black Terns are rare in spring, as the main migration route is through the center of the continent.

WHITE-WINGED TERN *Chlidonias leucopteris*

Review Species

Accidental. New Jersey's first White-winged Tern was seen just briefly at the South Cape May Meadows in May 1983 (Sibley 1997), but the second, a bird in basic plumage, spent the entire summer of 1989 at the same location. Although this species has occurred seven times in Delaware, just once since 1995, and has actually bred once in upstate New York (in a mixed pair with a Black Tern), these are the only two records for New Jersey.

10 MAY 1983, CAPE MAY, CAPE MAY CO.
4 JUN–25 AUG 1989, CAPE MAY, CAPE MAY CO. (RNJB 15:73, 84)

White-winged Tern is a Eurasian and African species that is a casual visitor to North America and has bred once in New York and twice in Ontario in mixed pairs with the closely related Black Tern. There are two records for New Jersey, the first a brief flyby, but the second, pictured here in first-summer, nonbreeding plumage, spent almost three months at Cape May, 4 June–25 August 1989. *Photograph by Kevin Karlson.*

WHISKERED TERN *Chlidonias hybrida*

Accidental. The two state records of Whiskered Tern have both been at Cape May. An individual found at the South Cape May Meadows on 12 July 1993 had probably been present for several weeks, but was not positively identified until that date (Sibley 1997); it represented the first record for North America. The bird remained for just one more day and then relocated to Little Creek and other nearby sites in Delaware, where it stayed for almost two months. The second, and only other record for the continent, was present at Cape May Point for five days in August 1998 (Crossley 1999).

12–13 JUL 1993, CAPE MAY, CAPE MAY CO. (RNJB 14:73, 88)
8–12 AUG 1998, CAPE MAY, CAPE MAY CO. (RNJB 25:67–68)

Whiskered Tern is another Eurasian and African tern; it has been found just twice in North America, both times in New Jersey. The first, in 1993, relocated to Delaware, where it spent almost two months, but the second—here—was present at Cape May in breeding plumage for five days in August 1998. *Photograph by Kevin Karlson.*

ROSEATE TERN *Sterna dougallii*

Rare to scarce spring migrant and summer visitor, rare fall migrant. Endangered Species in New Jersey. Most of the North American population of Roseate Terns nest on islands off eastern Long Island, NY, and Cape Cod, MA, but they migrate well offshore, both spring and fall, and only a few visit New Jersey. The species formerly nested in the state in small numbers, with a maximum of ten pairs in the 1970s, only one in 1980, and none since (Gochfeld et al. 1998). Most sightings are from mid-May to late July at preferred sites such as Cape May, Hereford Inlet, and Sandy Hook. Fall migrants are very rarely seen at Sandy Hook and Cape May in late August or early September.

Although much of the North American Roseate Tern population nests off eastern Long Island and in New England, it is a rare visitor to coastal New Jersey, mostly in May and June. The adult in breeding plumage (the bird on the right) is distinguished by its very white appearance, long thin black bill, and very long, white tail feathers that extend noticeably past the wingtips. First-summer Roseate and Common Terns, the two birds in the left composite photo, are readily separated by these same features. *Photographs by Kevin Karlson.*

COMMON TERN *Sterna hirundo*

Common but local summer resident, common spring and fall migrant. Common Terns, like so many other terns and herons, were decimated by egging and the millinery trade in the late 1800s, and their subsequent history has seen periods of recovery and decline. Spring migrants begin returning in late April. Many pass through during May, while the breeders begin to reestablish colonies at preferred sites from Cape May to Sandy Hook. The present population of about 3,300 in fifty-eight colonies represents a decline from about 9,400 birds in a similar number of colonies in 1989 (CWS). Common Terns begin to disperse from their breeding areas in mid-July, but the peak migration is from late August into early September. A few linger through October and, rarely, into November. There have been undocumented reports on five CBCs, but none is known to have successfully wintered.

ARCTIC TERN *Sterna paradisaea*

Very rare spring and fall migrant. Although Arctic Terns nest commonly in Maine and the Canadian Maritimes (formerly in Massachusetts, but now fewer than ten pairs), their migration route takes them so far offshore that they

8

are rarely seen even on pelagic trips to the Hudson Canyon. Although there have been more than seventy reports of this species, many of these have not been well documented to distinguish it from the very similar Common Tern. Arctic Tern was added to the Review List in 1996, and there have been eighteen accepted records, the majority occurring in May and June. Many of the summer records are of onshore one-year-old nonbreeders. Two were from pelagic trips far offshore, including fifteen or more at Hudson Canyon, 26 May 2003, but there are also two inland records.

Common and Arctic Terns can present some tricky identification problems. Common Tern is a familiar, local breeding species along the beaches and marshes of New Jersey from May to September, but Arctic Tern migrates far offshore and is very rare on land in the state. The top photo shows a blood-red bill without a black tip on the Arctic Tern on the left, and a more rounded head and proportionally longer tail in comparison with the Common Tern on the right. The shorter legs of Arctic Tern, which is usually evident when the two species are side by side, is not so apparent here. In the bottom photo, this first-summer Arctic Tern shows a very faint carpal bar and much paler primaries than a Common Tern of the same age would exhibit. *Photographs by Kevin Karlson.*

FORSTER'S TERN *Sterna forsteri*

Common but local summer resident, common spring and fall migrant, very rare winter resident. Specimen records suggest that Forster's Terns may have nested in Cape May County in the 1800s (Sibley 1997), but the species was considered a rare and irregular fall visitor until the 1950s, when the first confirmed breeding occurred at Brigantine in

1954 (Leck 1984). Numbers rapidly increased after that, and by 1979 there were about 1,300 nesting adults in the state (Galli and Kane 1981), growing to a maximum of 3,868 in 2004 (CWS). Forster's Terns become very common in fall as local populations are augmented by dispersing birds from the South and probably by migrants from the Great Lakes. They remain fairly common through November, and some linger into December to be tallied on CBCs (maximum of 99 in 2004). A few are found in midwinter in the southern counties on occasion (maximum 50 at Norbury's Landing on 15 February 1995), but they probably retreat from New Jersey to nearby states in colder weather and return during warm spells. By mid- to late March, the first spring migrants are already returning. Forster's Terns are regularly seen along the lower Delaware River, but are rare inland in the northern part of the state.

Forster's Tern was first confirmed nesting in New Jersey in 1954, but is now a common resident from March to November along the coast from the Hackensack Meadowlands to Cape May and Cumberland counties. In breeding plumage, as shown here, it is easily distinguished from Common Tern by the silvery-gray primaries; its white, not gray, body; and its slightly thicker orange, not red-orange, bill with a black tip. *Photograph by Kevin Karlson.*

ROYAL TERN *Thalasseus maximus*

Common fall and uncommon spring migrant, rare and very local summer resident. Royal Terns were not definitely recorded in New Jersey until 1933 (Stone 1937), when they began appearing as late summer and fall visitors. Since the 1950s they have been regular, as first the adults and then

juveniles disperse from their southern breeding colonies in late June and July. Beginning in the 1980s, Royal Terns began to be seen in small numbers in late April, and increased courtship activity led to the first confirmed nesting at Barnegat Bay in 1988 (Gochfeld et al. 1989). There were no further known breeding attempts until 2007, when a colony of thirty pairs set up housekeeping at Hereford Inlet in the company of Common Terns and Black Skimmers (Fritz 2008). Over a hundred pairs nested there in 2008, but the nesting area was destroyed by storms in 2009 and no nests were found. Royals Terns linger into November in the fall and have been found on four CBCS, but there is no evidence of overwintering.

Royal Tern has only recently begun nesting in the state at Stone Harbor, but is a common postbreeding visitor from southern Atlantic states from midsummer through the fall. It is most common from Ocean County south to Cape May County, but is regular north to Raritan Bay and along the Delaware Bayshore to Cumberland County. In full breeding plumage, bill color can be quite variable, as shown here. The full black cap is worn for only a few months in spring, and most birds have a completely white forehead by the time they arrive in New Jersey. Most local breeding birds have one by July. *Photograph by Kevin Karlson.*

SANDWICH TERN *Thalasseus sandvicensis*

Very rare spring, and rare summer and fall visitor. There were only two records of Sandwich Tern in New Jersey prior to 1955 (Fables 1955), but the rapid rise in the numbers of Royal Terns has been accompanied by an increase in the frequency of Sandwich Tern sightings. They are still very rare in spring, with nearly annual records in late May or early June, but occur annually in small numbers (fewer than ten per season) from late June to September, mainly at Cape May and Stone Harbor, but rarely at Island Beach and very rarely at Sandy Hook. The latest date is 2 October 2004.

BLACK SKIMMER *Rynchops niger*

Fairly common but local summer resident, fairly common spring and fall migrant, very rare in winter. Endangered Species in New Jersey. Black Skimmers were nearly extirpated from New Jersey by egg taking during the late 1800s, but began to recover after 1915 (Stone 1937), reaching a maximum of 2,000+ pairs in the early 1970s, but only 1,130 in 1976 (Gochfeld and Burger 1994). As a beach-nesting species, they are subject to the same pressures and vagaries of nature that confront many terns and plovers, and recent data (CWS) indicate a further decline. The skimmers that frequent the Hackensack Meadowlands and Hudson County shore in summer come from nesting colonies in New York Harbor. Large groups gather in late September and early October in coastal Cape May and Atlantic counties, but most have departed before November. A few, sometimes small flocks, linger into December, when they have been recorded on eleven CBCs since 1973, and there are about a half-dozen midwinter records. Black Skimmers begin returning to their breeding locations in mid-April.

Black Skimmer was nearly extirpated from New Jersey during the nineteenth century but recovered to become a fairly common coastal breeding species. As a beach nester, it is under constant pressure from human activities, predators, and the vagaries of nature. Its unique feeding habit of skimming the surface with the lower mandible is a delight to watch. *Photographs by Kevin Karlson.*

Family Stercorariidae: Skuas and Jaegers

GREAT SKUA *Stercorarius skua*

Accidental. There have been five accepted records of the North Atlantic–breeding Great Skua in New Jersey, all in winter and all well offshore. Several other reports have been accepted as pertaining to "skua sp.," and some may refer to this species, especially one in winter. Separation of Great and South Polar skuas, both of which are known to occur in the northwestern North Atlantic, is difficult, especially in the worn plumage involved in some of the photographed reports, and the possibility remains that one of the other two Antarctic species may have occurred off New Jersey (Lehman 1998c). Careful documentation of skua sightings is essential to establish the frequency of occurrence of Great Skua.

2 DEC 1978, HUDSON CANYON PELAGIC
1 DEC 1991, 100 MI. EAST OF CAPE MAY (AR 1998)
14 DEC 1991, HUDSON CANYON PELAGIC (AR 1999)
19 FEB 1995, 28 MI. SOUTHEAST OF CAPE MAY (AR 1999)
9 DEC 2000, OFF BRIELLE, MONMOUTH CO. (NJBRC 2001-059)

SOUTH POLAR SKUA *Stercorarius maccormicki*

Rare late spring and summer visitor. There have been fourteen accepted reports of this skua of the southern oceans, thirteen from late May, one from late August, and all far offshore. A recent report of a bird seen just three miles east of Atlantic City by three experienced observers on 9 July 2010 has not yet been reviewed. Pelagic trips out of Massachusetts and North Carolina have shown that skuas, especially South Polar Skua, occur rarely but regularly from late spring through the summer in waters near or beyond the continental shelf. This species is probably more common off New Jersey than the records would indicate.

POMARINE JAEGER *Stercorarius pomarinus*

Uncommon spring and especially fall migrant far offshore, rare from shore, and very rare in early winter. Pomarine Jaegers are more highly pelagic than Parasitic Jaegers and far less common from shore. The difficulty of identifying nonadult jaegers complicates accurate determination of their near-shore status. Offshore, a few are seen regularly on late-spring pelagic trips, but they are more common on fall trips from late August into December. They have been recorded on four CBCs and were present offshore in midwinter when large foreign fishing fleets were present in the 1970s. Most records from land are associated with storms, including an amazing thirty-two at Cape May on 2 September 2006 following tropical storm Ernesto.

PARASITIC JAEGER *Stercorarius parasiticus*

Scarce spring and uncommon fall migrant and rare summer visitor onshore, more numerous a mile or more offshore. Southbound Parasitic Jaegers can be seen along the coast, most often in Cape May County, as early as midAugust, but the main push is in September and October, with diminishing numbers through November. The species is regular in small numbers, especially when onshore winds and masses of migrating terns are present. This is by the far the most likely jaeger to be seen from shore and is less common far offshore than Pomarine Jaeger, though it is still seen on most pelagic trips in spring and fall. Small numbers of spring migrants are regularly seen in Cape May from late April to late May, but the few occasionally encountered in June and July are probably nonbreeders.

Parasitic is by far the most likely jaeger species to be seen from shore, and individuals are often seen over the "rips" at Cape May from late August to October harassing terns and gulls. Jaegers, particularly immature birds, can be very difficult to identify, but the light-morph adult shown here is in full breeding plumage. *Photograph by Kevin Karlson.*

LONG-TAILED JAEGER *Stercorarius longicaudus*

Very rare spring and scarce-to-rare fall migrant offshore, casual from shore. There have been about sixty reports of Long-tailed Jaeger in New Jersey, the majority of them far offshore and some involving multiple birds. Most likely to

be seen offshore between mid-August and mid-September, when many of the birds are juveniles. About twenty have been seen from shore or even onshore on the immediate coast, often associated with stormy weather, but none inland. The difficulty of identifying jaegers is exemplified by the juvenile that spent 14 September 1991 at Cape May Point loafing around Bunker Pond with Laughing Gulls. It was identified by the many observers present, including some of New Jersey's best, as a Parasitic Jaeger. Study of the excellent photographs taken belatedly revealed that the bird was, in fact, a Long-tailed.

Family Alcidae: Alcids

DOVEKIE *Alle alle*

Fairly common but irregular winter visitor offshore, very rare from land. Dovekies are rarely seen from shore in New Jersey, but are regularly encountered five miles or more from land from late November into March. Numbers vary from year to year, but the infrequency of pelagic trips makes their status difficult to assess. Although pelagic totals of dozens to a few hundred are normal, the peak count was 1,650 on a trip to Hudson Canyon 11 February 2006 (P. Guris, pers. comm.). Beached Dovekies were apparently much more common in the early 1900s, as Stone (1937) reported records for eight of fourteen winters from 1921 to 1934. A major incursion of birds occurred 19 November 1932 all along the Atlantic coast, and dozens were found at more than fifty locations in New Jersey on that and subsequent days, including some far inland in Sussex and Morris counties (Murphy and Vogt 1933). One observer estimated that 100,000 Dovekies flew by Lavalette, Ocean County, in four hours (Nichols 1935).

Dovekie is a fairly common but irregular visitor to the offshore waters of New Jersey during the colder months, but is rarely seen from land. When they do come close to shore, it is usually in November or December. This may be storm related or due to other causes, such as food deficiency or illness. This individual was at Cape May, 16 December 2007. *Photograph by Richard Crossley.*

COMMON MURRE *Uria aalge*

Review Species

Scarce and irregular winter (December to March) visitor offshore, casual from land. Common Murres nest as far south as the Bay of Fundy, but the first New Jersey record was of one found dead at Avon, Monmouth County, 3 February 1946 (Fables 1955). Since then, there have been eleven additional records from land and eleven from between about five and thirty-five miles offshore. Only two of the twelve since 1993 have been from shore, but the frequency with which they have been encountered on winter pelagic trips (e.g., ten in four groups on 8 February 2009), suggests that Common Murre may be a more regular visitor than earlier history would indicate. Veit and Guris (2008) have reviewed the evidence of an increase in abundance of this species and other alcids off New Jersey and neighboring states.

THICK-BILLED MURRE *Uria lomvia*

Review Species

Rare winter visitor. Thick-billed Murre breeds no closer to New Jersey than the Gulf of St. Lawrence, but historically it was the "common" murre of our coastal waters and even the Delaware River. Stone (1908) wrote that "apparently a few occur every year off the coast in winter, and in some seasons they are rather plentiful." By the mid-twentieth century they had become much rarer, although still of more frequent occurrence than their close cousin. Thick-billed Murre was added to the Review List in 1996 and there have been ten accepted records since then, seven from land, but one of those "records" refers to eight different individuals along the coast of northern Monmouth County, 29 January–16 March 2005. This species, too, has increased in recent years (Veit and Guris 2008).

Identification of the larger alcids, especially Common and Thick-billed Murres—both rare in New Jersey waters—can be very difficult under the adverse conditions where they are commonly encountered offshore from a boat. From land, where Thick-billed is more frequently seen, it's a bit easier. This Thick-billed Murre in nonbreeding plumage, seen in January 1991 at Manasquan Inlet, is distinguished from Common Murre by its shorter, heavier bill with decurved culmen (less prominent in first-year birds) and prominent white gape mark, and the more limited amount of white on the throat and sides of the head. *Photograph by Kevin Karlson.*

RAZORBILL *Alca torda*

Uncommon to fairly common offshore winter visitor, rare to scarce from land. Razorbill is the most frequently seen alcid in New Jersey, and small numbers are seen annually from shore. They have been seen as early as late October, but most occur between early December and early March. Razorbills tend to stay five or more miles from land, and they are routinely encountered on pelagic trips in winter, but numbers can vary widely from year to year, although they have shown a dramatic increase during the last two decades (Veit and Guris 2008). From shore they can sometimes be very rare, with only a few reports all winter, while in other years there may be dozens of sightings.

Review Species

BLACK GUILLEMOT *Cepphus grylle*

Very rare winter visitor. Although Black Guillemot breeds commonly as far south as the coast of Maine, it is the least frequently encountered eastern alcid in New Jersey. There have been fifteen accepted records, all from shore, starting with the first at Cape May, 10 December 1929 (Underdown 1930), and including one inland at Boonton Reservoir, 26 November 1939 (Fables 1955). All but one of the birds appeared in late November or December, although two remained into January. There has been a marked increase in occurrence of Black Guillemot in recent years, with eight records since 1998.

Black Guillemot is the least often seen of the eastern alcids that visit New Jersey, although there has been an increase in the frequency of occurrences since 1998. All of the records are of birds in winter plumage, and all but two have been one-day wonders. This bird was an exception, and it was seen by many during its six-week stay at Barnegat Light, Ocean County, December 2005–January 2006. *Photographs by Kevin Karlson.*

LONG-BILLED MURRELET *Brachyramphus perdix*

Accidental. Surprisingly, this Asian vagrant has occurred more than a dozen times in the Northeast, so its arrival in New Jersey was anticipated. It was discovered at Sandy

Hook around noon on 18 January 2007 and seen by many that day. Unfortunately, the weather deteriorated rapidly on the morning of the second day, and the crowds that came the third day were disappointed (Barnes 2009).

8–19 JAN 2007, SANDY HOOK, MONMOUTH CO. (NJBRC 2008-019)

Review Species

Long-billed Murrelet is an alcid native to northeastern Asia, but it has shown up more than a dozen times in northeastern North America, as well as numerous times in the interior of the continent. New Jersey's only record is of this individual that was present for two days at Sandy Hook and seen here on the first day, 8 January 2007. *Photograph by Jim Gilbert.*

ATLANTIC PUFFIN *Fratercula arctica*

Uncommon winter and spring visitor offshore, accidental from shore. Atlantic Puffin was formerly considered a Review List species in New Jersey, as there have been only five records from shore, all but one prior to 1955. However, winter pelagic trips have shown that it is an uncommon, but regular, winter visitor well offshore, especially twenty to ninety miles from land. There have even been a few late May–early June records, presumably nonbreeders, from the Hudson Canyon off Ocean County.

Order Columbiformes

Family Columbidae: Pigeons and Doves

ROCK PIGEON *Columba livia*

Common and widespread permanent resident. The ubiquitous and familiar Rock Pigeon (formerly known as Rock Dove) was introduced into North America by colonists in the early 1600s (Johnston 1992) and has spread from coast to coast. In New Jersey they are common everywhere but in the heart of the Pine Barrens. They are partial to man-made structures, such as bridges, barns, and buildings, but are less common in suburbia than in urban and some rural (e.g., agricultural) areas. On average, almost 20,000 Rock Pigeons are found on statewide CBCs.

BAND-TAILED PIGEON *Patagioenas fasciata*

Review Species

Accidental. There are just two records of this strong-flying denizen of mountainous and foothill areas of the western U.S., occurring twenty-seven years apart at opposite ends of the state. The first was seen by only two observers at a hawk-banding station in Sussex County, but the second lingered for three days at a backyard in West Cape May.

29 SEP 1980, STOKES STATE FOREST, SUSSEX CO. (RNJB 7[1]:7; AR 1991)
16–18 JAN 2007, WEST CAPE MAY, CAPE MAY CO. (NJBRC 2008-001)

Band-tailed Pigeon is a widespread species in North America that wanders occasionally to the East. In New Jersey, there are two records, one from the Kittatinny Mountains and the second, shown here, which spent three days at a Cape May backyard, 16–18 January 2007. *Photograph by Kevin Karlson.*

EURASIAN COLLARED-DOVE *Streptopelia decaocto*

Review Species

Rare but increasing stray from south and west of New Jersey. Eurasian Collared-Doves were introduced into the Bahamas in the mid-1970s and, after gaining a foothold in southern Florida by the mid-1980s, have spread explosively across most of the United States and southern Canada, except in the Northeast (Romagosa 2002). Some populations are likely the result of local releases, however. Although it is presumably just a matter of time before Collared-Doves colonize New Jersey, it has not yet happened. Following the first sighting at Cape May in 1997 (Lehman 1998b), there have been a total of fifteen accepted records of Collared-Dove in the state as of mid-2010, twelve of them in the period 2005–2009.

WHITE-WINGED DOVE *Zenaida asiatica*

Review Species

Rare but increasing vagrant from the southern or southwestern U.S. White-winged Dove was first found in New Jersey at West Cape May, 24 April 1981 (RNJB 7[3]:54; NJPF), and there are now thirty-one accepted records, seventeen of them since 2002. Most of the sightings have been from spring (April–May) or late fall (November–early December), but there are records for every month but October. All have been on or near the coast, with Cape May County accounting for the overwhelming majority.

White-winged Dove is a bird of the desert Southwest and southern Great Plains that has expanded its range eastward along the Gulf Coast to include southern Florida. It is known to wander widely as a vagrant and has appeared in New Jersey more than thirty times since the first occurrence in 1981. This individual was spotted in South Seaville, Cape May County, 6 May 2003. *Photograph by Kevin McGowan.*

MOURNING DOVE *Zenaida macroura*

Very common and ubiquitous permanent resident, though there are major seasonal movements of some subsets of the population. Mourning Dove is one of New Jersey's and North America's most widespread and abundant nesting species. They can be found in every corner of the state and may be observed courting and nesting in almost any month except, perhaps, December and January. Winter numbers are apparently augmented by migrants from the North, but no clear migration patterns are evident. Mourning Dove's abundance is indicated by the average of about 17,000 recorded on statewide CBCs.

PASSENGER PIGEON *Ectopistes migratorius*

Extinct. The tragic demise of the Passenger Pigeon is well known. It is estimated to have been the most abundant land bird in North America at one time, with a population of perhaps 3 to 5 billion. Passenger Pigeons were abundant migrants in New Jersey in colonial times, but a combination of habitat destruction and human disruption of nesting colonies caused their rapid decline, and they were considered rare in the state by the mid-1800s (Stone 1937). The last record for New Jersey was of one shot from a flock of ten at Morristown, 7 October 1893 (Fables 1955). A report listed in Fables of one shot at Englewood in 1896 turned out to have involved a Mourning Dove (Bull 1964).

COMMON GROUND-DOVE *Columbina passerina*

Review Species

Accidental. There are three accepted records of this vagrant from the southern U.S. that occurs regularly north only to South Carolina. The first was shot near Camden in the autumn of 1858 by the taxidermist John Krider, but the specimen is lost (Turnbull 1869). Although there were two plausible, but undocumented, reports in the intervening years, more than a century would pass before a sight record in 1984. More recently, a one-day-only bird was well photographed near Stone Harbor.

NOV 1858, NEAR CAMDEN, CAMDEN CO.
4 SEP 1984, HIGBEE BEACH, CAPE MAY CO. (AR 1998)
6 OCT 2009, NUMMY ISLAND, CAPE MAY CO. (NJBRC 2010-075; NJPF)

There have been just three records of Common Ground-Dove, a declining species of the South, in New Jersey, and only one of them was documented by a photograph. This bird was present for less than an hour at Nummy Island near Stone Harbor, 6 October 2009. *Photograph by Bob Abrams.*

Cinnamon Teal are common breeding birds west of the Rocky Mountains, but are the rarest of the native dabbling ducks in eastern North America. There are only three accepted records for New Jersey, including this drake that spent two weeks in Northfield, Atlantic County, 20 March–3 April 2001. *Photograph by Kevin Karlson.*

A highlight of the winter season is a visit to Barnegat Light State Park, where a flock of twenty to thirty Harlequin Ducks can be found regularly. Although they are occasionally seen at other sites along the coast, nowhere else are they so approachable and easily photographed. The female in the left foreground is being courted by six handsome males. *Photographs by Kevin Karlson.*

Long-tailed Duck is a common winter resident along the New Jersey coast, especially at estuaries such as Barnegat Inlet. The beautifully patterned males in winter plumage, shown here in flight and on the water, can often be heard yo-deling their distinctive "upup ow owel.EP" courtship call during the late winter and early spring. *Photographs by Kevin Karlson.*

This Yellow-nosed Albatross, New Jersey's only record, was first seen flying along the Garden State Parkway in Cape May County! It was relocated two days later along the Delaware Bayshore, where it was seen by many observers at several sites, including Reeds Beach, Cape May County, where this stunning photograph was taken on 23 May 2001. Rare as this species is along the North Atlantic coast, its appearance over land and in Delaware Bay is even more re-markable. *Photograph by Tonya Toole.*

The first occurrence of Roseate Spoonbill in New Jersey was a young bird seen briefly in Linden, Union County, in August 1992. More recently, individuals, both subadults, have appeared at Forsythe NWR in 2007 and 2009, each for extended stays. This bird was photographed at the latter site on 14 August 2007. *Photograph by Joe Delesantro.*

Ospreys declined severely during the mid-twentieth century due to a combination of habitat loss, persecution, and poor reproduction caused by pesticide residues. Fortunately, this trend was reversed primarily through the efforts of the New Jersey Endangered and Nongame Species program following the banning of DDT. By 2009, almost 500 pairs were nesting in the state, mainly along the Atlantic Coast and Delaware Bayshore. This bird nested in North Wildwood, Cape May County, in 2002. *Photograph by Kevin Karlson.*

Cooper's Hawk is now a common migrant and fairly common year-round resident in New Jersey, a major improvement from the 1970s, when it was considered threatened as a breeding bird. As with most hawks, the immature
plumage differs markedly from that of the adult. Most migrants that pass through the state are immatures, such as the
one pictured here at Cape May Point in October 2005. *Photograph by Kevin Karlson.*

Black Rail is one of the most elusive and sought-after breeding birds in New Jersey. It is normally a shy denizen of salt
and brackish marshes, heard almost only at night and rarely seen. This individual, however, spent a week at the South
Cape May Meadows in June 2009, calling in the day time and occasionally crossing the path in full view. *Photograph by
Karl Lukens.*

Pacific Golden-Plover nests in Siberia and extreme western Alaska and winters mainly in the Eastern Hemisphere, with small numbers in California and Mexico. It has occurred in migration in six northeastern states, including New Jersey. This molting second-life-year bird was present for almost two weeks at a sod farm in Deerfield Township, Cumberland County, 4–16 September 2001. ID criteria for this bird are discussed in Appendix D. *Photographs by Angus Wilson.*

Piping Plover is an Endangered Species in New Jersey, where its beach-nesting habit puts it in conflict with human activities and exposes it to predators. As of 2010, only about 120 nesting pairs remain in the state. This male and two young chicks were photographed in Cape May in July 1997. *Photograph by Kevin Karlson.*

Red-necked Stint is an Asian sandpiper that also breeds in small numbers in western Alaska. It has been confirmed just three times in New Jersey, all in late summer. In winter plumage it is difficult to distinguish from Semipalmated Sandpiper, but typically shows longer wings and more attenuated rear body structure. In worn breeding plumage, shown by this bird at Wildwood Crest, Cape May County, 30 August 2008, it looks very different. *Photograph by Richard Crossley.*

Curlew Sandpiper is a fairly common Eurasian species that is a regular vagrant to North America. It occurs in New Jersey in small numbers almost every year, usually in May or July and August. This bright male in full breeding plumage was photographed in May 2005 at Nummy Island near Stone Harbor. *Photograph by Kevin Karlson.*

Buff-breasted Sandpiper is an uncommon, but regular, migrant through New Jersey in late summer and early autumn. The birds' preferred habitat is sod farms and grassy edges of reservoirs and impoundments, but they also occur in low dunes along beaches. Almost all of the birds that pass through the state are juveniles, such as the one pictured here. *Photograph by Kevin Karlson.*

A rare and declining denizen of the Arctic, Ivory Gull has occurred just five times in New Jersey. Most of these have been very brief visits, but the juvenile bird found in Cape May on 27 November 2009 remained for two weeks. It was enjoyed by many observers as it flew around the harbor and perched at close range. *Photographs by Kevin Karlson.*

Snowy Owl is an almost annual visitor to New Jersey from the high Arctic, where it breeds. In most years there are only a few individuals present, but up to a dozen have been found during irruption years. They are usually found near the coast, with a majority of birds being immatures. The one pictured here is probably a first-year male and was photographed at Stone Harbor on 24 December 2007. *Photograph by Kevin Karlson.*

Barred Owl is one of the most widely distributed owls in North America, but is considered a Threatened Species in New Jersey, where it is uncommon and found primarily in wet woodlands. It is the only one of our owls, other than the very different Barn Owl, with dark eyes, and it lacks the ear tufts of the more familiar Eastern Screech- and Great Horned Owls. *Photograph by Kevin Karlson.*

Green Violet-ear is a large hummingbird native to the highlands of Mexico and Central and South America. It occurs almost annually in summer in Texas and nearby states. New Jersey's only record, a bird at a feeder for two days in Locust, Monmouth County, was also the first for the northeastern United States. It was photographed on the morning of the second day, 24 August 2005, just prior to its departure. *Photograph by Scott Elowitz.*

Red-bellied Woodpecker is a relative newcomer to New Jersey, having first nested here in the 1950s. It spread rapidly throughout the state, however, and is now the second most common woodpecker, after the smaller Downy. Although the name is misleading, it really does have a reddish patch on the belly. *Photograph by Kevin Karlson.*

Loggerhead Shrike was once an uncommon, but regular, migrant through New Jersey, mainly in August and September, but the northern migratory population in the East has almost entirely disappeared, and this species in now a very rare occurrence in the state. The bird shown here was one of the rare spring records: 6 May 2008 at Sandy Hook. *Photograph by Tom Boyle.*

Brown-headed Nuthatch is a resident species as near as southern Delaware, but is essentially nonmigratory. There are only two records for New Jersey, this juvenile bird present for six days at Cape May Point, 23–28 July 2005, and another individual at Cape May Point for four days in April 2010. *Photograph by Scott Elowitz.*

Varied Thrush is a bird of Alaska and the Pacific Northwest that wanders to eastern North America in small number every fall and winter. It has occurred in New Jersey more than twenty times, including this female that visited a River Vale, Bergen County, backyard for two consecutive winters in 2004 and 2005, shown here in December 2005. *Photograph by Kevin Watson.*

Black-throated Gray Warbler is a species fairly common in the dry, mixed oak and juniper woods of western North America that migrates to western Mexico for the winter. It has occurred as a vagrant many times throughout the eastern part of the continent, with twenty-one accepted records in New Jersey. This male, probably a first-year bird, spent most of January 2007 in a backyard in Evesham Township, Burlington County, and established only the second winter record for the state. *Photograph by Scott Elowitz.*

Yellow-throated Warbler is an attractive and widespread species of the southeastern United States that steadily expanded its range northward during the latter part of the twentieth century. The sexes are very similar in appearance, with the female only slightly duller. Two subspecies nest in New Jersey, southeastern *dominica* and interior *albilora*, pictured here. *Photograph by Lloyd Spitalnik..*

American Tree Sparrow nests in the far north of Canada and Alaska, but comes south to brighten a winter's day of birding in New Jersey. This attractive species, sometimes called the "winter Chippie" because of its resemblance to Chipping Sparrow, is much more common in the northern part of the state than in the south. *Photograph by Kevin Karlson.*

Le Conte's Sparrow is a small, shy and secretive but brightly patterned species of grassy meadows and marshy edges. Although it was not recorded in New Jersey until 1976, it has occurred with increasing frequency in recent decades and is almost annual, mainly in late fall. This individual was photographed at Cape May in October 1997. *Photograph by Kevin Karlson.*

Male Baltimore Oriole is one of the most beautiful birds in North America, and the adult female can be quite colorful as well. The species is a widespread migrant and summer resident in New Jersey and occasionally tries to overwinter, often at feeders. *Photograph by Lloyd Spitalnik.*

Order Psittaciformes

Family Psittacidae: Parakeets and Parrots

MONK PARAKEET *Myiopsitta monachus*

Fairly common, but very local, introduced resident. Monk Parakeets are native to southern South America, but they have been widely introduced in the United States, despite efforts by various state wildlife and agricultural authorities to contain them. A long-established colony in the Edgewater, Bergen County, area, numbers in the hundreds and has spread to neighboring communities. The birds are protected by the support of the local citizenry. The fate of a small colony recently established in Carteret, Middlesex County, remains to be seen. Monk Parakeet was added to the official State List by the NJBRC in 2008.

CAROLINA PARAKEET *Conurpsis carolinensis*

Extinct. Neither Turnbull (1869) nor Stone (1908, 1937) makes any mention of Carolina Parakeet in New Jersey, but Eaton (1936) cites an account of a flock that caused considerable damage to an apple orchard in East Orange, Essex County, during several hot summers in the 1850s. On the basis of this report and the inclusion of New Jersey in the species' former range on the AOU Check-list, both Kunkle (1959) and the NJBRC have included it on the State List.

Order Cuculiformes

Family Cuculidae: Cuckoos

YELLOW-BILLED CUCKOO *Coccyzus americanus*

Fairly common summer resident, spring and fall migrant. Spring migrant Yellow-billed Cuckoos may appear as early as late April and early May, but the main movement is from mid-May into early June. They are widely distributed as nesting birds in New Jersey, but populations fluctuate from year to year depending on the abundance of their preferred foods, mainly caterpillars, cicadas, and grasshoppers. As breeders, they are absent from the barrier islands, salt marsh, and heavily urbanized areas, but are fairly common in second-growth woodlands, thickets, and forest edges. Fall migration begins in late July, peaks in August, and diminishes through September, although the occasional stragglers can be found until the end of October, and exceptionally into the first days of November. The Yellow-billed Cuckoo population has declined significantly throughout its range in recent decades (Hughes 1999).

Yellow-billed Cuckoo is a fairly common, but elusive, migrant and summer resident in New Jersey. It taunts birders with a loud guttural call as it sits motionless on a branch before quietly slipping away. Numbers fluctuate greatly from year to year in response to the abundance of food. *Photograph by Kevin Karlson.*

BLACK-BILLED CUCKOO *Coccyzus erythrophthalmus*

Uncommon summer resident, spring and fall migrant. Black-billed Cuckoos are rare before the beginning of May, and although they are very inconspicuous in migration, the main movement is from mid-May to early June. The birds prefer more densely wooded areas than their Yellow-billed cousins, but are often in scrubby habitats as well, and can be found throughout the state where suitable conditions prevail. Breeding is apparently correlated with an outbreak of insects, especially caterpillars and cicadas, and Black-billed Cuckoos are known to wander erratically during the nesting season, presumably in search of such bounty. Fall migration begins in late July and is essentially complete by the beginning of October, but the cuckoos' secretive natures make them difficult to detect. A few have been seen as late as the beginning of November. Like the preceding species, numbers have declined dramatically across their range in recent decades (Hughes 2001).

GROOVE-BILLED ANI *Crotophaga sulcirostris*

Review Species

Accidental. New Jersey's only ani was originally identified as Smooth-billed, but subsequent examination of photographs and the written details of the observers convinced the records committee that the bird was the far more likely Groove-billed Ani. This species is a well-known wanderer and has occurred in Virginia and Maryland; the three ani records for Nova Scotia were most likely this species (Mlodinow and Karlson 1999).

9 OCT 1997, SANDY HOOK, MONMOUTH CO. (NJBRC 1997-070; NJPF)

In the United States, Groove-billed Ani breeds only in southern Texas, but it is known to wander far from there and from western Mexico and has occurred in more than half of the fifty states and several Canadian provinces. New Jersey's only record was of a bird present for just one day at Sandy Hook, 9 October 1997. *Photograph by Al Pochek.*

Order Strigiformes

Family Tytonidae: Barn Owls

BARN OWL *Tyto alba*

Uncommon and local (and probably declining) summer resident, uncommon fall migrant and winter resident; distribution poorly known. Barn Owls are almost exclusively nocturnal, do not have a characteristic territorial call, and may nest at almost any time of the year, so their presence in an area often goes undetected. The Atlas indicated that the New Jersey population is concentrated along the Delaware Bayshore, the Hackensack Meadowlands and lower Hudson River, and parts of the Piedmont and Highlands (Walsh et al. 1999). Many adult birds apparently do not migrate (Marti et al. 2005) and are vulnerable to severe winters,

but fall banding records from Cape May indicated a regular dispersal of juveniles and some adults (Duffy and Kerlinger 1992). It is likely that the species has been negatively affected by the disappearance of many farms and barns, and the concomitant reduction in prey availability.

Family Strigidae: Typical Owls

EASTERN SCREECH-OWL *Megascops asio*

Fairly common and widespread resident. Eastern Screech-Owls are resident throughout New Jersey, but are more common from the Piedmont north. The Atlas found them sparsely distributed throughout the Pine Barrens and the Inner Coastal Plain, but common in Cumberland and Salem counties. Because they are cavity dwellers and highly nocturnal in their foraging activities, Screech-Owls are seldom seen during the day. In winter, however, they will often sit in the entrance to their roost site to sun themselves on a cold, clear day. The numbers recorded on statewide CBCs have increased from an average of fewer than 200 to more than 400 since the 1970s, primarily due to increased observer effort.

Eastern Screech-Owl is our most common small owl and can be found in almost any woodland habitat throughout the state, although it is more common in the north. It comes in two color morphs, rufous and gray, which are about equally common and may occur in the same brood. A gray-morph adult is pictured here. *Photograph by Lloyd Spitalnik.*

GREAT HORNED OWL *Bubo virginianus*

Fairly common and widespread resident. Great Horned Owls are found in woodlands throughout the state, wherever they can find appropriate nest sites. They do not build their own nests but use old hawk and crow nests, and they can often be seen in late winter or early spring sitting on a nest exposed by a lack of foliage. Great Horned Owls are less common in the Pine Barrens and urban areas of northeastern New Jersey and are nocturnal unless disturbed from a roost. As with Eastern Screech-Owls, the numbers on statewide CBCs have increased since the 1970s from an average of about 110 to about 300, due to increased observer effort.

SNOWY OWL *Bubo scandiacus*

Very rare to rare migrant and winter visitor, accidental in summer. One or more Snowy Owls visit New Jersey almost every winter, usually along the Hudson River, at the Hackensack Meadowlands, or on the coast from Sandy Hook to Cape May. In years of big flights, a dozen or more may be found. Especially in such years, some may be present inland, primarily in agricultural fields. Some individuals move on in a day or two, whereas many remain in a given area for weeks or months. The earlier arrivals have been in November and most have departed by late February, although some birds occasionally linger into March. On 30 August 2009, a Snowy Owl, not a juvenile, was photographed near Liberty SP, Hudson County. Whether or not it summered in the area is not known. (*See photo page 146.*)

NORTHERN HAWK OWL *Surnia ulula*

Review Species

Accidental. There are two accepted records of this diurnal owl of the boreal forest, both from the early twentieth century. One was shot during the winter of 1904 in Essex County and was in a private collection, but the specimen has been lost (Eaton 1936, Bull 1964); another was seen in New Brunswick in 1926 (Brooks 1927). The only record of Hawk Owl near New Jersey in recent decades was one present in February and March 1991 in Wayne County, PA, just forty miles northwest of High Point.

WINTER 1904, ESSEX CO.
19 DEC 1926, NEW BRUNSWICK, MIDDLESEX CO.

BARRED OWL *Strix varia*

Uncommon and somewhat local resident. Threatened Species in New Jersey. Barred Owls prefer swampy woodlands with trees large enough to provide the cavities that they use for nesting. Like most wetland species, their numbers declined during much of the 1900s due to habitat loss, but have shown some recovery in recent decades. The Atlas showed that their stronghold in the state is the Kittatinny Mountains, Kittatinny Valley, and the Highlands in the north and Cumberland and Cape May counties in the south. Atlantic and Burlington counties and the wooded swamps of Morris and western Essex counties also have healthy populations. On average, about twenty Barred Owls are recorded on the CBCs. (*See photo page 146.*)

LONG-EARED OWL *Asio otus*

Uncommon migrant and winter resident, rare and local summer resident. Southbound Long-eared Owls may arrive as early as mid-October, and banding studies at Cape May showed early November to be the peak migration time. They winter throughout much of New Jersey, but their secretive nature makes numbers difficult to assess. The owls sometimes form communal roosts of a dozen or more in areas where abundant prey is available (Marks et al. 1994). Most wintering birds have departed by the beginning of April, and only the small and scattered breeding population remains for the summer. Both historical reports and the Atlas have indicated that Long-eared Owl is one of the rarest of the regularly occurring breeding birds, with most records from Burlington, Hunterdon, Morris, and Sussex counties (Walsh et al. 1999, Bosakowski et al. 1989a). Bosakowski et al. (1989b) documented an apparent long-term decline in the numbers of both wintering and nesting birds in the state.

SHORT-EARED OWL *Asio flammeus*

Uncommon migrant and winter resident, formerly nested in very small numbers. Endangered Species as a breeding bird in New Jersey. Short-eared Owls arrive at their wintering sites from late October into November, and most have departed by the end of March, although a few linger through April. Numbers vary from year to year, with the

highest counts usually in midwinter. They are typically seen hunting over the coastal marshes in southern New Jersey and over open fields in the north just after sunset, but they can also be found hunting at dawn and during the day under overcast conditions. Short-eared Owls nested in small numbers along the coast from Salem County to Barnegat Bay and Newark Bay at least through the 1920s (Stone 1937), and Fables (1955) considered it a decreasing permanent resident. They were seen at two sites in Barnegat Bay and one at Tuckahoe WMA during June 1979 (RNJB 5[4]:60), but the last known possible nesting was at Supawna Meadows NWR, Salem County, where a pair was present from 28 March to 2 June 1989 (RNJB 15[3]:54).

Short-eared Owl is primarily a winter resident in New Jersey, and is most often seen hunting at dusk over salt marshes along the coast or farm fields in the northern part of the state. Its mothlike flight pattern is so distinctive that Short-eared can be identified at a great distance. *Photograph by Kevin Karlson.*

BOREAL OWL *Aegolius funereus*

Review Species

Accidental. New Jersey's only Boreal Owl was found moribund at the Raritan Arsenal next to a building that it had apparently struck during the night. It died after a week and was carefully buried by the finder, a young boy who kept pointing out to his elders that it resembled this species. Three months later it was dug up, in surprisingly good condition, and taken to the Newark Museum, where its identity was confirmed. The specimen now resides in the American Museum of Natural History.

1 NOV 1962, BONHAMTOWN, MIDDLESEX CO. (*AMNH #835288)

NORTHERN SAW-WHET OWL *Aegolius acadicus*

Uncommon migrant and winter resident, rare and local summer resident. Northern Saw-whet Owls are small, secretive, nocturnal, and rarely encountered in the field, even with diligent searching. Fall banding studies at Cape May Point have shown that they can be fairly common migrants in some years, with a peak flight in early to mid-November (Duffy and Kerlinger 1992). Data from winter roadkills and birds brought to rehabilitators suggest that substantial numbers of Saw-whet Owls winter in New Jersey, especially in major flight years (Loos and Kerlinger 1993, Sutton 1996), but few are recorded on CBCs (nine on average). There are no data on spring migration, but the presence of calling birds in late spring at multiple locations in the Pine Barrens, the Highlands, and the Kittatinny Mountains has long led to the suspicion of breeding. This was confirmed in 1986 with the discovery of a free-flying juvenile in Passaic County (Benzinger 1987) and in Burlington County during the Atlas (Dasey 1999). More recently, a brood of flightless young was found in a Screech-Owl box in Somerset County in 2008 (L. Soucy, pers. comm.).

Northern Saw-whet Owl is the smallest and least known of our regularly occurring owls but is probably more common than field encounters would lead one to believe. It is shy, secretive, and nocturnal by nature and vocalizes infrequently, so it often escapes detection. Banding studies, however, have shown that these owls can be fairly common in migration in most years. *Photograph by Kevin Karlson.*

Order Caprimulgiformes

Family Caprimulgidae: Nighthawks and Nightjars

LESSER NIGHTHAWK *Cordeiles acutipennis*

Accidental. A nighthawk discovered roosting at Cape May Point SP at noon on 25 November 2007 was carefully scrutinized and photographed and determined to be a Lesser Nighthawk, the first for New Jersey. It remained for the rest of the day, to the delight of the many who came from all parts of the state. At dusk it took flight, made a couple of circles, and disappeared, never to be seen again (O'Brien 2008). The only other records of the species for the Northeast are from Ontario (1974) and West Virginia (2008), both in late April. One was found on Bermuda in December 1965.

25 NOV 2007, CAPE MAY PT., CAPE MAY CO. (NJBRC 2009-090; NJPF)

Review Species

outer primary shorter than next inner primary

Lesser Nighthawk is a bird of the Southwest that has occurred just three times in northeastern North America. One of these was a bird discovered at Cape May Point State Park on 25 November 2007, where it spent the day but departed at dusk. ID criteria for this species can be found in Appendix D. *Photograph by Kevin Karlson.*

COMMON NIGHTHAWK *Cordeiles minor*

Uncommon spring and fall migrant, scarce and local summer resident. Common Nighthawks were formerly more common migrants in New Jersey, especially in the early fall, but their numbers have declined dramatically in recent decades. As breeding birds, historically they were ground nesting birds and Stone (1908) considered them common, but by 1937 Stone (1937) called them "local or rare breeding birds" in the northern counties. Many took to nesting on gravel rooftops in towns and cities, but by the 1980s Leck (1984) and Boyle (1986) suggested that they were confined to the Pine Barrens and the urban areas of northeastern New Jersey. The Atlas found the urban population

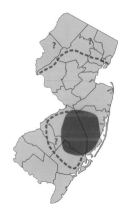

substantially reduced and the greatest concentrations in the Pine Barrens and the Kittatinny Valley province, although the recent lack of observations suggests that they may no longer nest in the latter area. The last few decades appear to have witnessed a substantial decline in the breeding population of Common Nighthawk in the state, as has been documented for neighboring New York (Medler 2008) and many other areas in the East. Various reasons have been postulated for this decline, including pesticide spraying and a switch from gravel roofing to less attractive substrates.

CHUCK-WILL'S-WIDOW *Caprimulgus carolinensis*

Uncommon and local summer resident, very rare spring and fall migrant. The first breeding record of Chuck-will's-widow in New Jersey was at Cape May Point, where a female with two young was found on 21 May 1922 (Fables 1955); curiously, Stone (1937) makes no mention of this event. From this beginning they slowly expanded their range up the Delaware Bayshore and the Atlantic coast, reaching Oceanville, Atlantic County, by 1973 and Island Beach SP by 1978 (Leck 1984). The Atlas found the limits of Chuck-will's-widow's range to be southern Salem County on the Bayshore and northern Ocean County on the coast, with a few records from the Pine Barrens. They have been found as far north as Sandy Hook and rapidly colonized part of Long Island, NY, during the late 1970s and early 1980s, but have since disappeared from most of the island (Mitra 2008). Migrants are rarely encountered, but they arrive on the breeding grounds in late April and apparently depart by early September (Sibley 1997).

A southern species that first appeared in New Jersey in the early twentieth century, Chuck-will's-widow slowly expanded its range up the Delaware Bayshore and the Atlantic Coast, but has not penetrated far inland. Since it is larger than its cousin Whip-poor-will, it has displaced them in these coastal zones. *Photograph by Kevin Karlson.*

WHIP-POOR-WILL *Caprimulgus vociferus*

Whip-poor-will is a fairly common but declining summer resident of the Pine Barrens and the Outer Coastal Plain, scarce spring and fall migrant. It is a very local and uncommon breeding bird in the Highlands and along the Kittatinny Ridge. As with other nightjars, Whip-poor-will populations have shown dramatic declines during recent decades in the Northeast, including northern New Jersey. Two potential explanations for this are the succession of old farmland and second-growth woodland to more mature forests, plus urban and suburban sprawl (Benzinger and Van de Venter 1995). The species migrates through in spring and fall, but is seldom encountered due to its strictly nocturnal habits.

Whip-poor-will populations in New Jersey and elsewhere in the Northeast have declined dramatically in recent decades, but the species remains fairly common in the Pine Barrens of southern New Jersey. Whip-poor-will roosts mainly on the ground, but when perched in trees, it sits longitudinally on a branch, as do all nightjars. This migrant bird was photographed in Cape May in September. *Photograph by Kevin Karlson.*

Order Apodiformes

Family Apodidae: Swifts

CHIMNEY SWIFT *Chaetura pelagica*

Common and widespread, but declining, summer resident, common spring and fall migrant. Chimney Swifts return to New Jersey in mid-April, with the peak migration during the following few weeks. Throughout the summer they are common, especially around human habitation, as they now

nest almost exclusively in chimneys and similar structures. Unfortunately, as older chimneys deteriorate and newer ones are less suitable for nest sites, Chimney Swift populations have declined throughout their range in recent decades (Cink and Collins 2002), with an average annual decline on Breeding Bird Survey routes of 2.8 percent in New Jersey since 1966 (Sauer et al. 2008). They often form large roosts in August and September, such as the annual gathering of up to 4,000 at a school in Ridgewood, Bergen County, before departing for South America. Migrants peak in early September, but stragglers are seen through October into early November.

Family Trochilidae: Hummingbirds

GREEN VIOLET-EAR *Colibri thalassinus*

Review Species

Accidental. There is just one record for this vagrant from Central America, a bird that visited a feeder in Locust, Monmouth County, on the afternoon of 23 August 2005. It was present after dawn the next morning, to the joy of many observers, but departed before seven a.m., never to be seen again (Barnes 2006). Although there are more than fifty occurrences of the species north of the Mexican border, mainly from Texas, this was the first for the northeastern U.S (Howell 2002), the next closest being in eastern West Virginia. (*See photo page 147.*)

23–24 AUG 2005, LOCUST, MONMOUTH CO. (NJBRC 2006-074)

RUBY-THROATED HUMMINGBIRD *Archilochus colubris*

Fairly common and widespread summer resident, fairly common spring and fall migrant. Male Ruby-throated Hummingbirds arrive from their wintering grounds in mid- to late April, followed by the females two weeks later. After courtship and mating, the female alone builds the nest, lays the eggs, and raises the young. She may raise two or even three broods (Robinson et al. 1996), and birds have been seen sitting on nests in late August at Cape May (pers. obs.). Ruby-throated Hummingbirds are least common in highly urban areas, on the Inner Coastal Plain, and on the barrier islands. Peak movement of southbound migrants is late August to early September, but increasingly a few are lingering through October and even into December, with four recent CBC records.

Ruby-throated Humming-
bird is a fairly common summer resident throughout the
state, arriving in April and
departing mainly in September, although an increasing
few are lingering later in the
year. The male is stunning
with his beautiful, iridescent
gorget. *Photograph by Kevin
Karlson.*

BLACK-CHINNED HUMMINGBIRD *Archilochus alexandri*

Accidental. All four of New Jersey's Black-chinned Hummingbirds have been immature birds, as expected, that
showed up at feeders in late fall. Because of the difficulty of
separating this species from the common Ruby-throated
Hummingbird, a few of which sometimes linger into November and even December, good photographs, meticulous
descriptions, and banding, if possible, are needed to con-
firm the identity (Crossley 1997). Three of the records are
from near the coast, but one is from the Highlands of Sussex County.

Review Species

10–15 NOV 1996, VILLAS, CAPE MAY CO. (NJBRC 1996-092; NJPF)
27–29 OCT 2001, CAPE MAY, CAPE MAY CO. (NJBRC 2002-049; NJPF)
20–27 NOV 2005, BARNEGAT LIGHT, OCEAN CO. (NJBRC 2006-059;
  NJPF)
30 OCT–1 NOV 2006, VERNON, SUSSEX CO. (NJBRC 2007-049; NJPF)

Black-chinned Hummingbird is a common summer
resident in much of the American West, but has
strayed east in autumn and winter on numerous
occasions. All four of New Jersey's records have
been immature birds in fall, such as the female
shown here in North Cape May, Cape May County,
in November 1996. Immatures and females are
very similar to Ruby-throated Hummingbirds. They
are best separated by a combination of characteris-
tics, including the broader, rounded, more recurved
tips to the outermost primaries. ID criteria for separating this bird from Ruby-throated are provided
in Appendix D. *Photograph by Kevin Karlson.*

CALLIOPE HUMMINGBIRD *Stellula calliope*

Casual. The first of New Jersey's six Calliope Hummingbirds arrived at a Wildwood Crest feeder 23 November 1996, but was identified "after the fact." Despite some discrepancies, it was initially dismissed as an odd Rufous/Allen's. As it lingered into December, it was captured and taken to a rehabilitation center, then transported to California in late January. The bird was identified as a female Calliope from photographs taken at the feeder and in the hand (Lehman 1997). Subsequently, there have been five additional records, all at feeders in October or November including an adult male at Eldora, Cape May County, 2–6 October 2007. The 1996 Calliope was the first for the Northeast, but since then the species has appeared in Connecticut, Maine, Massachusetts, New York, Pennsylvania and Maryland.

Calliope Hummingbird, the smallest North American bird, is a summer resident of mountains in the western U.S. In recent years, this species has appeared in eastern states with increasing frequency in fall and winter. There are now six records for New Jersey, only one of which involved an adult male, photographed here at Eldora, Cape May County, 2 October 2007. *Photograph by Don Freiday.*

RUFOUS HUMMINGBIRD *Selasphorus rufus*

Rare, but increasingly regular, visitor, almost always at feeders. New Jersey's first Rufous Hummingbird, an adult male, was present at New Lisbon, Burlington County, 2–3 July 1991, but there have now been eighteen accepted records of the species and another twenty-four records accepted as Rufous/Allen's Hummingbird, most of which are surely Rufous. Only adult males of the two species can be reliably separated in the field, so most of the accepted records have been identified in the hand. There have now been three other adult male Rufous, all in summer. Rufous and Rufous/Allen's Hummingbirds have been found from

July to early December, with most reports coming from October and November. Many have lingered at feeders into December, five into January, and one to 10 February. The growing trend of "western" hummingbirds appearing in the East in autumn can only partly be due to feeders being left out later in the season.

ALLEN'S HUMMINGBIRD *Selasphorus sasin*

Accidental. There are now three records of Allen's Hummingbird in New Jersey, all from southern Cape May County. The first, an immature female, was identified by capturing and measuring the wing and tail dimensions (O'Brien and Gustafson 2002). Both of the other records are of immature males, also captured, measured, and banded. Nonadult male Rufous and Allen's Hummingbirds are almost impossible to separate in the field, so many are best identified only as "Rufous/Allen's." Allen's has occurred once in Massachusetts, twice in Delaware, and more recently in Pennsylvania and Maryland, but now appears annually in the southeastern U.S.

Review Species

12 NOV 2000–2 JAN 2001, CAPE MAY, CAPE MAY CO. (NJBRC 2001-064)

14 NOV 2003–11 JAN 2004, CAPE MAY, CAPE MAY CO. (NJBRC 2004-050)

3 NOV–19 DEC 2004, VILLAS, CAPE MAY CO. (NJBRC 2005-046)

Allen's Hummingbird is a summer resident of western California and southwestern Oregon. Like many other western hummingbirds, it has shown an increasing pattern of fall and winter vagrancy to the eastern U.S. in recent years. Immature and female birds are very difficult to separate from the closely related Rufous Hummingbird, and all three of New Jersey's records have been confirmed using measurements obtained in the hand by banders. The first was this immature female present at a Cape May feeder for almost two months and photographed on 20 December 2000. *Photograph by Kevin Karlson.*

Order Coraciiformes

Family Alcedinidae: Kingfishers

BELTED KINGFISHER *Ceryle alcyon*

Fairly common spring and fall migrant, uncommon but widespread summer resident, uncommon winter resident. Belted Kingfishers are present year-round through most of New Jersey, but their nesting distribution is limited by the availability of vertical banks or cliffs for nest sites, and a nearby source of food (Walsh et al. 1999). Consequently, they are scarce as breeding birds in the Pine Barrens and on most of the barrier islands. Fall migration is mainly from late August to mid-October, but many stay to winter in the state, wherever open water is available. CBC totals have remained consistently in the 300 to 500 range in recent decades. Spring migration peaks in April, with summering birds returning and northbound birds passing through.

Belted Kingfisher is a noisy and conspicuous year-round resident of the state, although it becomes much less common in winter. The male, shown here, is distinguished from females by having only the single, blue band, whereas the female has a second, rufous band. *Photograph by Kevin Karlson.*

Order Piciformes

Family Picidae: Woodpeckers

RED-HEADED WOODPECKER *Melanerpes erythrocephalus*

Scarce, local, and erratic summer resident, scarce and irregular migrant and winter resident. Threatened Species in New Jersey. Although Red-headed Woodpeckers were once common breeding birds in much of eastern North

America, they suffered serious declines by the beginning of the twentieth century (Bull 1964, Kaufman 1996). Their historical status in New Jersey is less clear. Stone (1908) made no mention of any decline and later (1937) stated that the species "has always been rare and exceedingly erratic in its occurrence east of the Delaware and Hudson Rivers." Today, Red-headed Woodpeckers nest sporadically and unpredictably in northwestern New Jersey and the Pine Barrens, less frequently in Cape May and Cumberland counties. During fall migration, mainly September–October, individuals may be encountered anywhere in the state, but are most frequent near the coast when a single season might see two or three at Sandy Hook and a dozen or more at Cape May. Numbers of wintering birds vary widely from year to year, at least partly in response to acorn abundance, and the Great Swamp CBC has produced more than forty on two separate occasions. Northbound migrants are occasionally seen in late April and May, mainly along the coast.

The handsome Red-headed Woodpecker is a scarce and erratic resident and migrant in New Jersey. It prefers open oak woodlands with mature trees for nesting holes and an abundance of acorns. Loss of nest cavities to aggressive European Starlings has greatly reduced the breeding population in the East since the 1880s. *Photograph by Kevin Karlson.*

RED-BELLIED WOODPECKER *Melanerpes carolinus*

Common and ubiquitous resident. Red-bellied Woodpecker is a relatively recent addition to New Jersey's resident avifauna. Until the 1950s, when the first nestings occurred in Salem and Cape May counties, they were considered accidental stragglers from the South (Stone 1937, Fables 1955). From there, they spread rapidly north, reaching Princeton

by 1962 and Sussex County by 1976 (Walsh *et al.* 1999). Today, Red-bellied is the second commonest woodpecker after Downy, and it can be found throughout the state, although infrequently on the barrier islands. Their population expansion is reflected in the increase in CBC totals, which averaged about 120 in the mid-1970s, but almost 2,000 in the first decade of the twenty-first century. (*See photo page 148.*)

YELLOW-BELLIED SAPSUCKER *Sphyrapicus varius*

Uncommon spring and fall migrant, uncommon winter resident, scarce and local summer resident. Fall migrant Yellow-bellied Sapsuckers are first seen in mid-September, but the main flight is usually during the first half of October, when the birds may be fairly common along the coast, but much less so inland. Because they are usually silent and somewhat shy in migration and in winter, they are often overlooked. They are found throughout the state in winter, more frequently inland, and CBC totals have shown a steady increase in recent decades from an average of about 20 in the mid-1970s to more than 200 in some recent years. Sapsuckers are inconspicuous in spring migration, which peaks in April. Prior to 1998, there was only one confirmed nesting record for Yellow-bellied Sapsucker in New Jersey. In June 1998, a pair was found feeding young along the Kittatinny Ridge in High Point SP. Since then, the breeding population in that area has grown to perhaps several dozen pairs in the park and adjacent Stokes State Forest.

DOWNY WOODPECKER *Picoides pubescens*

Very common and ubiquitous resident. The familiar Downy Woodpecker, New Jersey's most abundant woodpecker, can be found just about anywhere in the state, although it is less common on the barrier islands than elsewhere. Stone (1908) described them as second in abundance to Northern Flicker, a situation that is surely not the case today. Although some authors (Cruickshank 1942, Veit and Peterson 1993, Sibley 1997) have reported an apparent small migration in the fall, Jackson and Ouellet (2002) argue that, while there may be some unidirectional dispersal, there is no evidence of true migration in the species. The abundance of Downy Woodpeckers in the state is indicated by the CBC average of more than 2,000.

HAIRY WOODPECKER *Picoides villosus*

Fairly common and widespread resident. Hairy Woodpeckers are much less common in New Jersey than their smaller cousin, the Downy, but are almost as widely distributed, being absent or nearly so from the barrier islands and uncommon in parts of the Pine Barrens and Cape May County. In eastern North America, there has been a slow, but steady, decline in populations in the past century, perhaps due to forest fragmentation and their reliance on larger, more mature woodlands (Kaufman 1996, Jackson et al. 2002). Boyle (1986) suggested that numbers had declined in recent years, but CBC totals have remained relatively constant since 1970 when adjusted for observer hours.

RED-COCKADED WOODPECKER

Picoides borealis

Review Species

Accidental. The presence of this woodpecker on the New Jersey State List is due to a specimen, an adult male of the nominate race, apparently collected at Hoboken some time prior to 1866 by a C. Galbraith. Some authorities have expressed doubts concerning the correctness of the locality, but Bull (1964) wrote that "there appears to be no reason to question that it was actually taken in New Jersey," and both the AOU and the NJBRC have accepted that view. The range of this species declined dramatically during the twentieth century, but it nested as far north as Dorchester County on the Eastern Shore of Maryland as recently as the 1950s (Stewart and Robbins 1958).

BEFORE 1866, HOBOKEN, HUDSON CO. (*AMNH #44035)

AMERICAN THREE-TOED WOODPECKER

Picoides dorsalis

Review Species

Accidental. One report of this species of the boreal forest has been accepted, a leisurely close-range study by an experienced observer at West Englewood, Bergen County, in February 1918 (Cruickshank 1942). Although Fables (1955) and Bull (1964) relegated the sighting to the hypothetical list, the NJBRC agreed with Cruickshank's verdict.

5 FEB 1918, WEST ENGLEWOOD, BERGEN CO. (NJBRC AR 1996)

BLACK-BACKED WOODPECKER *Picoides arcticus*

Review Species

Surprisingly, there have been sixteen accepted records o
this usually sedentary boreal woodpecker. The first wa
collected at Englewood, Bergen County, on 29 Novembe
1923 and is a specimen in the American Museum of Natu
ral History. Six of the records have come from Berger
County, including one to three birds at Oradell Reservoi
every other winter from 1956–1957 to 1960–1961. Be
tween 1950 and 1969 there were twelve different sighting
of Black-backed Woodpecker, but there has been only one
since, an adult feeding on a dead Scotch pine in Princeton
on 5 and 9 April 1983. Such southward movements in thi
species appear to be much less frequent since the 1960
throughout the Northeast.

Black-backed Woodpecker is
a mostly sedentary resident
of northern boreal forests,
but there are a surprising sixteen records for New Jersey,
a majority from the 1950s
and 1960s. Since 1969, there
has been just one occur-
rence, this male photo-
graphed at Princeton, Mercer
County, 9 April 1983. *Photograph by Tom Southerland.*

NORTHERN FLICKER *Colaptes aureus*

Common and widespread resident, very common migran
along the coast, especially in fall. Northern Flicker remain
one of our most familiar and common birds, although long
term Breeding Bird Surveys and CBCs indicate a steady de
cline in the population over the past fifty years, due in par
to competition with Starlings for nest cavities (Wiebe and
Moore 2008). As predominantly ground feeders, flickers mi
grate from the northern parts of their range, resulting in
sometimes-spectacular flights along the coast in late Sep
tember into October and much less noticeable flights in
late March to early April. During winters with heavy snow

cover, many withdraw from the northwestern part of the
state or become regular visitors to feeding stations.

PILEATED WOODPECKER *Dryocopus pileatus*

Uncommon and somewhat local resident. Stone (1937)
considered Pileated Woodpeckers to be extirpated from
most of state by the beginning of the twentieth century, as
they retreated in the face of advancing civilization. Griscom
(1923) noted their rediscovery in the northernmost counties by the early 1920s, and Bull (1964) added that they
had "increased greatly." They are most common in the Kittatinny Mountains and Valley and the Highlands, but are
found throughout the Piedmont in relatively mature second-growth forest. Occasional sighting from Cumberland
and western Cape May counties in recent decades suggest
a small population exists there, where there is localized
suitable habitat. More recently, there have been scattered
reports from eastern Monmouth County, perhaps scouts
from the Piedmont looking for new territory, and from
other sites, such as Cape Island, that are far from potential
breeding areas.

Order Passeriformes

Family Tyrannidae: Tyrant Flycatchers

OLIVE-SIDED FLYCATCHER *Contopus cooperi*

Scarce spring and fall migrant. Olive-sided Flycatchers are
late spring migrants, arriving from their South American
wintering grounds from mid-May to early June, and are
encountered primarily in the northern part of the state and
at Cape May. Conversely, the return flight from breeding
territories in northern New York, New England, and Canada, is relatively early and runs from early August to
mid-September. There have been a couple of early October
records recently, and Walsh et al. (1999) cite an early November report. Olive-sided Flycatchers have declined dramatically in recent decades (4 percent per year on Breeding
Bird Surveys, 1966–1996), probably due in part to extensive deforestation of their wintering areas in the forests of
the Andes (Altman and Sallabanks 2000). An active birder
is lucky to find more than one or two a year in the state.

EASTERN WOOD-PEWEE *Contopus virens*

Common and widespread summer resident, fairly common spring and fall migrant. Eastern Wood-Pewees arrive on their breeding grounds in New Jersey from early to mid-May, with migrants passing through into early June. During the nesting season, their plaintive call can be heard in almost any woodland throughout the state, with the exception of the barrier islands and highly urbanized areas. Pewees head south from late August to early October, with a peak in mid-September. A few individuals have been seen as late as the beginning of November, but there are no winter records (and none for anywhere in the U.S.). Although Breeding Bird Surveys showed a significant decrease in some parts of their range during the late 1900s, this has not been noticeable in New Jersey.

YELLOW-BELLIED FLYCATCHER *Empidonax flaviventris*

Scarce spring and uncommon fall migrant. Yellow-bellied Flycatchers are one of the more sought-after of the regular migrants that pass through New Jersey. The fall passage, running from mid-August to late September, is concentrated primarily in the middle of that period, when one is lucky to encounter more than one or two in a day. An exceptionally late bird was present the last week of October 2005 at Bay Head, Ocean County. Spring migration, which is mostly to our west, occurs during mid- to late May, but an active birder is fortunate to find even one in a season.

ACADIAN FLYCATCHER *Empidonax virescens*

Fairly common but somewhat local summer resident, scarce spring and fall migrant. Acadian Flycatchers have long been established breeders in wet woodlands of the southern counties and parts of the Pine Barrens (Stone 1908), but they largely disappeared from the northern part of New Jersey, New York, and New England around 1900, for unknown reasons (Whitehead and Taylor 2002). Although Bull (1964) considered them rare north of the Raritan River, they recolonized the northern counties during the second half of the twentieth century and are now fairly common breeders in hemlock glens in the Kittatinny Mountains and the Highlands and along the upper Delaware River. Acadian

Flycatchers arrive on their breeding grounds between late April and mid-May, but migrants may occur into early June. They are seldom reported in fall migration, but most have departed or passed through by early September.

ALDER FLYCATCHER *Empidonax alnorum*

Uncommon and local summer resident, scarce spring and uncommon fall migrant. The history of Alder Flycatcher in the state is confused by the fact that it and Willow Flycatcher were considered conspecific as Traill's Flycatcher until 1973. Northern New Jersey is the southeastern limit of its breeding range, and here it has a patchy distribution, mainly in overgrown fields and swamps from the Great Swamp NWR and Troy Meadows north and west to the Delaware River and New York State, frequently at the same site as Willow Flycatcher. The two species are difficult to separate other than by voice, but fall migrants appear to pass through from mid-August to late September. Alder Flycatchers are late migrants in spring, arriving on the breeding territories in mid-May, with passage birds continuing into early June.

WILLOW FLYCATCHER *Empidonax traillii*

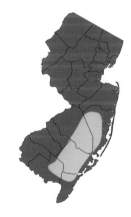

Fairly common but local summer resident, uncommon spring and fall migrant. The history of Willow Flycatcher in New Jersey is confused by the fact that it and Alder Flycatcher were considered conspecific as Traill's Flycatcher until 1973. Willows are widely distributed in the northern part of the state, where they nest in thickets, shrubby areas, and overgrown fields. During the twentieth century, they expanded their range southward, mainly avoiding the Pine Barrens, all the way to southern Cape May County, where they were unknown in Stone's time (Stone 1937). Willow Flycatchers arrive at their breeding grounds in mid- to late May and probably move south in August and early September, although the difficulty of distinguishing the species from Alder Flycatcher other than by voice makes the dates uncertain.

LEAST FLYCATCHER *Empidonax minimus*

Uncommon and local summer resident, uncommon spring and fairly common fall migrant. Least Flycatcher is con-

fined primarily to the northwestern corner of New Jersey as a breeding bird and has retreated from some sites, such as the Great Swamp, where it was formerly a regular nester. A variety of banding and Breeding Bird Survey data indicate a substantial decline in the northeastern population in recent decades (Tarof and Briskie 2008), especially in New Jersey (Sauer et al. 2008). Least Flycatchers arrive on their breeding grounds beginning in early May, with most migrants passing through in the middle of the month. The most common Empidonax migrants, they can be found moving as early as late July, with a peak from late August to mid-September. A few linger into late October, and there is even a recent record of one that stayed in Cape May until late December.

PACIFIC-SLOPE/CORDILLERAN FLYCATCHER

Empidonax difficilis/occidentalis

Review Species

Accidental. These two species were formerly lumped as Western Flycatcher, and this sight record by two observers familiar with the species was accepted as that by the NJ-BRC in 1990. Following the decision of the AOU to split Western into two species of flycatcher, the record was accepted on the State List revision of 1996 as Pacific-slope/Cordilleran Flycatcher.

16 NOV 1981, FORSYTHE NWR, ATLANTIC CO. (NJBRC AR1996)

EASTERN PHOEBE *Sayornis phoebe*

Fairly common and widespread summer resident, fairly common spring and common fall migrant, rare winter resident. Eastern Phoebes are short-distance migrants, arriving on their breeding grounds throughout the state from mid-March to early April. Stone (1937) knew of no nesting records south of the central Pine Barrens or lower Delaware River, but phoebes expanded their range during the twentieth century to include most of New Jersey. They remain scarce in the urbanized areas, on the barrier islands, in coastal wetlands, and in most of southern Cape May County. Fall migration peaks in early to mid-October, but stragglers remain into December, when they are increasingly found on CBCs. Scattered January and February reports show that some survive the winter.

Eastern Phoebe is a familiar sign of spring, especially in the northern part of the state, where it is one of the first migrant passerines of the season, typically arriving in late March. It likes to breed near water, often building its nest under a bridge. *Photograph by Kevin Karlson.*

SAY'S PHOEBE *Sayornis saya*

Casual. Since the first appearance of Say's Phoebe in New Jersey at Tuckerton in 1948, there have been sixteen accepted records, one in winter, two in spring, and the rest in the fall. Half of the sightings have occurred since 1999 and all but four have been one-day wonders. As expected, most records are from the coast, but there are three from inland sites in Bergen, Passaic, and Monmouth counties.

Review Species

Say's Phoebe is a widespread species of western North America, but wanders casually to the East Coast, primarily in fall. All but three of New Jersey's sixteen records have been on or near the coast, this one near Goshen, Cape May County, 24–27 October 1999. *Photograph by Kevin Karlson.*

VERMILION FLYCATCHER *Pyrocephalus rubinus*

Review Species

Accidental. A first-spring male was discovered at the Wetlands Institute, Stone Harbor, on the afternoon of 13 May 2002. It was seen again briefly the following morning, but then disappeared in the strong winds that had come up. Remarkably, it was found again the next day at Stone Harbor Point, about a mile south of the Wetlands Institute. It remained for only an hour, and then flew off to the north, never to be seen again. Prior to this report, there had been at least nine confirmed records of Vermilion Flycatcher from the Northeast, including one from each of the states surrounding New Jersey, so the appearance was long anticipated (Karlson 2003).

13–15 MAY 2002, STONE HARBOR, CAPE MAY CO. (NJBRC 2003-028; NJPF)

Vermilion Flycatcher ranges from the southwestern U.S. desert to southern South America, but is well known to wander in fall and winter to the southeastern U.S. There are now at least a dozen records for the Northeast, mostly in spring and fall, including one from New Jersey. This male was seen briefly on three consecutive days at Stone Harbor, 13–15 May 2002. *Photograph by Jenny Harrington.*

ASH-THROATED FLYCATCHER *Myiarchus cinerascens*

Review Species

Rare. Ash-throated Flycatcher is a rare, but increasingly encountered, late autumn–early winter stray from the western U.S. All accepted records have occurred between late October and mid-January, with most between early November and mid-December, and many involve birds that linger for days or even a few weeks. Most are found along or near the coast, but there are nine inland records, as well. Between the first bird—at Assunpink WMA in December 1984—through 1999, there were just fifteen sightings, but the period from 2000 to 2008 produced an additional twenty-seven accepted records. The year 2009 yielded only two, however, so the species remains on the Review List.

Ash-throated Flycatcher is another widespread Southwestern species with a propensity for widespread vagrancy. In some recent years, there have been as many as four or five records in New Jersey, all from late fall and early winter. The bird is more likely to be encountered after October than its cousin, Great Crested Flycatcher, which is a widespread breeding bird from late April to September. This bird was photographed in Cape May in November 1998. *Photograph by Kevin Karlson.*

GREAT CRESTED FLYCATCHER *Myiarchus crinitus*

This flycatcher is a fairly common and familiar summer resident throughout the state, being absent only from the highly urbanized areas of the northeast and the barrier islands. It is especially common in the Pine Barrens, where its characteristic "weep" call is omnipresent from late April through the summer. During migration, it can be encountered anywhere in New Jersey but is more common along the coast in autumn through early October. A few have exceptionally lingered into December, but this species is actually less expected in late autumn and early winter than is the Ash-throated Flycatcher.

SULPHUR-BELLIED/STREAKED FLYCATCHER
Myiodynastes luteiventris/maculates

Accidental. An individual of this tropical American genus was discovered at Higbee Beach, Cape May County, in October 2006. Unfortunately, it stayed for only a few minutes and was seen by just a handful of birders (Armistead and Feenstra 2007). Careful notes and descriptions made at the time convinced the NJBRC that the bird was either Sulphur-bellied Flycatcher, which summers north to southeastern Arizona, or Streaked Flycatcher, a widespread species that has not yet been documented north of Mexico. Although the former is a known, but accidental, vagrant to the Northeast and by far the more likely to occur in New Jersey, the limited observation did not allow time to distinguish conclusively between the two species.

Review Species

13 OCT 2006, CAPE MAY, CAPE MAY CO. (NJBRC 2007-078)

WESTERN KINGBIRD *Tyrannus verticalis*

Rare fall and very rare spring and early summer migrant, accidental in winter. Western Kingbirds were very rare in New Jersey during the first third of the twentieth century, and Stone (1937) knew of only one record for Cape May County. They became much more regular after that time, perhaps as a result of the eastward expansion of their breeding range (Gamble and Bergin 1996), with seasonal totals varying from a few to more than twenty, including eight at West Cape May, 24 November 1984 (Walsh et al. 1999). Since the 1980s, however, sightings have averaged only three or four per year. Most records are from the coast from mid-September to early December, but they were also recorded on sixteen individual CBCs in eleven years from 1975 to 2007. A few have survived into late January, but none has been recorded thereafter. Western Kingbirds are very rare visitors in spring and early summer.

EASTERN KINGBIRD *Tyrannus tyrannus*

Common and widespread summer resident, common fall and fairly common spring migrant. Eastern Kingbirds breed throughout New Jersey, and are one of the most widely distributed species in the state, as well as being the commonest flycatcher. Breeding Bird Survey data indicate that the species has declined in abundance in much of eastern North America in recent decades (Murphy 1996), and

Eastern Kingbird, seen here perched and in flight, is one of our most common and widespread flycatchers, although its numbers have declined substantially in recent decades. It is almost always found nesting near water. *Photographs by Kevin Karlson.*

the decline continues in New Jersey at a serious rate (Sauer et al. 2008), but the species continues to show a conspicuous presence. Eastern Kingbirds are early fall migrants, mainly mid-August to mid-September, and sometimes form spectacular concentrations at Cape May (e.g., 5,000 at Higbee Beach, 20 August 1987). A few are seen during early October, but there are no winter records. Spring migrants arrive as early as late April, but the main passage is in mid-May.

GRAY KINGBIRD *Tyrannus dominicensis*

Casual. As expected for this species, all but two of the twelve accepted records were found on or near the coast. There are two May and one July sightings from Cape May, but the rest are from September and October. Gray Kingbird nests along the Gulf Coast from Mississippi east and along the Atlantic coast of Florida north to Georgia, sporadically to South Carolina. It is, however, a well-known wanderer and has occurred in most of the northeastern states and eastern Canadian provinces.

Review Species

Gray Kingbird is a summer resident of the southeastern coast from Georgia to Mississippi but sometimes strays well to the north. Most of the twelve records in New Jersey are from September and October, but there is one from early July and two from May, including the one shown here on 22 May 2006. *Photograph by Richard Crossley.*

SCISSOR-TAILED FLYCATCHER *Tyrannus forficatus*

Rare, primarily spring, visitor from the southwest. Almost seventy years passed between the first record (a specimen) of Scissor-tailed Flycatcher in New Jersey in April 1872 and the second in September 1941, but the species has appeared much more frequently since the mid-twentieth century. There are now more than forty accepted records, including one or more almost annually since 1982, with a maximum of six birds in 1994. The majority of occurrences

are along the coast, and more than two-thirds have been in the late April–June time frame. Another eight have been in the fall, and there is even one December record of a bird that remained for the Assunpink CBC in 2004.

Scissor-tailed Flycatcher is a common species of the southern Great Plains but, like many flycatchers, is prone to wander and has occurred in all forty-eight contiguous United States and most Canadian provinces. Since the early 1980s it has occurred almost annually in New Jersey, primarily in late spring, but this long-tailed adult spent more than two weeks at Mercer County Park in September and October 1984. *Photograph by Jim Williams.*

FORK-TAILED FLYCATCHER *Tyrannus savana*

This striking flycatcher is an annual vagrant to the East Coast of North America, especially the Northeast, and a very rare visitor to New Jersey. There are now nineteen accepted records for the state, half of them in the decade of the 1990s. The first was shot near Bridgeton, Cumberland County, around 1812, while the second was shot in Camden in 1832 and painted by John James Audubon. Most of the Fork-tailed Flycatchers that occur in the eastern U.S. and Canada are believed to be of the highly migratory nominate race that breeds in southern South America and winters in the north of that continent. A pattern of overshoots for northbound migrants and reverse migration for intended southbound migrants has been proposed, but the span of dates (19 August–12 December) seems too wide for the latter proposal to adequately explain all the fall occurrences (McCaskie and Patten 1994). The five spring records are from early May to early June.

Fork-tailed Flycatcher occurs from central Mexico to southern South America, with the southern populations being migratory. These austral migrants are typically the source of the vagrants that show up along the East Coast of North America annually in very small numbers, and this subspecies (*T. s. savana*) has a darker back and less head/back contrast than generally nonmigratory birds from Mexico to Panama (*T. s. monachus*). There are nineteen accepted records of this species in New Jersey, mostly in the fall and mainly during the 1990s, but none after 2001 until an adult male was seen at Cape May, 2 May 2010. This handsome bird was at Cape May, 12–16 December 1994. *Photograph by Kevin Karlson.*

Order Passeriformes

Family Laniidae: Shrikes

LOGGERHEAD SHRIKE *Lanius ludovicianus*

Very rare spring and fall migrant, casual in winter. Endangered Species in New Jersey. Loggerhead Shrikes apparently never nested in New Jersey, but they were formerly uncommon, but regular, fall (mainly mid-August to early October) migrants and rare spring migrants (March to early April). They occurred mainly along the coast in fall, especially at Cape May, where Stone (1937) reported that they were seen daily in small numbers (up to six), while inland reports were more common in spring. Loggerhead Shrikes have declined dramatically throughout their range since the mid-twentieth century (Yosef 1996, Sauer et al. 2008), and they have become very rare or casual in New Jersey at any season. Since the species was added to the Review List in 1996, there have been just seven accepted records, four in spring, one in winter, and three in fall (one of the latter returning from the previous winter). (*See photo page 149.*)

Review Species

Records since 1996

NORTHERN SHRIKE *Lanius excubitor*

Rare and irruptive winter visitor. Although Northern Shrikes have been recorded as early as late October and as late as mid-April, they are mainly winter visitors from late November to early March. New Jersey is near the southern limit of their range, and, as an irruptive species, numbers may vary dramatically from year to year, apparently in response to weather conditions, prey availability, and the number of shrikes (Cade and Atkinson 2002). In some years, about once a decade, there are no reports, whereas in others there may be dozens, as in the major flight of 1995–1996 when at least sixty individuals were seen around the state (Kane 1996). The majority of Northern Shrike sightings are from the northern third of the state, but there are many records from the remainder of the state as far south as Cape May Point.

Family Vireonidae: Vireos

WHITE-EYED VIREO *Vireo griseus*

Fairly common and widespread summer resident, uncommon and inconspicuous spring and fall migrant, casual in winter. Shriner (1897) wrote that White-eyed Vireos "are to be found during the summer all over New Jersey," but Griscom (1923) found that the species had greatly decreased in numbers in the northern part of the state and were "rare or uncommon in most of its former range." The birds remained common, as they are today, in the southern two-thirds of the state, but have only gradually returned to the higher elevations of northern New Jersey, where they are still uncommon. White-eyed Vireos arrive at the nesting grounds in the second half of April, and most depart during August and September. A few remain into October, especially in the southernmost counties, and individuals were found on ten CBCs between 1984 and 2009. There are a few midwinter records.

BELL'S VIREO *Vireo bellii*

Casual vagrant. There have been six accepted records of Bell's Vireo in New Jersey, all but one from Cape May and all in the fall or early winter. The first, a female of the nominate midwestern race (as are most or all of the other New

Jersey records), was taken as a specimen at Island Beach, 15 September 1959, and is now in the AMNH (Jehl 1960). All of the remaining records occurred during a twelve-year period from 1994 to 2005, including single birds found in December 1996 and 2001 that lingered for four weeks into the following January. Interestingly, the first confirmed record of Bell's Vireo in neighboring New York was captured and banded ten days after the 1959 New Jersey bird (Bull 1964).

Bell's Vireo has occurred in New Jersey just six times, five of them in late fall or early winter at Cape May between 1994 and 2005. All records are known or presumed to belong to the Midwestern race, which nests as far east as western Ohio. This individual spent five days in Cape May and was photographed on 30 October 1994. *Photograph by Kevin Karlson.*

YELLOW-THROATED VIREO *Vireo flavifrons*

Uncommon and somewhat local summer resident, uncommon spring and fall migrant. Yellow-throated Vireos nest around the edges of mixed or deciduous woodlands, often near water. They were restricted to the northern part of the state until about the middle of the twentieth century (Fables 1955). Although they have declined in abundance in that area, particularly in the northeast, they extended their range southward to central New Jersey and, by the 1970s, to Cumberland and northern Cape May counties, but are still scarce in the Pine Barrens. Yellow-throated Vireos arrive in late April to early May, with some migrants continuing to the end of May. Southbound birds, usually only a few per day even at migrant hot spots, move through in late August and early September, with only the occasional straggler to

the end of the month. They are very rare after September, and there are no confirmed records after mid-October, when confusion with bright Pine Warblers is likely.

CASSIN'S VIREO *Vireo cassinii*

Accidental. This vireo was considered a subspecies of Solitary Vireo (V. solitarius) until genetic studies during the 1990s led to the separation of that species into three (Goguen and Curson 2002). The existence of a specimen of Vireo s. cassinii from New Jersey was discovered in the collection of the AMNH by Phillips (1986) and more recently examined by Buckley (Buckley and Mitra 2003). This was the first record for the East Coast.

11 NOV 1933, BARNEGAT, OCEAN CO. (NJBRC 2005-054; *AMNH #417404)

BLUE-HEADED VIREO *Vireo solitarius*

Uncommon and local summer resident, uncommon spring and fairly common fall migrant, casual in winter. Formerly known as a race of Solitary Vireo, Blue-headed Vireos nest in small numbers in coniferous (especially hemlock) and mixed woods along the Kittatinny Mountains and the northern parts of the Highlands. They are relatively short-distance migrants and return to New Jersey in mid- to late April, with some passing through into mid-May. Likewise, they are late migrants in fall, with a peak from late September to mid-October. Some stragglers remain into December, and they have been recorded on nine CBCs from 1983 to 2009. There are at least two midwinter records.

Blue-headed Vireo is part of the Solitary Vireo complex and was formerly known by that name. It is a fairly common migrant through New Jersey, arriving earlier in spring and departing later in fall than most of the other vireos. Small numbers breed locally in hilly forested areas of the northwestern counties. *Photograph by Kevin Karlson.*

WARBLING VIREO *Vireo gilvus*

Fairly common and widespread summer resident in the northern half of New Jersey, uncommon spring and fall migrant. Warbling Vireos reportedly declined in numbers in the early 1900s (Bull 1964), but today they are easily found singing within their breeding range wherever there are large trees near ponds or streams. They are absent from the Pine Barrens, but recent summer sightings in the southern counties suggest a possible attempt at range expansion. Spring migrant Warbling Vireos arrive from early to mid-May, while fall migrants are concentrated between mid-August and early September. Few are seen in late September, and they are very rare in October. Stone (1937) knew of no records for Cape May County, but they are now very uncommon, but regular, migrants there.

PHILADELPHIA VIREO *Vireo philadelphicus*

Uncommon fall migrant and rare spring migrant. Southbound Philadelphia Vireos are found from late August into early October, with a noticeable peak in mid-September. The majority of occurrences are along the coast at migrant traps such as Sandy Hook and Cape May, but there are many sightings inland, as well. In spring, they migrate up the central part of North America and are rarely encountered in New Jersey. There are usually only one or two reports of Philadelphia Vireo in May, and many long-time birders have never seen one at that season. A well-described individual was seen on the Sandy Hook CBC in 1993, but there are no other records after the third week of October.

RED-EYED VIREO *Vireo olivaceus*

Common and widespread summer resident, common fall and fairly common spring migrant. Red-eyed Vireos are one of the most common songbirds breeding in the woodlands of eastern North America (Cimprich et al. 2000), and this has long been true in New Jersey (Stone 1908). During the second half of the twentieth century, Breeding Bird Surveys indicated a substantial decline in populations, perhaps due to forest fragmentation, but the species remains a plentiful summer resident. Red-eyed Vireos are very common migrants in fall, mainly mid-August to late September, with a few lingering into October and occasionally early No-

vember. In spring, they are less common but arrive any time from late April to late May, mainly during the first half of May. There are no winter records.

Family Corvidae: Jays and Crows

BLUE JAY *Cyanocitta crestata*

Common and ubiquitous resident, fairly common spring and common fall migrant. The familiar Blue Jay is a common and conspicuous (except while nesting, when they can be very quiet) species throughout New Jersey. They can also be very common migrants along the coast from late September into October. Although Stone (1937) did not find Blue Jays to be noteworthy in passage at Cape May, it is now not unusual to see over a thousand there on a good day in early October. Numbers of fall migrants may vary from year to year, in part due to the quality of the mast crop to the north. A smaller, but still noticeable, return flight occurs in late April and May. Although most of New Jersey's Blue Jays are permanent residents, an analysis of banding records suggests that as many as 10 percent migrate to or from the state (Stewart 1982).

The noisy and aggressive Blue Jay is a familiar sight at feeding stations and a common year-round bird everywhere in the state. Some of our breeding birds probably migrate in fall, especially during years with low acorn crops. Migrant flocks are regularly seen along the coast and along the ridges in fall and spring. Birds from the north also account for part of our winter population. Although it is sometimes vilified as a bully and nest robber, it is surely one of the most handsome species. *Photograph by Kevin Karlson.*

AMERICAN CROW *Corvus brachyrhynchos*

Common and ubiquitous resident, fairly common migrant.
Noisy and gregarious, American Crows are a common
daily presence almost anywhere in New Jersey and are well
known for the large winter roosts in which they often
gather. They are highly susceptible to West Nile disease
(Komar et al. 2003), and their numbers declined significantly during the early 2000s in the Northeast (McGowan
2008, Sauer et al. 2008). The statewide CBC total dropped
from an average of about 35,000 during the 1990s to just
10,000 in 2003. They have partially recovered in recent
years, with CBC totals averaging about 20,000. In the late
fall, American Crows are conspicuous migrants along the
mountain ridges, less so at Cape May.

FISH CROW *Corvus ossifragus*

Common and widespread summer resident, fairly common
migrant and winter resident. Stone (1908) wrote that Fish
Crows were restricted to the Atlantic coast and lower Delaware River, and Bull (1964) contended that they were "almost exclusively confined to tidewater" as breeding birds
and doubted inland reports. By 1986, Boyle noted, they
were uncommon, but increasing, inland even away from
river systems. The Atlas found Fish Crows widespread as
nesters, but absent or scarce from parts of the Pine Barrens
and Kittatinny Ridge and Valley regions (Walsh et al.
1999). During the winter, they withdraw from parts of
northern New Jersey, remain in reduced numbers inland,
and locally withdraw from the immediate coast, but concentrate along the Delaware River from Trenton south.
Some Fish Crows migrate south in autumn, and their return presence along the coast in March and April is an-
nounced by their nasal call.

COMMON RAVEN *Corvus corax*

Scarce and local, but increasing, permanent resident, scarce
fall migrant along the mountain ridges. Common Ravens
nested in small numbers in the Pine Barrens in Atlantic,
southern Burlington, and Ocean counties until at least
1905 (Stone 1908), but their disappearance there coincided
with serious declines in both New York and Pennsylvania.
For many years it was "one of the rarest of migrants" (Fa-

bles 1955), mainly along the Kittatinny Mountains, but in 1991 a pair was seen carrying nesting material on the New Jersey side of the Delaware Water Gap. Within a few years, a small population was established along the entire Kittatinny Ridge that then spread slowly south and east, by the mid-2000s reaching such unlikely places as Secaucus, Bergen County; Chimney Rock, Somerset County; and Lakewood Naval Air Station, Ocean County. Occasional sightings south of their current range suggest that further expansion may be anticipated. True wanderers have been found casually south to Cape May.

Family Alaudidae: Larks

HORNED LARK *Eremophila alpestris*

Uncommon to fairly common but local winter resident, uncommon fall and scarce spring migrant, scarce and local summer resident. From a relatively small breeding range in the northwestern part of New Jersey, Horned Larks expanded their nesting range rapidly during the first half of the twentieth century to include almost every county in New Jersey, taking advantage of open farmlands and barrier beaches. They retreated just as rapidly during the second half of the century, however, and are now limited to a few scattered airfields, protected barrier islands, and remnant farmland around the state. The breeding subspecies, *E. a. praticola*, probably migrates (at least partially) from New Jersey in fall, and is replaced in winter by the highly migratory *E. a. alpestris*, with flocks arriving from late October into December (Beason 1995). Winter flocks are nomadic and may be found in sandy dunes or fallow fields anywhere in the state. Horned Larks are very early spring migrants, with most wintering birds departing by late February or early March, while breeding birds may start nesting as early as March.

Family Hirundinidae: Martins and Swallows

PURPLE MARTIN *Progne subis*

Common and fairly widespread summer resident, especially south of the Piedmont, uncommon spring and fall migrant, except at a few staging areas. In New Jersey, Purple Martins nest exclusively in colonial martin houses provided by humans, and they require both open spaces and proximity to water to succeed. They are early migrants in fall, often gathering in mid- to late August at staging areas, of which the one at Mauricetown, Cumberland County, is the most prominent, attracting several tens of thousands annually. Some migrants pass through during September, but all are gone by the end of the month. Early spring migrants may arrive in late February to mid-March, but they invariably get caught by cold spells and probably do not survive. Most breeders return in early to mid-April.

BROWN-CHESTED MARTIN *Progne tapera*

Review Species

Accidental. New Jersey's only Brown-chested Martin was discovered on 6 November 1997 in Cape May, where it remained for ten days, to the delight of birders from all over the country (Lehman 1998). This was just the second documented record for North America, the other coming from Monomoy Island, MA, 12 June 1983 (Petersen et al. 1986). The species has since occurred in Arizona (2006), Connecticut (2006), and Massachusetts (2009).

6–15 NOV 1997, CAPE MAY, CAPE MAY CO. (NJBRC 1997-083; NJPF)

Brown-chested Martin is a migratory South American species that has been documented just five times in North America. New Jersey's only record, the second of the five, was present at Cape May for ten days in November 1997. *Photographs by Kevin Karlson.*

TREE SWALLOW *Tachycineta bicolor*

Very common fall and common spring migrant, common and widespread summer resident, rare to scarce in winter along the coast. Tree Swallows did not breed in northern New Jersey prior to the 1900s, but they spread to every

corner of the state during the twentieth century. The availability of nest boxes, originally provided for bluebirds and Wood Ducks, appears to have helped increase their numbers, as populations in some areas are still limited by the number of suitable cavities (Robertson et al. 1992). Spectacular concentrations of Tree Swallows gather along the coast in fall, starting in late July and peaking in late September to mid-October (maximum 500,000, Cape May, 30 September–1 October 1974). Numbers diminish through November, but some individuals or small flocks often attempt to winter, mainly in the south, and are sometimes successful. The first spring Tree Swallows usually arrive in mid-March, with the bulk of migrants in early to mid-April.

VIOLET-GREEN SWALLOW *Tachycineta thalassina*

Review Species

Accidental. There are just three records of this small swallow of western North America, all in late autumn. The first two stayed in the vicinity of Cape May Point for days and, despite being hard to find, were enjoyed by many. All of the records occurred within a seven-year time span.

7–13 NOV 1992, CAPE MAY PT., CAPE MAY CO. (AR 1993-1995)
16–29 OCT 1997, CAPE MAY PT., CAPE MAY CO. (NJBRC 1997-072)
14 NOV 1999, EAST POINT, CUMBERLAND CO. (NJBRC 1999-056)

Violet-green Swallow, closely related to Tree Swallow, is a common and widespread species of western North America that has occurred only a handful of times in the East. Three of those occurrences have been in New Jersey, two in Cape May and one in Cumberland County. The first, photographed distantly here on the day it was discovered, was present 7–13 November 1992. *Photograph by Bob Barber.*

NORTHERN ROUGH-WINGED SWALLOW
Stelgidopteryx serripennis

Fairly common and widespread summer resident, fairly common fall and uncommon spring migrant, very rare in winter. Stone (1908) reported that Northern Rough-winged

Swallows were "tolerably common" in southern New Jersey, but rare in the northern counties. By mid-century, however, they were considered fairly common breeding birds (Fables 1955, Bull 1964), although limited by the availability of nest cavities, and today they are much less common in the south, especially the Pine Barrens, than the north. Fall migration is complex, as most Northern Rough-winged Swallows begin to move in mid-July, with a peak from late July to early August. Modest numbers continue through September, and there is often another, smaller peak in mid-October, diminishing through November. In recent years, a flock of up to 125 birds have lingered along the Delaware River near Philadelphia through December into mid-January and are sometimes seen from the New Jersey side. Breeding birds typically arrive in early to mid-April, with migrants continuing into mid-May.

BANK SWALLOW *Riparia riparia*

Fairly common but local summer resident, fairly common spring and fall migrant. Bank Swallows can be found breeding throughout most of New Jersey, but have a very patchy distribution due to their nesting requirements. They nest colonially and excavate cavities in river banks, sand banks, and gravel pits. Because the latter two tend to be ephemeral, colonies may appear and disappear from year to year. Bank Swallows begin to return from their South American wintering grounds in early to mid-April, but the peak migration is in early to mid-May (Walsh et al. 1999). They are early migrants in fall, with a peak from mid-July to mid-August, but continue in diminishing numbers to mid-September. Some late migrants pass through in late September and early October, and rare strays are seen in early November.

CLIFF SWALLOW *Petrochelidon pyrrhonota*

Uncommon spring and fall migrant, scarce and local summer resident. Cliff Swallows are colonial breeders and build their nests in New Jersey on man-made structures such as bridges, culverts, and barns. They spread eastward across the country during the nineteenth century, but declined in New Jersey during most of the twentieth. A slight resurgence was seen in the 1980s and 1990s, but they remain scarce and local along the Delaware River north of

Trenton and at a few sites in the Kittatinny Valley and the Highlands. Small colonies have recently spread to several sites in Bergen County, as well as the Route 27 bridge over the Raritan River in Middlesex County. Most spring-migrant Cliff Swallows pass through from mid-April to mid-May, and the fall migration is mainly from mid-August to late September, with a peak in mid-September. Small numbers are seen at Cape May during October, and the rare straggler occurs in November.

CAVE SWALLOW *Petrochelidon fulva*

Rare to scarce fall and very rare spring vagrant. When New Jersey's first Cave Swallow appeared at Cape May, 20 April–4 June 1990 (Bacinski 1990) it was the first record for eastern North America north of Florida, except for four records from Nova Scotia. It was followed by the second occurrence, involving up to four birds, at Cape May in November 1992. Since then, the species has appeared in the late autumn (26 October–13 December) of every year but 1995, most often along the coast, typically peaking around mid- to late November, and with single-day totals exceeding two hundred birds at Cape May on a couple of occasions. The increase in New Jersey records has been mirrored by increasing numbers of reports from nearby states and provinces, and Cave Swallow, now an expected late-fall visitor to Cape May, was removed from the Review List in 2008 (Hanson 2008). There have been just four inland reports of one to three birds, all in November, and a coastal high count (away from Cape May County) of fifteen at Sandy Hook, 9 November 2008. All specimens of fall birds (many stay too long and die at roosts in December) belong to the southwestern subspecies *pelodoma*. There are just five spring records for New Jersey from 25 March to 4 June, all involving just one or two birds.

BARN SWALLOW *Hirundo rustica*

Common and ubiquitous summer resident, common spring and fall migrant. Barn Swallows have adapted well to the presence of human beings, and they build their nests exclusively on or under man-made structures. They typically form small colonies and can be found commonly throughout New Jersey except for a few areas in the heart of the

Pine Barrens. Spring migrants can arrive as early as late March, but the majority of birds pass through from late April to mid-May. Fall migrants are most common in August and early September, when they are especially abundant along the coast, with a high estimated count of 12,000 at Cape May, 19 August 1996. They become uncommon by the end of September, but a few stragglers linger through October and into November. Single Barn Swallows were seen on two different coastal CBCs in December 1984, but there are no midwinter records.

Barn Swallow is our most common and familiar swallow. It has adapted so well to the presence of human beings that it now nests exclusively on man-made structures. *Photograph by Kevin Karlson.*

Family Paridae: Chickadees and Titmice

CAROLINA CHICKADEE *Poecile carolinensis*

Common resident in the southern two-thirds of the state, where Black-capped Chickadee occurs only as a rare and irregular winter vagrant. The northern boundary of the Carolina's range is roughly defined by a line running from Lambertville on the Delaware River northeast along the Hunterdon-Mercer County line and southern Somerset County to about Millstone, then east to New Brunswick and along the Raritan River to Raritan Bay. Oddly, the species does not occur at Sandy Hook. Along the boundary there is a zone of overlap (perhaps five to fifteen miles wide) where individuals of both species may be encountered and where hybrids may occur, as has been demonstrated at Hopewell, Mercer County, where at least twenty-

five hybrids have been banded since 1992 (H. Suthers, L. Larson, pers. comm.). The difficulty in separating the two species and the fact that they learn each other's songs makes defining the exact range of either species nearly impossible (Sibley 1994).

BLACK-CAPPED CHICKADEE *Poecile atricapillus*

Common resident throughout the northern third of the state, where Carolina Chickadee does not occur. Also present on Sandy Hook. In some winters, irruptions of individuals from farther north augment the resident population and small numbers are reported south of the normal range. Whether the birds that venture farther south are New Jersey birds or the visitors from farther to the north is not known (Walsh et al. 1999). As noted under Carolina Chickadee, there is a zone of overlap with that species, which may vary from year to year, but Carolinas have never been encountered north of that zone (Sibley 1994).

The perky and confiding Black-capped Chickadee is a common species in the northern third of the state, as is its cousin, the Carolina Chickadee, in the southern two-thirds. Both are familiar visitors to feeders. The two species can be difficult to tell apart in the narrow zone of overlap, where they often learn each other's song and may interbreed. *Photograph by Kevin Karlson.*

BOREAL CHICKADEE *Poecile hudsonicus*

Casual visitor from the North. This irruptive species has occurred in New Jersey irregularly in the past, mainly from November to March. The first record for the state was a specimen obtained at Ramsey, Bergen County, 1 November 1913 (Fables 1955), followed by small influx of nine birds at Princeton and Plainfield in 1916–1917 (Stone 1937). Thirty-five years would pass before the next record in 1952, but there followed a period from 1952 to 1984 when Boreal Chickadee was seen in twenty-four different years, with major flights during the winters of 1961–1962, 1969–1970, and 1975–1976, the latter including at least fifty birds. The most southerly bird visited a feeder in Toms River, Ocean County, from 18 January to 21 February 1981. A single bird in 1987 was the last recorded sighting in New Jersey, and the species was added to the Review List in 1996.

Review Species

TUFTED TITMOUSE *Baeolophus bicolor*

Common to very common resident throughout the state. Historically, Tufted Titmouse was a southern species, and Shriner (1897) noted that "they are distributed from the middle of New Jersey southward." Its range expanded rapidly during the twentieth century. In 1955 Fables called it "a permanent resident through the state . . . while it is relatively scarce in most of the ridge country of Passaic, Sussex, and Warren Counties." Today the titmouse has extended its range far to the north and east of the borders of New Jersey.

Tufted Titmouse, a relative of the chickadees, is a southern species that expanded its range northward during the twentieth century. Formerly limited to the southern half of New Jersey, it is now common throughout the state and a familiar visitor to bird feeders. *Photograph by Kevin Karlson.*

Family Sittidae: Nuthatches

RED-BREASTED NUTHATCH *Sitta canadensis*

Irregularly scarce to fairly common migrant and winter resident, scarce and local summer resident. Red-breasted Nuthatches are known for their unpredictable irruptions at two- to four-year intervals, with major flights in August and September, and hundreds of individuals often remain for the winter. In other years, a much smaller flight occurs between October and November, and only a few dozen are found on CBCs and through the winter. They nest in conifers, and have been found breeding in many parts of New Jersey, but they are consistently found only in Norway spruce plantings in Sussex County and the Highlands. Nesting in other areas may be related to influxes of migrants from the preceding fall and winter, as is the case in Massachusetts (Veit and Petersen 1993). Spring migration following a fall irruption is noticeable in late April or early May (Walsh et al. 1999).

WHITE-BREASTED NUTHATCH *Sitta carolinensis*

Fairly common and widespread resident. White-breasted Nuthatches are familiar residents and breed throughout most of New Jersey in deciduous or mixed woodlands with trees large enough to provide nesting cavities. They appear to be more common and widespread than formerly (cf. Griscom 1923, Bull 1964), but are generally absent from salt marsh edges and parts of the coastal plain, as well as highly urban and deforested areas. Although

White-breasted Nuthatch is found throughout most of New Jersey, where it prefers deciduous or mixed woodlands. It is often detected by its nasal call before it is seen and is a regular visitor to feeding stations, including suet feeders, where it demonstrates its propensity to forage and feed upside down.
Photograph by Kevin Karlson.

White-breasted Nuthatches are primarily nonmigratory, there is evidence of occasional short distance or irruptive movements by some northern and western populations, but these appear to be very localized (Grubb and Pravosu-dov 2008), such as birds seen in southern Cape May County in fall and winter. This may account for the spikes seen in CBC numbers in certain years.

BROWN-HEADED NUTHATCH *Sitta pusilla*

Review Species

Accidental. A juvenile bird was present at Cape May Point, 23–28 July 2005 (Crossley 2006). Although Brown-headed Nuthatches nest as close as southern Delaware, within fif-teen miles of Cape May, this was the first accepted record for New Jersey. Amazingly, another Brown-headed Nut-hatch was discovered on 8 April 2010, just one block from the previous sighting, and was present for four days. Hypo-thetical reports cited in Fables (1955) and Leck (1984) were not accepted by the Historical Review Committee (Halliwell et al. 2000). (*See photo page 149.*)

23–28 JUL 2005, CAPE MAY PT., CAPE MAY CO. (NJBRC 2006-005; NJPF)
8–11 APR 2010, CAPE MAY PT., CAPE MAY CO. (NJBRC 2011-011; NJPF)

Family Certhiidae: Creepers

BROWN CREEPER *Certhia americana*

Uncommon spring and fall migrant, uncommon winter resident, scarce and local summer resident. Quiet and in-conspicuous, Brown Creepers are often overlooked. They are most often seen during fall migration, beginning in late September and peaking in mid- to late October, when banding records show that they are much more common than sight records would indicate (Walsh et al. 1999). Win-ter abundance varies somewhat with the severity of the sea-son, but CBC totals average about 200. Brown Creepers are early spring migrants and pass through largely unde-tected in early to mid-April. Although only one nesting lo-cation, in Sussex County, was known as of 1942 (Cruick-shank 1942), later authors and the Atlas have found the species broadly distributed in the northwestern part of the state. There are also scattered breeding records for the Piedmont, the Pine Barrens, and Cumberland County.

Family Troglodytidae: Wrens

ROCK WREN *Salpinctes obsoletus*

Accidental. A Rock Wren discovered in a residential area of Cape May Point, 2 December, 1992, remained for almost four months. This is the only record for New Jersey, but the species has occurred three times in Massachusetts and Virginia and once each in Maryland and western New York.

2 DEC 1992–28 MAR 1993, CAPE MAY PT., CAPE MAY CO. (RNJB 19[2]48, AR 95; NJPF)

Rock Wren is a widespread bird of western North America that ordinarily occurs no closer to New Jersey than western Kansas. The species has wandered east on occasion, including once to New Jersey. This individual spent almost four months at Cape May Point from December 1992 to March 1993. *Photograph by Richard Crossley.*

CAROLINA WREN *Thryothorus ludovicianus*

Common and widespread resident. Carolina Wrens have long been resident in southern New Jersey and the lower Hudson Valley (Stone 1908), but they took advantage of warmer conditions during the twentieth century to expand their range to include the entire state (Walsh et al. 1999), although they are decidedly less common in the northwestern counties. The devastating impact of severely cold winters with ice and snow on local populations has been well documented (Haggerty and Morton 1995), but they recover rapidly. Long term, the trend is clearly up, as evidenced by CBC data, which averaged about 250 individuals (~0.12 birds/party hour) in the late 1970s and early 1980s to more than 2,000 (~1.0 bird/party hour) in recent years.

The cheerful songs and calls of the Carolina Wren can be heard almost anywhere in New Jersey. It sings through-out the year, except during very cold or snowy periods. Once primarily limited to the southern counties, the species spread northward during the twentieth century to include the entire state. *Photograph by Kevin Karlson.*

BEWICK'S WREN *Thyromanes bewickii*

Accidental. There have been five accepted reports of Bewick's Wren in New Jersey. Three are banding records, two of which were also photographed. This species formerly nested as far east as central Pennsylvania, but declined rapidly there during the twentieth century and was extirpated before 1980 (Fingerhood 1992). A 1974 nesting in Ulster County, NY, the only one for that state, was far from any previously known breeding sites (Brooks 1998).

20 APR 1958, SUNRISE MT., SUSSEX CO. (AFN 12[4]:338)
10 OCT 1962, CAPE MAY, CAPE MAY CO. (AFN 17[1]:20; NJPF)
JUN 1964, WEST ORANGE, ESSEX CO.
11 OCT 1969, ISLAND BEACH SP, OCEAN CO. (AFN 24[1]:29)
4 MAY 1977, ISLAND BEACH SP, OCEAN CO. (AB 32[2]:187; NJPF)

Review Species

Bewick's Wren has almost completely disappeared from its former breeding range east of the Mississippi and is unlikely to be seen in New Jersey again. There are five records from the state, all prior to 1980. The last was this bird banded at Island Beach, Ocean County, 4 May 1977. *Photograph by William Pepper.*

HOUSE WREN *Troglodytes aedon*

Common and ubiquitous summer resident, common migrant, very rare in winter. Spring-migrant House Wrens begin to arrive in mid-April, and the males are busy setting up territories and building nests by mid-May. They are conspicuous by their noisy presence just about anywhere in the state through the summer. Southbound House Wrens begin to appear in numbers in August, with a peak in September, and are mostly gone from northern New Jersey by mid-October. Small numbers remain through November, and from five to ten are usually found on CBCs, mainly in the southern counties. A few have been found in January and February, apparently successfully overwintering.

WINTER WREN *Troglodytes troglodytes*

Uncommon fall migrant and winter resident, scarce to uncommon spring migrant, scarce and local summer resident. Most spring-migrant Winter Wrens pass through in a fairly narrow time window between late March and mid-April. Although Cruickshank (1942) predicted that they might someday be found breeding in northwestern New Jersey, it wasn't until 1962 that the first confirmed nesting occurred (Bull 1964). Today they are scarce and elusive breeders in the Kittatinny Valley and Mountains and in the Highlands, mainly in hemlock glens or on steep wooded slopes. The Atlas also found isolated pockets of nesting Winter Wrens along the Hudson River in Bergen County and the Delaware River in Sussex and Warren counties. Fall migration peaks in mid- to late October, when these shy birds are most often detected by their call note. Winter numbers are variable, but CBC totals show a distinct increase in recent decades, and they can be fairly common in very local pockets in the southern counties.

SEDGE WREN *Cistothorus platensis*

Rare fall migrant and winter resident, very rare spring migrant, very rare and local summer resident. Endangered Species in New Jersey. The Sedge Wren is an enigmatic, nomadic species with a lengthy breeding season that often involves extensive relocation within the nesting range and a mid- to late summer arrival at many sites (Herkert et al. 2001). Formerly an uncommon but regular breeder in the inland marshes and upland edges of salt marshes in New

Jersey, it all but disappeared as a nesting species during the late 1900s, due largely to habitat loss. During the Atlas, only one pair a year was located, all in different places. Few Sedge Wrens are encountered in the state in any given year, but fall migrants are found between late October and late November. Most recent records are from December and January, when an average of about four are reported on CBCs, mainly along the southern Atlantic coast and in Delaware Bay salt marshes. They are very rarely encountered in spring.

MARSH WREN *Cistothorus palustris*

Common but local summer resident, fairly common spring and fall migrant, rare to scarce winter resident. Marsh Wrens nest in both freshwater and saltwater marshes, preferring cattails inland and *Spartina* along the coast. They are apparently far less abundant than they were a century ago, before the extensive draining of inland marshes and ditching of coastal marshes, but they remain locally common where their preferred habitat persists. Marsh Wrens arrive at their breeding sites between late April and mid-May, and most depart during September and early October. Small numbers remain in the coastal marshes in the southern counties and the Hackensack Meadowlands, and an average of thirty to forty are seen on CBCs. The rare Marsh Wren that tries to winter inland in the north probably doesn't survive, but the coastal ones do unless the winter is unusually severe.

Family Regulidae: Kinglets

GOLDEN-CROWNED KINGLET *Regulus satrapa*

Common fall and fairly common spring migrant, fairly common winter resident, scarce and local summer resident. The fall migration of Golden-crowned Kinglets begins in late September and peaks in mid- to late October, when they can be locally abundant in some years at coastal sites, such as Sandy Hook and Cape May. Numbers of migrants and wintering birds vary from year to year, possibly due to the availability of food farther north and to reduced survival from a severe previous winter (Veit and Petersen 1993). Spring movement is early, with most passing through from late March to mid-April. Golden-crowned Kinglets were first discovered nesting in New Jersey in 1971 at Vernon, Sussex County, in Norway spruce groves. They have since been found nesting in spruce groves elsewhere in the northern part of the Highlands and along the Kittatinny Mountains, rarely in isolated groves in the southern Highlands. As these spruce groves mature and die out, the future of this kinglet as a New Jersey breeding bird is in doubt.

The two kinglets are our smallest passerines, and Golden-crowned Kinglet is the more colorful of the two. In the East, it breeds farther south and winters farther north than does Ruby-crowned Kinglet. The female Golden-crowned Kinglet, shown here, lacks the orange tones to the crown exhibited by the male. *Photograph by Kevin Karlson.*

RUBY-CROWNED KINGLET *Regulus calendula*

Common spring and fall migrant, scarce to fairly common winter resident. Immature Ruby-crowned Kinglets migrate before adults (Swanson et al. 2008) and may arrive as early as late August, but the majority passes through, sometimes in spectacular numbers along the coast, in mid- to late October. CBC numbers vary with the severity of the weather prior to the counts, but they may be fairly common, even in midwinter, in the southern counties and along the coast. A few are found in the northern part of the state in December, but they become rare to scarce after the new year. In spring, Ruby-crowned Kinglets are more common inland than along the coast and migrate a bit later than their Golden-crowned cousins, peaking from late April to early May (Walsh et al. 1999).

Family Sylviidae: Gnatcatchers

BLUE-GRAY GNATCATCHER *Polioptila caerulea*

Common spring and fall migrant, fairly common and widespread summer resident. Blue-gray Gnatcatchers were rare and local breeding birds in southern New Jersey at the beginning of the twentieth century and were accidental farther north (Stone 1908). The first nesting record in the north occurred in Sussex County in 1928, part of a gradual range expansion in eastern North America that has spread well beyond New Jersey (Elison 1992), and the species is now a common migrant as well as a widespread nester. Spring migrants may arrive in early April, but the peak flight occurs from mid-April to early May. The prolonged fall migration may begin in late July, with significant flights from mid-August to September and very few seen after mid-October. Up to four have been recorded on eleven different CBCs since 1976, but gnatcatchers are unknown in midwinter.

Family Turdidae: Thrushes

NORTHERN WHEATEAR *Oenanthe oenanthe*

Review Species

Very rare fall vagrant, one spring record. There have been twenty-two accepted records of Northern Wheatear in New Jersey, all but six on or near the coast, and all but one between 25 August and 12 November. Many have been one-day wonders, but nine have stayed longer, including the first at Cape May Point, 7–14 October 1951. The sole spring record is from Thompson's Beach, Cumberland County, 1 June 1981.

Northern Wheatear is a Eurasian species that also nests in Alaska and parts of northern Canada. Most North American breeders migrate south in fall via Asia or northern Europe, all to winter in Africa and the Middle East, but a few manage to get lost each year and show up along the East Coast. These records probably represent the subspecies *leucorhoa*, which breeds in Greenland and Nunavut. There are twenty-two accepted records for New Jersey, including this adult female at Cape May, 9 September 2008. *Photograph by Kevin Karlson.*

EASTERN BLUEBIRD *Sialia sialis*

Common fall and fairly common spring migrant, fairly common summer resident, uncommon winter resident. Eastern Bluebirds declined in numbers during the first two-thirds of the twentieth century due to competition with House Sparrows and European Starlings for nest cavities. In recent decades, however, the widespread erection of nest boxes has led to a dramatic recovery in the bluebird population, and they can now be found breeding in most parts of the state. Many Eastern Bluebirds migrate through or from New Jersey in fall, with a peak from late October to mid-November, when large flights may occur along the coast. Substantial numbers remain to winter throughout the state, however, and the CBC numbers have increased from an average of about 70 during the 1970s to more than 2,000 in the past decade. Bluebirds are early migrants, passing through mainly in March, and by April they are busy nest building.

Eastern Bluebird is a colorful and familiar (even to many nonbirders) bird of fields with adjacent woodlands and wooded swamps. Its numbers declined substantially during most of the twentieth century, but a strong recovery, assisted by nest-box programs, in the past several decades has resulted in healthy populations. The male, shown here, is bright blue above, while the female has more subdued plumage tones. *Photograph by Kevin Karlson.*

MOUNTAIN BLUEBIRD *Sialia currucoides*

Accidental. Only three reports of this handsome western thrush have been accepted from the several received. The first was an immature male photographed and seen by numerous observers at Forsythe NWR, 21 November 1982. Only three were on hand to enjoy the second bird at Cape May, and the third was seen by only one birder. This species has occurred once in Pennsylvania and Virginia, twice in Maryland, and ten times in New York.

Review Species

21 NOV 1982, FORSYTHE NWR, ATLANTIC CO. (RNJB 9[1]:14–15)
12 NOV 1988, CAPE MAY, CAPE MAY CO. (AR 1996)
29 DEC 2009, MERCER COUNTY PARK, MERCER CO. (NJBRC 2010-093)

Mountain Bluebird is a widespread bird of open country in western North America, nesting as far east as eastern Manitoba and wintering east to Kansas and Oklahoma. It is a well-known vagrant, however, and has occurred ten times in neighboring New York. The first of New Jersey's three records was this handsome male at Forsythe NWR, 21 November 1982. Photograph by *Jose Garcia*.

TOWNSEND'S SOLITAIRE *Myadestes townsendi*

Review Species

Accidental. All nine of New Jersey's Townsend's Solitaires have arrived in late fall or early winter (19 October–27 December), and five of them have occurred along the mountain ridges of Sussex and Warren counties. The first state record was at Sunrise Mountain, 17 November–14 December 1980. All three coastal birds have stayed for extended periods, including one at Heislerville, Cumberland County (27 December 1998–18 April 1999); one at Cedar Run, Ocean County (29 November–18 December 2004); and another at Sandy Hook (25 November 2007–23 March 2008).

Townsend's Solitaire is a bird of the forested mountains of western North America that descends to the lowlands in winter. It has a well-established pattern of vagrancy and has occurred many times in the Northeast, including nine times in New Jersey. Five of our records are from the mountain ridges in the northwest, while three are from coastal sites. This individual spent almost four months near Heislerville, Cumberland County, from December 1998 to April 1999. *Photograph by Kevin Karlson.*

VEERY *Catharus fuscescens*

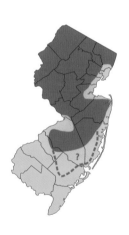

Common and fairly widespread summer resident, common fall and uncommon spring migrant. Veeries have long been common summer residents of the northern half of New Jersey (Stone 1908), but apparently extended their breeding range south during the twentieth century to include Monmouth County and parts of the Pine Barrens. They continue to be common in moist deciduous woodlands and wooded swamps within that range, but long-term Breeding Bird Survey data indicates a serious decline in numbers both in New Jersey (– 2.6 percent per year, 1966–2007) and continent-wide (Sauer et al. 2008, Bevier et al. 2005), perhaps related to destruction of their winter habitat in southern Brazil (Remsen 2001). Veeries are common nocturnal migrants in fall from mid-August to early October, with a peak in early to mid-September. In spring, they are rare before May, but are found migrating throughout that month. There is a recent late November record from Cape May, but there are none from winter.

GRAY-CHEEKED THRUSH *Catharus minimus*

Uncommon fall and scarce spring migrant. Gray-cheeked Thrushes are shy and inconspicuous migrants, especially in the fall, and are more likely to be heard at night than seen during the day. Most fall migrants occur from mid-September to mid-October, when nocturnal counts in double digits are not uncommon at Cape May. Banding records, e.g., fifty-three at Island Beach SP, 27 September 1963 (Leck 1984), suggest that the species is (or was) more common than field experience would lead one to believe. Spring migrants pass through from mid- to late May and can sometimes be heard singing at stopover sites, such as Garret Mountain. There are no confirmed winter records.

BICKNELL'S THRUSH *Catharus bicknelli*

Probably a regular spring and fall migrant in small numbers. Bicknell's Thrush is a relatively recent (1996) split from Gray-cheeked Thrush, and its status in New Jersey is poorly known. Separation of the two species in the field is very difficult unless the bird is singing, as there is a subtle, but distinct, difference in the songs and flight calls. Bicknell's Thrush was discovered in 1881 on Slide Mountain, NY, just fifty miles from High Point, and still breeds there (Rimmer et al. 2001). Most of the breeding range lies to the north and east of New Jersey, so much of the small population of this rare species probably pass through the state on the way to and from their wintering grounds in the Greater Antilles. The limited data suggest that the timing of migration is similar to that of Gray-cheeked Thrush.

SWAINSON'S THRUSH *Catharus ustulatus*

Fairly common fall and uncommon spring migrant. Swainson's Thrushes begin to arrive in New Jersey during fall migration in early September, with peak flights late in the month or in early October, and become scarce after mid-October. Highest numbers are obtained during nocturnal counts based on call notes, but this species has shown an unexplained decline in recent decades based on both Breeding Bird Survey and migration studies (Mack and Yong 2000, Sauer et al. 2008). Spring migrants are rare before early May, and peak numbers occur from mid- to late May, with a few stragglers into June. Swainson's Thrushes nest as close as the Catskill Mountains in southern New York, but have never been found breeding in New Jersey. There were eight reports on CBCs from 1983 to 1997, several with good details from experienced observers, but there are no midwinter records.

HERMIT THRUSH *Catharus guttatus*

Common fall and fairly common spring migrant, uncommon winter resident, scarce and local summer resident. Although Hermit Thrushes were first found breeding in New Jersey in the Highlands only in 1921 (Griscom 1923), they are now widespread, but scarce, in hemlock glens and dry ridge tops in the Kittatinny Mountains as well as the Highlands. They were found nesting in the Pine Barrens in 1981 and continue to nest there in very small numbers. Hermit Thrushes migrate later and are much less shy than the other *Catharus* thrushes, with peak numbers in mid- to late October. Migration continues through November, and good numbers remain for the CBCs except in the northwestern counties. Wintering birds are fairly common in the southern part of the state, although they are probably reduced by severe weather. Spring movement is mainly in April and early May, when the birds can sometimes be heard singing at migration stopovers.

WOOD THRUSH *Hylocichla mustelina*

Fairly common and nearly ubiquitous summer resident, uncommon fall and spring migrant. The song of the Wood Thrush is a familiar sound in woodlands throughout the state. Although the species has suffered significant declines over much of its range in recent decades, the numbers in New Jersey do not seem to have been so severely affected

The beautiful song of the Wood Thrush is still a familiar sound in woodlands throughout much of the state, although it has declined significantly in recent decades. The male can be heard singing from the time of his arrival on the breeding grounds in late April until August, but he becomes quiet when busily feeding young. *Photograph by Kevin Karlson.*

except in areas where the understory has been destroyed by deer. Wood Thrushes begin to arrive on their breeding grounds in late April, with migrants passing through to mid-May, and return south after the nesting season in September and early October. Despite their abundance to the north of New Jersey, they are uncommon as migrants. There have been ten reports on CBCs since 1975, several well documented and a couple photographed, but there are no midwinter records.

AMERICAN ROBIN *Turdus migratorius*

Abundant migrant, common and ubiquitous summer resident, common winter resident. The familiar American Robin, surely our best-known bird, nests in every corner of New Jersey, from suburban yards to mature forests. Although many are present all year, the fall migration peaking from late October to early November can result in spectacular flights at coastal sites, such as the estimated 1.25 million seen on the morning of 7 November 1999 (Obercian 2000). Robins remain common in winter, but largely withdraw from the northwestern part of the state, especially in snowy winters. Spring migration is protracted, with migrants passing through from February to May, but most local breeding birds are on territory by early April.

VARIED THRUSH *Ixoreus naevius*

Review Species

Very rare vagrant from western North America. There have been twenty-three accepted records of Varied Thrush in New Jersey, most of them occurring in the years 1976–1987 (ten) and 2000–2005 (seven). Unlike those of many other western vagrants, all but two of the records are from well inland. All are from late fall through the winter, including three that have lingered into April. The majority have been present for days or weeks, and a few have even stayed for three to four months. (*See photo page 150.*)

Family Mimidae: Mockingbirds and Thrashers

GRAY CATBIRD *Dumetella carolinensis*

Common and ubiquitous summer resident, common migrant, scarce to uncommon winter resident. Gray Catbirds can be found during the nesting season any place in New

Jersey where there are thickets, overgrown fields, shrubby areas, or gardens. Migration is often obscured by the presence of so many breeders, but peak flights in the fall occur from mid- to late September. In winter, catbirds are found in small numbers along the coast and in the southern counties. One or two are found on most of the CBCs in the northern part of the state, but it's doubtful that many survive the entire winter. Spring migrants arrive between late April and mid-May.

NORTHERN MOCKINGBIRD *Mimus polyglottos*

Common and nearly ubiquitous resident, uncommon migrant. Northern Mockingbirds underwent a dramatic range expansion during the twentieth century. Stone (1908) described them as a "very rare summer resident," and even in the early 1950s they were considered thinly distributed in southern and eastern New Jersey (Fables 1955). They reached Sussex County in 1958 (Bull 1964) and are now common throughout the state, except for the higher elevations in the northwest and the heart of the Pine Barrens, where they are uncommon. Although generally considered permanent residents, some Northern Mockingbirds are migratory, and small groups or individuals have been documented moving along the Palisades both spring and fall (Walsh et al. 1999) and at Cape May in the fall (Sibley 1997).

Northern Mockingbird is a southern species that expanded its range dramatically during the twentieth century. A very rare resident in southern New Jersey at the beginning of the twentieth century, it became widespread and common throughout most of the state by the end of the century. Its loud, varied song is often heard all night long in spring and summer during calm, warm weather conditions. *Photograph by Kevin Karlson.*

SAGE THRASHER *Oreoscoptes montanus*

Accidental. Three of the New Jersey records of this bird of the West have been one-day wonders, but the Sandy Hook bird stayed a second day and was enjoyed by dozens of birders. The Barnegat Light, Spring Lake, and Sandy Hook sightings fit the typical time frame for western vagrants and other East Coast occurrences of this species, but the Forsythe NWR record is very unusual for the spring.

Review Species

27 NOV 1949, BARNEGAT LIGHT, OCEAN CO. (AFN 4[3]:196)
30 OCT 1990, SPRING LAKE, MONMOUTH CO. (RNJB 17(1):16; NJPF)
27 APR 2004, FORSYTHE NWR, ATLANTIC CO. (NJBRC 2005-025; NJPF)
20–21 OCT 2009, SANDY HOOK, MONMOUTH CO. (NJBRC 2010-079; NJPF)

Sage Thrasher is a western species that casually wanders to the East. All four of New Jersey's records have come from the Atlantic Coast, but only one at Sandy Hook stayed around long enough to be seen by many observers. It was photograph here on 20 October 2009, the first day of its two-day visit. *Photograph by Tom Boyle.*

BROWN THRASHER *Toxostoma rufum*

Fairly common and widespread, but declining, summer resident, uncommon spring and fall migrant, scarce winter resident. Brown Thrashers nest in thickets and shrubbery, especially around overgrown fields and woodland edges, and are fairly common throughout New Jersey where that habitat is available. Clearing of forests in pre–twentieth-century times facilitated the range expansion and population increase of the species, but recent data indicate a major decline in numbers throughout its range (Cavitt and Haas 2000), including New Jersey, where Breeding Bird Survey trends show a drop of 4.9 percent per year from 1966 to

2007 (Sauer et al. 2008). Thrasher migration is obscured by the presence of breeding birds, but peaks from mid-September to mid-October in the fall and late March to mid-April in the spring. Most Brown Thrashers leave New Jersey for the winter, but some remain in the southern counties and along the coast, with CBC totals averaging about a hundred a year.

Family Sturnidae: Starlings

EUROPEAN STARLING *Sturnus vulgaris*

The introduced European Starling is a very common to abundant permanent resident throughout the state. During the Breeding Bird Atlas, it was absent only from a few parts of the Pine Barrens where there are large, unbroken tracts of woodland (Walsh et al. 1999). Following the initial release in New York City in 1890–1891, it spread rapidly across the state, reaching Cape May in 1909, and by the 1930s was one of the commonest birds in southern New Jersey (Stone 1937). As an aggressive cavity nester, it is believed to have a significant negative effect on the breeding success of other species such as Eastern Bluebird and woodpeckers. Large feeding flocks form in fall and winter, often with blackbirds mixed in, and gather at noisy nighttime roosts. Migratory flocks are also regularly seen along the coast in autumn.

Family Motacillidae: Wagtails and Pipits

AMERICAN PIPIT *Anthus rubscens*

Fairly common fall and uncommon spring migrant, scarce to uncommon winter resident. American Pipits are late migrants in the fall, with some recorded in late September, but the largest flights are seen from mid-October to November at grasslands and farm fields throughout the state. Numbers appear to have declined in recent decades (Walsh et al. 1999), but CBC totals are highly variable (93 in 2006, 949 in 2007) and don't show a long-term downward trend as in some parts of the country (Verbeek and Hendricks 1994). In winter, most pipits are found in the southern tier of counties, but in some years a few remain in fields in a belt across north-central New Jersey (see map). The spring migration occurs mainly inland and peaks during April, with occasional stragglers through early May or even later.

Family Bombycillidae: Waxwings

BOHEMIAN WAXWING *Bombycilla garrulus*

Casual winter and early spring visitor. There have been fifteen accepted records of Bohemian Waxwing in New Jersey, some involving multiple birds (up to nine). The first three birds occurred in 1962, but there were only three other sightings until one in 1998 and another in 1999. After a short gap, 2004 was the big year, with a total of ten to twelve birds at four different sites, three along the coast. The largest single flock of nine birds was at Island Beach, 23–25 December 2007, followed by a group of three or four at Sandy Hook and another inland in early 2008. Whether this recent increase in sightings will continue remains to be seen.

Review Species

CEDAR WAXWING *Bombycilla cedrorum*

Common but erratic resident and migrant. The flocking and unpredictable nomadic behavior of Cedar Waxwings is typical of animals that feed primarily on specialized foods such as sugary fruits that are patchily distributed both in season and location (Witmer et al. 1997). Because of their wandering, exact times of migration are difficult to specify, but peak fall flights usually occur along the coast in September and October, while spring migration peaks from mid-May to June. Cedar Waxwings nest later than most songbirds, typically July and August in New Jersey, and they may be found anywhere in the state, but not necessarily the same place two years in a row. CBC numbers vary widely, and Cedar Waxwings tend to become less common, especially in the northern counties, in midwinter and early spring.

Family Parulidae: Wood-Warblers

BLUE-WINGED WARBLER *Vermivora pinus*

Fairly common spring and fall migrant, fairly common and widespread summer resident. Blue-winged Warblers expanded their breeding range in New Jersey during the 1900s to include the Kittatinny Mountains and Valley and the Highlands, where they are now widely distributed and where their presence has apparently contributed to the decline of the Golden-winged Warbler. They also nest in most of the Piedmont and at many sites throughout the Pine Bar-

rens and the Outer Coastal Plain, especially Monmouth and Cape May counties. Spring migration runs from late April to mid-May, with local breeders arriving first, whereas the fall migration peaks in mid- to late August, with only a few remaining to mid-September, exceptionally as late as early October. Hybrids with Golden-winged Warbler are scarce, but sometimes detected in migration at various sites or during the nesting season in the area where the ranges overlap in northwestern New Jersey. The "Brewster's" types are more frequently encountered than the "Lawrence's" types.

GOLDEN-WINGED WARBLER *Vermivora chrysoptera*

Scarce fall and rare spring migrant, rare summer resident. The range of the Golden-winged Warbler has undergone expansion and contraction for at least 150 years in response to deforestation and reforestation, among other factors (Confer 1992). Although they were formerly common in the northern counties of New Jersey (Griscom 1923, Bull 1964), the Atlas found them limited to a small portion of the Kittatinny Mountains and the Highlands (Walsh et al. 1999). Today there are very few breeding pairs left in the state, as they have declined precipitously across the entire southern extent of their range in the face of competition and hybridization with Blue-winged Warblers, forest succession, and other causes (Confer 1992, Sauer et al. 2008). Most Golden-winged Warblers nest north and west of the Appalachian Mountains, and they are scarce fall migrants mainly in late August and early September, with the latest birds recorded in early October. Breeding birds arrive in early to mid-May, as do the few migrants seen away from the nesting areas.

TENNESSEE WARBLER *Vermivora peregrina*

Uncommon fall migrant, scarce to uncommon spring migrant. Tennessee Warblers have been shown to experience dramatic population explosions and collapses in response to spruce budworm infestation cycles in the boreal forest, as occurred in 1910–1920, 1945–1955, and 1968–1985 (Bolgiano 2004). This boom-to-bust cycle has been readily apparent to long-time birders in New Jersey, who could expect to see and hear 50 to 100 or more on a good flight day in mid-May 1975–1980, but are now delighted to find one or two in 2010. Likewise, the high fall count of 250 at Higbee Beach, 11 September 1988, compares with a daily maximum of 8 at the same site in 2009. Spring migration is almost entirely in May, peaking mid-month, while fall migration is primarily late August to mid-September. There have been several recent late November records and there is one CBC record of a moribund bird on the Lower Hudson count from December 1975.

ORANGE-CROWNED WARBLER *Vermivora celata*

Scarce fall and very rare spring migrant, rare winter resident. Orange-crowned Warblers are the latest fall migrants among our regular warblers. They are rare in late September, with most records from early October into December. About twenty are reported to Jersey Birds or the Rare Bird Alerts in an average season (others no doubt go unreported), mostly from the coast, and many of them stay around for the CBCs. Up to twenty have been reported in the state in a single year on CBCs, with an average of nine per year, but one year (2003) had none. A few Orange-crowned Warblers are found along the coast later in winter, mainly at Cape May and Sandy Hook, but even fewer are detected as migrants in spring, and those few are usually seen in late April and early May.

NASHVILLE WARBLER *Vermivora ruficapilla*

Uncommon spring and fall migrant, scarce and very local summer resident. A few southbound Nashville Warblers arrive in late August, but the main flight is from mid-September to mid-October. Although they are not common, one can expect to encounter five to ten on a good flight day. Of the eastern warblers that winter primarily south of the U.S., Nashville is the most likely to be encountered in early winter, and a total of twenty-nine individuals has been found on CBCs from 1992 to 2008. One successfully wintered at Cape May in 2007–2008, but there do not appear to be any other records after early January. Spring migrants are concentrated mainly in the first half of May. Nesting Nashville Warblers in New Jersey are scarce and have been found in two very different habitats —brushy bogs and dry mountain ridge tops in the northern Highlands and the Kittatinny Mountains.

VIRGINIA'S WARBLER *Vermivora virginiae*

Accidental. A Virginia's Warbler was captured in a mist net, banded, and photographed at Island Beach in 1962. Another reported banding record in 1966 was not documented by photograph and has not been accepted by the Records Committee. The only other records for the Northeast are from Rhode Island and three Canadian provinces, Ontario, Nova Scotia, and Labrador.

6 OCT 1962, ISLAND BEACH SP, OCEAN CO. (AFN 17[1]:21; NJPF)

Virginia's Warbler breeds mainly in the Great Basin and southern Rocky Mountain States and winters in southern Mexico. Nevertheless, it has shown up at least five times in northeastern North America, including once in New Jersey. This individual was banded and photographed at Island Beach, Ocean County, 6 October 1962. *Photograph by Francis Hornick.*

NORTHERN PARULA *Parula americana*

Common spring and fall migrant, fairly common summer resident. Historically, Northern Parula was a common breeding bird in the Pine Barrens and southern counties (Stone 1908) and a rare and local nester in the northwestern part of New Jersey (Griscom 1923). By 1955 they had been extirpated from the northern areas and become rare in the south, where the *Usnea* lichen they used for their nests disappeared, apparently due to air pollution. Beginning in the late 1970s, they began to recolonize parts of the south and the north, especially along the Delaware River. Since then, the population has continued to grow and expand to cover much of the state. Northern Parulas are one of the more common spring migrant warblers, with the main passage from the end of April through the middle of May. In autumn, they may be found beginning in late August, but the main flight is through September into early October, and a couple of birds are reported annually in early November. Individuals were reported on five CBCs from 1981 to 2001, and one attempted to overwinter at a Lambertville, Hunterdon County, feeder in early 2007, but disappeared after a hard freeze.

Northern Parula nearly disappeared as a breeding bird in New Jersey during the middle of the twentieth century but has recovered strongly. The blending of the yellow lower mandible with a yellow throat is unique to parulas. *Photograph by Kevin Karlson.*

YELLOW WARBLER *Dendroica petechia*

Common and widespread summer resident, common spring and fall migrant. Yellow Warblers are familiar and common nesting birds throughout most of New Jersey, although less so in the Pine Barrens, where the brushy habitat near water that they require is less available. In prime habitat, such as Great Swamp, Troy Meadows, and upland edges of salt marshes, they can be abundant breeders. Yellow Warblers arrive on territory in late April, with migrants passing through into mid-May. Southbound birds are among the earliest migrant warblers, beginning in mid-July, peaking in early to mid-August, and continuing in declining numbers

Yellow Warbler is the most widespread and one of the most common North American wood-warblers. The bright yellow adult male is easily distinguished from the slightly duller female by its reddish streaks on the underparts. *Photograph by Kevin Karlson.*

through September into early October as individuals from an enormous breeding range work their way south. There are a few records for early November, and there is one well-documented CBC record from DeKorte Park, 20 December 1987, but there are no other winter records.

CHESTNUT-SIDED WARBLER *Dendroica pensylvanica*

Fairly common migrant and fairly common, but somewhat local, summer resident. Most Chestnut-sided Warblers in New Jersey nest north and west of the Piedmont, where they favor second-growth woodlands, edges, and over-grown fields. This species is one of the few songbirds that has benefited from human activities, and its population has greatly expanded since the early 1800s (Richardson and Brauning 1995), although there has been some apparent decline across much of its range since the 1960s. This has been evident in New Jersey as well (Sauer et al. 2008). Northbound Chestnut-sided Warblers pass through New Jersey primarily in early to mid-May, when they are more common inland than along the coast. The reverse is true in fall, when they first arrive in mid-August, peak from late August to mid-September and are rare after September. There are a few records for late October.

Although strikingly different in plumage, Chestnut-sided Warbler is closely related to Yellow Warbler but has a much more restricted range. It nests in second-growth woodlands in the northwestern part of New Jersey. The female is similar to the male, shown here, but has less bold facial markings and a shorter chestnut stripe on the sides. *Photograph by Kevin Karlson.*

MAGNOLIA WARBLER *Dendroica magnolia*

Fairly common to common spring and fall migrant, scarce and local summer resident. Magnolia Warblers, in their handsome black and yellow breeding plumage, are one of the most common migrant spring warblers in New Jersey, with most passing through in mid- to late May. A very few stay to nest in the northwestern corner of the state, primarily in spruce plantings along the Kittatinny Mountains. Fall migration begins in late August, with a peak in early to mid-September and diminishing numbers from late September into mid-October. There is one well-documented CBC record from Boonton, 23 December 1984, but no midwinter reports.

CAPE MAY WARBLER *Dendroica tigrina*

Uncommon spring and fall migrant. Cape May Warbler, like Tennessee and Bay-breasted warblers, is one of the boreal forest breeders known to undergo large population swings tied to the spruce budworm cycles (Baltz and Latta 1998). At the turn of the twentieth century, there were only a few specimens or sight records for New Jersey (Stone 1908), but the three major outbreaks of budworms since then have produced occasional large flights. Spring migrants pass through during May, when a birder can hope to see two or three individuals on a good flight day compared to the maximum of 1,000+ at Sandy Hook, 19 May 1984. Cape May Warblers are more numerous in the fall, but the season total of 122 birds at the daily-staffed Morning Flight Survey at Higbee Beach in 2009 still falls well short of the single-day totals obtained several times during the 1980s (Sibley 1997). A few birds have been recorded as late as early November, and individuals have been reported on eight CBCs since 1973; one survived the winter at Princeton in 1990 (RNJB 16[2]:27), and another made it through the season at a suet feeder in Columbia, Warren County, in 2000 (RNJB 26[2]:70).

The handsome male Cape May Warbler is much more brightly colored than the female. This species is an uncommon migrant, spring and fall, on its way to and from boreal forests, where it breeds, and the Caribbean region, where it winters. The population undergoes large swings in response to outbreaks of spruce budworm. *Photograph by Kevin Karlson.*

BLACK-THROATED BLUE WARBLER
Dendroica caerulescens

Common fall and fairly common spring migrant, scarce and local summer resident. Black-throated Blue Warblers migrate through New Jersey in spring from late April to late May and can be found at many places throughout the state. Small numbers remain to nest on laurel-covered hillsides in the Kittatinny Mountains and the Highlands. Fall migration begins in late August and continues strongly through September into early October, then diminishes gradually during the remainder of the month. Numbers can be impressive along the coast—for example, an estimated one thousand Black-throated Blue Warblers at Higbee Beach, 12 September 1992 (Sibley 1997). A few linger through early November, but there are no winter records.

The male Black-throated Blue Warbler, shown here, and the female differ so much in appearance that Alexander Wilson and John James Audubon thought they were separate species. It is one of our more common migrant wood-warblers and is a scarce breeding bird in the northwestern part of the state. Like Cape May Warbler, it winters in the Caribbean. *Photograph by Kevin Karlson.*

YELLOW-RUMPED WARBLER *Dendroica coronata*

Abundant fall and common spring migrant, fairly common winter resident, scarce and local summer resident. Yellow-rumped Warbler is one of the rarest breeding warblers in New Jersey and was first confirmed as a nesting species in 1979 in the Highlands (Bacinski 1980). Since then, they have been found in limited numbers in coniferous woodlands in the Highlands and the Kittatinny Mountains. Spring migrant yellow-rumps arrive in late April and early May, and are common throughout the state at that time. In fall, they are by far the most abundant migrant warbler, passing through from mid-September into December, with massive flights numbering in the tens of thousands often occurring in early to mid-October. Many Yellow-rumped Warblers winter in New Jersey, especially along the coast, with recent CBCs averaging about 5,000. Birds in the northern counties and inland become much scarcer as the winter progresses. The "Audubon's race" of this species, *D. c. audubonii,* has been reported more than a dozen times in the state, mainly in late fall, and was added to the Review List in 1996. There have been two accepted records of this subspecies since then.

BLACK-THROATED GRAY WARBLER

Dendroica nigrescens

Review Species

Casual. Since the first appearance of this western warbler in New Jersey at Tuckerton, 23 September 1956, there have been twenty-one accepted records. All but two have oc- curred in fall or early winter, except for one at Mickleton, Gloucester County, in April 1957 and one at Marlton, Bur- lington County, 1–28 January 2007. The majority of re- ports are from the coast, but there have been eight inland sightings. (*See photo page 150.*)

BLACK-THROATED GREEN WARBLER *Dendroica virens*

Fairly common spring and fall migrant, uncommon and lo- cal summer resident. The first spring-migrant Black- throated Green Warblers are seen in late April, but they are most common during the first half of May. In northern New Jersey, they nest primarily in eastern hemlock groves and, to a lesser extent, white pine/deciduous woods, in the Kittatinny Mountains and the Highlands, and this popula- tion is at risk, as the woolly adelgid continues to kill most hemlocks (Morse and Poole 2005). The birds were first re- corded breeding in Atlantic white cedar swamps in the Pine Barrens in 1935 (Stone 1937), and the Atlas confirmed the continued presence of a small and scattered nesting popu- lation there. Southbound migrants appear as early as mid- August, but the main flight is from mid-September to the beginning of October, with diminishing numbers through- out that month and into the first week of November. There is a recent late November record from Cape May and a well-documented sighting on the 26 December 1982 Boon- ton CBC, but none after that date.

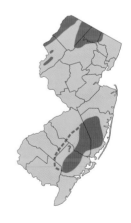

Review Species

TOWNSEND'S WARBLER *Dendroica townsendi*

Accidental. There have been ten accepted records of this attractive western warbler in New Jersey, all since December 1971. Six of the sightings occurred in the period between December 1977 and November 1988; there were none in the 1990s, and only three since then. There are four inland records and six coastal ones, including three from Sandy Hook. Most of the records are from early winter, but there is one from April and one from May.

BLACKBURNIAN WARBLER *Dendroica fusca*

Uncommon to fairly common spring and fall migrant, scarce and local summer resident. As a breeding bird in New Jersey, the beautiful Blackburnian Warbler has a limited and patchy distribution in coniferous woods in the Kittatinny Mountains and the northern Highlands. During migration, they are found throughout the state, with peak spring flights in mid-May and fall movement from late August to mid-September, with the latest records in mid-October.

The strikingly beautiful Blackburnian Warbler is one of the jewels among North American birds. A scarce breeding bird at the higher elevations of northern New Jersey, it is a widespread and fairly common migrant, especially in fall. The male, shown here, has a flaming orange throat and face, while the female's color is a more subdued yellow-orange. *Photograph by Lloyd Spitalnik.*

YELLOW-THROATED WARBLER *Dendroica dominica*

Fairly common but local summer resident, scarce spring and fall migrant. New Jersey is at the northern limit of the breeding range of Yellow-throated Warbler along the Atlantic Seaboard, and the species is infrequently encountered in migration, although it is an occasional spring overshoot in areas north of the nesting range. Two subspecies breed in the state. Nominate *D. d. dominica* was first discovered nesting at Cape May in 1922 (Fables 1955). This form, which prefers white pine plantations and mixed oak–pitch pine woodlands, has spread gradually northward to include much of Cape May, Cumberland, and Atlantic counties. The Interior or Sycamore subspecies, *D. d. albi-lora*, was found nesting at Bull's Island in 1954 and has spread slowly in small numbers in both directions to just reach Mercer and Sussex counties. It is occasionally found inland along rivers, but seems to have retreated from many former breeding sites. Yellow-throated Warblers are early spring migrants, arriving on their breeding territories in late March or early April. Most probably depart during August, but a few migrants are seen at Cape May through September. There is one winter record from Margate, Atlantic County, 16–19 January 1998. (*See photo page 151.*)

PINE WARBLER *Dendroica pinus*

Common and fairly widespread summer resident, uncommon spring and fall migrant, rare winter resident. Pine Warblers are common and nearly ubiquitous breeders in the Pine Barrens and the Outer Coastal Plain. In northern New Jersey, they have a widespread but very patchy distribution in pine woodlands or plantations, occupying only a small percentage of the area shown on the map. Pine Warblers are very early migrants, arriving on the nesting grounds in the Pine Barrens as early as mid-March, but still passing through in early May in the north. Fall migrants may be seen at nonbreeding sites from late August to early November, and from one to nineteen have been seen on CBCs, with as many as eight different areas recording the species in one year. A few are found in midwinter at suet feeders or sheltered sites.

PRAIRIE WARBLER *Dendroica discolor*

Common and fairly widespread summer resident, fairly common spring and fall migrant, casual in early winter. Prairie Warblers have long been common nesting birds in the Pine Barrens and dry brush clearings and second growth in southern New Jersey. They expanded their range into the northern part of the state, where they are partial to overgrown fields with red cedars, during the mid-twentieth century (Bull 1964). They are absent from the Inner Coastal Plain and much of the Piedmont. Prairie Warblers arrive on their breeding grounds in late April and early May, with mi-

grants passing through during the first half of May. In fall, migrants mingle with breeders to peak from late August to mid-September and are mostly gone by the end of the month. A few stragglers linger into November, and Prairie Warblers have been recorded on CBCs in four years, with a maximum of eight on four counts in 1999. One survived at Cape May to at least mid-January 1998 (Walsh et al. 1999).

PALM WARBLER *Dendroica palmarum*

Common fall and fairly common spring migrant, rare to scarce winter resident. Palm Warbler is one of the latest regular migrant warblers to arrive in the fall, beginning in early September, but with peak numbers from late September to mid-October. A modest coastal flight continues into December, and one to two dozen are found on CBCs, mainly along the coast. A few of these apparently survive the winter, especially in Cape May County. Spring migrants first appear in late March or early April, peak in mid-April, and have largely departed by the end of the first week in May. Spring birds are almost all of the eastern "Yellow" subspecies, whereas the majority of fall migrants are of the duller "Western" subspecies.

BAY-BREASTED WARBLER *Dendroica castanea*

Uncommon spring and fall migrant. Bay-breasted Warbler is another of the species that has shown wide population swings correlated with outbreaks of spruce budworm in the boreal forest where it breeds (Williams 1996). Peak numbers in migration were encountered during the 1970s and 1980s, followed by a noticeable decline, but they are still apparently more common today than at the beginning of the twentieth century (Stone 1908). In spring, Bay-breasted Warblers are rare before May, with maximum numbers seen in mid- to late May, while the fall migration starts in late August and continues through September, with only the rare straggler seen after early October.

BLACKPOLL WARBLER *Dendroica striata*

Common spring and fall migrant throughout the state, but especially along the coast in autumn. Although some Blackpolls arrive in early May, the bulk of the spring migration is in mid- to late May, with some stragglers still passing through during the first week of June. The first fall birds arrive in late August, but the main push of migrants is from mid-September to mid-October (Walsh et al. 1999). Some linger into November, and there are two CBC records since 1981. Much of the fall migration is believed to take place offshore, as birds depart the coast from between Nova Scotia and North Carolina on a direct path to northern South America. While this hypothesis is controversial (Murray 1989), Brady (1992) witnessed a spectacle in the early morning hours of 15 October 1991 when an estimated 9,000 Blackpolls flew by in the lights of the boat on a pelagic trip seventy miles off Barnegat Light. Blackpoll Warbler does not breed in New Jersey, but it does so on the top of Slide Mountain, NY, only fifty miles north of High Point.

CERULEAN WARBLER *Dendroica cerulea*

Scarce and local summer resident, rare to scarce spring and fall migrant. Cerulean Warblers increased as breeding birds in New Jersey during the last half of the twentieth century (Walsh et al. 1999), even as their numbers declined in the Ohio and Mississippi River valleys (Hamel 2000), but their breeding range in New Jersey appears to have shrunk somewhat during the past decade. They nest in mature, deciduous woodlands primarily along the Kittatinny Mountains and in the Highlands, south along the Delaware River, the Delaware Water Gap, and formerly to Bull's Island, and are most common in Stokes State Forest and High Point SP. Cerulean Warblers arrive on the breeding grounds from late April to early May, and occasional migrants are seen to mid-May. In fall, they pass through from early August to early September, when a few migrants are encountered at Cape May, but rarely elsewhere.

Cerulean Warbler has a very patchy distribution across its breeding range in the eastern United States, just reaching New Jersey in the northwest corner. It has declined substantially in recent decades and is rarely seen in migration. The male, shown here, and female have a similar plumage pattern, but the male is sky blue above, with a dark breast-band, while the female is a unique blue-green above. *Photograph by Lloyd Spitalnik.*

BLACK-AND-WHITE WARBLER *Mniotilta varia*

Common spring and fall migrant, fairly common and wide-spread summer resident. Black-and-white Warblers are common breeding birds in most of northern New Jersey, although they have declined in recent years, and are less common in the more deforested parts of the Piedmont and Inner Coastal Plain. They are also common in the Pine Barrens and much of the Outer Coastal Plain, an apparent increase in numbers during the past century compared to what Stone reported in 1908. Spring migrants may appear as early as mid-April, but most pass through during the first half of May. Fall migration is more protracted, with some seen by early August, the main flight from late August to mid-September, and small numbers seen regularly through early October. Black-and-white Warblers winter as far north as North Carolina, and have been recorded on a total of ten individual CBCs in seven different years, but there are no midwinter reports.

One of the earliest migrant warblers to return in the spring, Black-and-white Warbler is a familiar migrant and fairly common summer resident, especially in the northern part of the state. Its peculiar habit of creeping along tree trunks and limbs like a nuthatch is unique among North American wood-warblers. In late summer and early fall, immature birds such as this young male augment the breeding population. *Photograph by Kevin Karlson.*

AMERICAN REDSTART *Setophaga ruticilla*

Common and fairly widespread summer resident, common spring and fall migrant. American Redstarts are very common breeding birds in the woodlands of northern New Jersey, but are less common with a somewhat patchy distribution in the southern two-thirds of the state, being nearly

absent from the southwestern counties. In spring, they begin to arrive in late April or early May, with peak numbers
in mid-May. Fall American Redstarts are among the most
numerous migrant songbirds, passing through from early
August to early October, with a peak in the first half of
September. A few may be seen as late as early November,
and there is a recent 15 December record for Avalon, but
no winter reports.

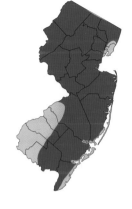

American Redstart is a butterfly of the bird world. The male, in his black and orange dress, and the female, in her gray, greenish, and yellow attire, flit actively
through the trees, flicking their tails to show off the colors. A widespread species
in North America, it is one of our most common breeding and migrant warblers. *Photograph by Kevin Karlson.*

PROTHONOTARY WARBLER *Protonotaria citrea*

Fairly common but local summer resident, scarce spring and
fall migrant. Prothonotary Warblers first nested in New Jersey in 1924 (Stone 1937), then spread gradually through
much of the southern part of the state. They nest in cavities
in swamps and wet deciduous lands and can be found almost anywhere that habitat is available in the range shown.
In the northern part of the state, they have nested at numerous sites, such as Whittingham WMA in Sussex County,
Great Swamp, and Princeton, but have failed to establish
sustainable numbers. Central New Jersey is the northern
limit of their breeding range on the eastern seaboard, so they
are seldom seen in migration, except for small numbers at
Cape May in August and as spring overshoots in the northern counties. Prothonotary Warblers arrive on territory in
late April or early May and depart from late July to late August, with very few stragglers detected in early September.

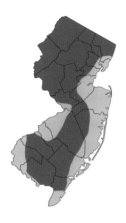

WORM-EATING WARBLER *Helmitheros vermivorum*

Fairly common but somewhat local summer resident, uncommon spring and fairly common fall migrant. Worm-eating Warblers choose two very different habitats for nesting in New Jersey. In the north they prefer wooded hillsides, often with steep slopes, whereas in the south they select wet deciduous woodlands. They can be quite common in the northwestern counties, although they have declined in recent years, but are still thinly distributed in the southern part of the state, where they were first found nesting during the early 1980s in Cumberland County (Sutton and Sutton 1986). Spring migrants arrive in late April, with some passage into mid-May, while the first southbound migrants can be seen as early as late July. The bulk of the fall flight is from mid-August to early September, and Worm-eating Warblers are rare after mid-September.

Review Species

SWAINSON'S WARBLER *Limnothlypis swainsonii*

Very rare. There have been eighteen accepted records of Swainson's Warbler in New Jersey, all but two along the coast and all but two in spring or early summer. A number of reports of singing birds have not been accepted due

Swainson's Warbler is an uncommon species of the southeastern U.S. that formerly nested as close as southern Delaware. It has occurred in New Jersey eighteen times, and several males have stayed for a month or more, singing and trying, unsuccessfully, to attract a mate. This individual was photographed at Jakes Landing, Cape May County, 4 May 2002. *Photograph by Elaine Crunkleton.*

to possibility of confusion with Hooded Warbler or Louisiana Waterthrush. The first state record was a bird banded at Linwood, Atlantic County, 23 May 1968, and prior to 2000 there were only eight more, including three banded. The eight years from 2000 to 2007, however, produced an additional nine records, six of them from Cape May.

OVENBIRD *Seiurus aurocapilla*

Common and very widespread summer resident, fairly common spring and fall migrant. In New Jersey, Ovenbird is the most common woodland breeding songbird, and has long been so (Stone 1908). Although their numbers have declined over much of their range in recent decades due to forest fragmentation and development (Van Horn and Donovan 1994), the loud, ringing song of the Ovenbird remains a common sound in our woodlands. Breeding birds arrive on their territories beginning in mid- to late April, but northbound migrants continue through mid-May. They start to head south in mid-August, with peak numbers in early to mid-September, but small numbers continue to migrate through during most of October. Ovenbirds have been found on nine CBCs since 1974, and there is a recent mid-January record from Hunterdon County.

NORTHERN WATERTHRUSH *Seiurus novaboracensis*

Common fall and fairly common spring migrant, uncommon and local summer resident. Northern Waterthrush is a bird of wooded swamps and bogs and can be found breeding throughout most of northwestern New Jersey where suitable habitat is available. They have also been found in summer in a few white cedar swamps in the Pine Barrens, within the dashed lines on the map, but the population seems to be very small and dispersed. Northbound Northern Waterthrushes arrive beginning in late April, with migrants continuing through most of May. In fall, they are among the earliest of migrant songbirds, with passage beginning in mid-July and continuing through September. A few are seen in early October, but they are rare after mid-month. They have been seen on a couple of CBCs, but there are no midwinter records.

LOUISIANA WATERTHRUSH *Seiurus motacilla*

Fairly common but somewhat local summer resident, uncommon fall and scarce spring migrant. Louisiana Waterthrushes have long been common breeding birds in northern New Jersey (Griscom 1923), but their presence in much of the southern part of the state, albeit in small numbers, seems to represent a recent range expansion (Walsh et al. 1999). Unlike their Northern Waterthrush cousins, Louisiana Waterthrushes prefer running water and nest along wooded streams. In spring, they are the earliest of the migrant warblers that winter south of the U.S., with a few arriving on territory during the last few days of March. Likewise, Louisiana Waterthrushes are among the earliest of migrant songbirds to depart in fall, with southbound birds seen in mid-July and the peak movement in early August. They are very rare after the end of August.

KENTUCKY WARBLER *Oporornis formosus*

Uncommon and local summer resident, scarce spring and fall migrant. Kentucky Warblers require wet woodlands with a dense understory for nesting, and they can be found in much of southern New Jersey, where suitable conditions exist. Their distribution in the central and northern parts of the state is very patchy and inconsistent, with some sites being used for years and then abandoned. Because Kentucky Warblers are near the northern limit of the breeding range in New Jersey, relatively few are seen in migration. Most nesting birds arrive on territory in early to mid-May and depart by mid-August.

CONNECTICUT WARBLER *Oporornis agilis*

Casual spring migrant and uncommon but regular fall migrant throughout the state. Due to its secretive nature, this species may be more numerous than birding experience would predict. Banding results, in particular, point to a much higher frequency of occurrence than those encountered in the field. Connecticut Warblers were apparently much more common in fall migration during the early part of the twentieth century (Stone 1937). Peak flight is in mid-September, but the birds should be looked for from early September to mid-October. In spring, Connecticut Warblers migrate up the Central Flyway and are seldom encountered in New Jersey.

Connecticut Warbler is one of the most sought-after of fall migrants in the state, but is uncommon and shy. This immature exhibits the strong, unbroken eye-ring that helps distinguish it from the similar Mourning Warbler and accidental MacGillivray's Warbler. It lacks the gray hood of an adult male or the grayish hood of an adult female. *Photograph by Lloyd Spitalnik.*

MOURNING WARBLER *Oporornis philadelphia*

Uncommon spring and fall migrant. Mourning Warblers are among the most sought-after and latest of the regular migrant spring warblers, typically not appearing before mid-May, but with a few passing through into the first ten days of June. Fall migration occurs mainly from mid-August to mid-September, but stragglers have been found into early October, and there is a recent (22 October 2006) record from Cape May. Oddly, Stone (1937) knew of no records in Cape May County, where the single-day high count is now twelve, twice in late August (Sibley 1997). Mourning Warblers nest as close to New Jersey as the Catskill and Pocono mountains, but the only known breeding attempt was a male that sang on territory for three weeks in Passaic County in June 1996, but apparently never attracted a mate.

MACGILLIVRAY'S WARBLER *Oporornis tolmiei*

Review Species

Accidental. An immature bird of this species was discovered at "The Beanery" (Rea Farm) in Cape May, 12 November 1997, where it remained for two months. This is the only New Jersey record of this western wood-warbler and one of fewer than a dozen in the northeastern U.S. Although the bird survived several periods of sub-freezing

weather, it disappeared during a spell of unusually mild temperatures and may have fallen victim to a predator (Karlson 1998).

12 NOV 1997–11 JAN 1998, CAPE MAY, CAPE MAY CO. (NJBRC 1997-086; NJPF)

MacGillivray's Warbler is the western counterpart of the eastern Mourning Warbler and is a very rare vagrant to eastern North America. This immature, the only record for New Jersey, shows the bold, white eye-arcs, complete grayish hood, and whitish throat that distinguish it from an immature Mourning Warbler. It spent two months at "The Beanery" in Cape May, 12 November 1997–11 January 1998. *Photograph by Kevin Karlson.*

COMMON YELLOWTHROAT *Geothlypis trichas*

Common and ubiquitous summer resident, common spring and fall migrant, rare winter resident. Common Yellowthroats are one of the most common and widely distributed breeding birds in New Jersey. With the widespread destruction of wetlands, on which they depend for nesting, they have declined in abundance throughout their range, including New Jersey (Guzy and Ritchison 1999, Sauer et al. 2008). However, their ability to use a variety of habitats from the understory of moist woods to the edges of marshes and wet woods has helped them remain a familiar summer resident. In spring, most Common Yellowthroats arrive in late April or early May, with migrants passing through to mid-month. Local breeders remain into September, when their numbers are augmented by large flights of northern migrants later in the month and into early October. Most are gone by the end of October, but a few stragglers remain through November and December. About five to ten are found annually on CBCs (maximum thirty-six in 1984), but they are very rare after mid-January.

HOODED WARBLER *Wilsonia citrina*

Fairly common but somewhat local summer resident, scarce spring and fall migrant. Hooded Warblers nest primarily in three regions in New Jersey: the mountains of the northern counties, the cedar swamps of the Pine Barrens, and the wooded swamps of Cumberland and Cape May counties (Leck 1984). In most of these areas, they are closely associated with a dense understory of mountain laurel, and they can be locally abundant in prime habitat. New Jersey is near the northern edge of their range east of the Appalachians, so Hooded Warblers are infrequently encountered in migration. They arrive on territory in late April or early May, and depart after the nesting season from mid-August to late September, with only a few seen in early October. There are no winter records.

One of our most attractive warblers, the Hooded Warbler is a widely distributed and fairly common breeding bird in New Jersey. Although it usually stays hidden in the dense undergrowth that it prefers, the male, pictured here, often sings from a perch ten to twenty feet above the ground. The female is similar, but usually shows less black on the crown and lacks the black throat of the male. *Photograph by Kevin Karlson.*

WILSON'S WARBLER *Wilsonia pusilla*

Uncommon spring and fall migrant. Most northbound Wilson's Warblers pass through in mid- to late May and are more likely in the northern part of New Jersey than in the south. They are also more frequently reported in spring than in fall, perhaps because the males are readily detected by their song. In fall, the earliest migrants appear in late August, but most are found in early to mid-September, with only a few stragglers after early October. Wilson's Warblers have been found on CBCs in five different years, including singles on three counts in 2004, but there are no midwinter records.

CANADA WARBLER *Wilsonia canadensis*

Fairly common spring and fall migrant, uncommon and local summer resident. Canada Warblers nest in wet woodlands with a dense understory in northwestern New Jersey. Although they were found breeding in several places in the Pine Barrens in the 1980s, they have apparently withdrawn from there and from much of their former range in the state. For example, at Black River WMA, Morris County, where the species was a common breeder in the early 1980s, it was absent twenty years later. Canada Warblers have shown a serious decline in the Northeast in recent decades, perhaps due to habitat destruction on their wintering grounds in South America (Conway 1999, Sauer et al. 2008). They are fairly late migrants in spring, passing through from mid- to late May, but they return early, with southbound birds seen by early August and a peak flight during the latter part of that month. Small numbers continue through to mid-September, but they are rare after that.

Canada Warbler, like Connecticut Warbler and a few other Neotropical migrant warblers, is a long-distance migrant, wintering in South America as far down as central Peru. In New Jersey, it is a fairly common migrant but nests only in the northwestern part of the state. The male, shown here, is bright yellow below and gray above, with a bold black necklace. The female's plumage is a more washed-out version of the male's. *Photograph by Lloyd Spitalnik.*

YELLOW-BREASTED CHAT *Icteria virens*

Uncommon and somewhat local summer resident, uncommon to scarce spring and fall migrant, very rare winter resident. As breeding birds in New Jersey, Yellow-breasted Chats are concentrated in the southern tier of counties from Gloucester and Salem to Cape May. They do nest sparingly and sporadically throughout most of the rest of the state west of the Pine Barrens and the northeastern counties. New Jersey is near the northern limit of their breeding range in the East, so not only does the population fluctuate, but they are seldom seen in migration. Yellow-breasted Chats return to the breeding grounds by mid-May. Their tendency to become quiet and inconspicuous by late July, and the dispersal of some individuals to the northeast, makes the fall migration difficult to ascertain. Chats are reported occasionally throughout the fall, and one or more are reported on CBCs every year, but only a few have successfully overwintered.

Family Emberizidae: New World Sparrows

GREEN-TAILED TOWHEE *Pipilo chlorurus*

Review Species

Casual winter visitor from the West. There are just seven accepted records of this species in New Jersey. Most of the occurrences have been at feeders and all have been present for extended periods, two for almost five months. Unlike the majority of western vagrants, none of the Green-tailed Towhees have been found near the immediate coast. The earliest arrival date is 20 November, and the latest departure date is 20 May. The most recent record occurred 1 January–10 May 2009, almost twenty-four years after the previous one.

Green-tailed Towhee is a fairly common species of the western United States. It is a short-distance migrant but has strayed to the East on numerous occasions. There are seven records for New Jersey, although just one since 1985. Most have stayed for months, like this bird that visited the McDevit feeder in Collings-wood, Camden County, from 1 January to 10 May 2009. *Photograph by Tom Johnson.*

SPOTTED TOWHEE *Pipilo maculatus*

Casual. There have been six records of Spotted Towhee, formerly (until 1995) considered conspecific with Eastern Towhee, the first being a specimen taken at Metuchen, Middlesex County, 24 December 1952. Individuals were banded at Ramsey (October 1959) and Island Beach (October 1987), followed by birds at Cape May (December 1994–March 1995) and Salem County (March 1995). The only recent record is a female discovered at Palmyra Cove Nature Park on 26 November 2009 that remained to the end of April.

Spotted Towhee is the western counterpart of our familiar Eastern Towhee and has been recorded six times in the state. The most recent was this female, discovered at Palmyra Cove Nature Park, Burlington County, on 26 November 2009 and which remained until at least May 2010, having survived numerous snow storms. *Photograph by Jonathan MacCornack.*

EASTERN TOWHEE *Pipilo erythrophthalmus*

Common and widespread summer resident, common spring and fall migrant, uncommon but apparently increasing winter resident. Eastern Towhees can be found breeding throughout New Jersey except in highly urbanized areas lacking the thickets and shrubs they require for nesting. They are abundant in the Pine Barrens and on the drier ridges of the Highlands and Kittatinny Mountains. Spring migrants from the South reach New Jersey by early April, with peak numbers occurring from late April to early May. Fall migration begins in September and continues into mid-November, when towhees become scarce in the northern part of the state. Eastern Towhees are recorded on the majority of CBCs in the state (an average of 300 a year), and many survive the winter in the southern third of New Jersey.

CASSIN'S SPARROW *Aimophila cassinii*

Review Species

Accidental. There is just one accepted record of this sparrow of the southern High Plains and southwestern U.S., a bird trapped at Island Beach in September 1961 that died in the hands of the banders. This species, whose erratic nesting and migration patterns continue to puzzle ornithologists, has occurred just three other times on the Atlantic coast, in New York (2000), Maine (1990), and Nova Scotia (1974).

22 SEP 1961, ISLAND BEACH SP, OCEAN CO. (AFN 16[1]:18); (*AMNH #366768)

BACHMAN'S SPARROW *Aimophila aestivalis*

Review Species

Accidental. New Jersey's first Bachman's Sparrow was a specimen collected at the unlikely location of Fort Lee, Bergen County, in 1918. This record coincided with the peak of a rapid expansion of the species' breeding range in the early twentieth century as far north as central Ohio and southwestern Pennsylvania (Dunning 2006). The second occurrence was a singing male in the Pine Barrens of Burlington County in 1957. With the contraction of the breeding range of this denizen of the pine flatwoods of the southeastern U.S. during the remainder of the twentieth century, a repeat of these appearances is unlikely in the near future.

9 MAY 1918, FORT LEE, BERGEN CO. (*USNM #442569)
16 JUN 1957, ATSION, BURLINGTON CO. (AFN 11[5]:396)

AMERICAN TREE SPARROW *Spizella arborea*

Common winter resident in northern New Jersey, uncommon to scarce in the south, common fall and fairly common spring migrant. In fall, the first American Tree Sparrows usually arrive in late October or early November, and numbers build through early winter. The number of wintering birds varies considerably depending on the severity of the season, with more birds farther south in snowy winters, but CBC totals have shown a clear decline in recent decades from an average of 4,900 from 1973 to 1982 (2.1

birds/party hour) to 2,500 from 1999 to 2008 (0.9 bird/party hour). Tree Sparrows are much more common in the northern part of the state and are scarce in the southern coastal region. In spring, most have departed by early April. (*See photo page 151.*)

CHIPPING SPARROW *Spizella passerina*

Common and nearly ubiquitous summer resident, common spring and fall migrant, uncommon winter resident. Chipping Sparrows are the most familiar of our breeding sparrows and nest everywhere in New Jersey except some highly urbanized areas, salt marshes, and on some of the barrier islands. They are common migrants in spring, arriving between late March and early May, with a peak in mid- to late April. Fall migrants augment the local breeding birds beginning in early October, with peak passage in late October to early November. High counts of 1,000 to 1,500 have been estimated at Cape May in late October. Chipping Sparrows are uncommon in winter, mainly in the southern counties, but have increased substantially in recent decades. This is reflected in CBC totals, which averaged about 60 per year during the 1980s and about 270 in the most recent ten years. Exact totals are uncertain because of the frequent misidentification of Tree Sparrows as Chipping Sparrows in winter.

CLAY-COLORED SPARROW *Spizella pallida*

Scarce fall and very rare spring migrant, very rare winter resident. Clay-colored Sparrows are scarce, but increasing, fall migrants, sometimes found inland although far more likely along the coast. They have become far more regular since the mid-1950s (Kunkle et al. 1959), likely a result of the extension of their breeding range during the late twentieth century to include all of southern Ontario, southwestern Quebec, and western and northern New York (Knapton 1994, Smith 2008). Clay-colored Sparrows occur mainly from mid-September to November, but they have been recorded on twenty-two different CBCs in twelve years between 1981 and 2009, and there have been more than a dozen midwinter reports in the past two decades. They are much less common in spring, about one every three to five years, but usually appear in May, and singing males have lingered into June and July on several occasions.

Clay-colored Sparrow is a bird of open country in the central part of the continent, but gradually extended its breeding range east during the twentieth century to western New York and Quebec. Perhaps because of this range expansion it occurs more frequently now than prior to the 1950s (birders are also
more aware of how to identify it). It is distinguished from nonbreeding Chipping
Sparrow by the strong dark moustache, pale lores, dark lower border to the
cheek patch, and brownish versus grayish rump (not visible here). *Photograph by
Kevin Karlson.*

FIELD SPARROW *Spizella pusilla*

Fairly common summer resident, common spring and fall
migrant, fairly common winter resident. Field Sparrows
nest in brushy, overgrown fields and can be found breeding
throughout New Jersey where this necessary, but declining,
habitat is available. They are absent as nesters from most
of the urbanized parts of the Piedmont and from most of
the barrier islands and salt marshes. Field Sparrows can be
common fall migrants, starting in early October, peaking in
late October to early November, and continuing into December. Many stay to winter, especially in the southern part
of the state, but they become scarce in the northwest.
Northbound movement in spring is less obvious than fall,
as a combination of wintering birds and arriving and departing migrants probably overlap (Walsh et al. 1999).

VESPER SPARROW *Pooecetes gramineus*

Scarce fall and rare spring migrant, rare and local summer
resident, very rare winter resident. Endangered Species as a
breeding bird in New Jersey. Vesper Sparrows were probably rare in the East prior to European settlement, but by

about 1900 they were considered common breeding birds throughout the eastern portion of their range, including all of New Jersey (Jones and Cornely 2002, Stone 1908). By the middle of the twentieth century they had begun a rapid decline that has only accelerated during the last several decades. Due to urbanization, second-growth succession, and a change in farming practices, the dry, grassy fields they use for nesting are no longer available. Sadly, in recent years Vesper Sparrows have been found nesting only in two small areas in Warren and Sussex counties. The small number of fall migrants is usually encountered in October and November, both inland and along the coast, and on average about five are seen on CBCs, mainly in the southern counties. Only a handful of spring migrants is seen from late March to mid-April.

LARK SPARROW *Chondestes grammacus*

Rare fall and very rare spring migrant, very rare in winter. Migrant Lark Sparrows may show up any time from mid-August to early November, with about five to ten seen in any given year; they are far more likely along the coast than inland. One or two show up in early winter most years, and the species was recorded on seventeen different CBCs in eleven years from 1981 to 2008. There have been several records of Lark Sparrows successfully overwintering, and a recent bird in Salem County, 18 March to at least 10 April 2006, probably spent the winter there. Reports of spring migrants are very unusual, with only about one or two per decade.

BLACK-THROATED SPARROW *Amphispiza bilineata*

Review Species

Accidental. The three records of this attractive southwestern sparrow are widely separated in time and space. The first visited a New Brunswick feeder for almost six months in 1961–1962 and was seen by hundreds of observers. Next was a bird discovered in a North Arlington cemetery in 1974, while the most recent individual spent three months at a Cherry Hill feeder, arriving in December 1992.

30 OCT 1961–23 APR 1962, NEW BRUNSWICK, MIDDLESEX CO. (AFN 16[1]:15)
14 DEC 1974–19 JAN 1975, NORTH ARLINGTON, BERGEN CO. (RNJB 1[1]:3; NJPF)
12 DEC 1992–MID-FEB 1993, CHERRY HILL, CAMDEN CO. (RNJB 19[2]:44; NJPF)

Black-throated Sparrow is a handsome bird of the deserts of the western U.S. Although it normally winters from southern California and western Texas south to central Mexico, it has appeared several times in the Northeast, including three times in New Jersey. All three visitors to the state have stayed for extended periods of time. This individual was found at a cemetery in North Arlington, Bergen County, 14 December 1974–19 January 1975, pictured here on 20 December. *Photograph by Dick Burk.*

LARK BUNTING *Calamospiza melanocorys*

Casual. This unique sparrow of the Great Plains is a rare but regular vagrant to the East Coast. There are only six accepted records for New Jersey, but there have been numerous other, poorly documented sightings, some of which were probably correct. Interestingly, all of the accepted occurrences have been in the very narrow time window between 27 August and 18 September. The first was at Cape May, 16 September 1956, and the longest staying bird was at Piscataway, Middlesex County, 27 August–3 September 1989.

Review Species

Lark Bunting is a large sparrow of the Great Plains, with a large, blue-gray bill. Adult males are all black with white wing patches in breeding plumage, but immatures and females, such as the bird shown here, are brown and heavily streaked, with less conspicuous white in the wings. All six accepted records have been of birds in this plumage. This bird was present at Stone Harbor, 15–16 September 2000. *Photograph by Kevin Karlson.*

SAVANNAH SPARROW *Passerculus sandwichensis*

Common fall and fairly common spring migrant, fairly common winter resident, scarce and local summer resident. Threatened Species as a breeding bird in New Jersey. Savannah Sparrows nest in man-made habitats, such as farm fields, airports, and pastures, and they have a very patchy distribution as a result. With the disappearance of many of these sites, they are seriously threatened as a breeder in the state. Savannah Sparrows are common fall migrants throughout the state beginning in early September, peaking in mid-October, and continuing into December. They winter in good numbers except in northernmost New Jersey, and an average of about 500 are recorded on CBCs. Spring migrants move north mainly in April, leaving only the breeding birds behind. The large, pale *princeps* race ("Ipswich Sparrow") that breeds on Sable Island, Nova Scotia, is an uncommon winter resident along the coast from late October to early April.

GRASSHOPPER SPARROW *Ammodramus savannarum*

Uncommon and local summer resident, rare fall and very rare spring migrant, casual in winter. Threatened Species as a breeding bird in New Jersey. Grasshopper Sparrows nest in dry, weedy fields, pastures, and airports and are broadly, but thinly, distributed through much of the state where suitable habitat is available. They have declined severely in New Jersey and other eastern states as their nest sites have been destroyed for developments, succession, and changes in agricultural practices, such as early-season mowing (Vickery 1996, Walsh et al. 1999). Grasshopper Sparrows respond well to habitat improvement, and efforts to preserve grasslands will continue to benefit the species. Despite their presence as a breeding species here and farther north, they are seldom encountered in migration. Fall birds pass through in October and November, and spring migrants arrive in late April and early May. Grasshopper Sparrows have been recorded on ten CBCs since 1983, and one lingered to 10 January 1994 at Cape May.

HENSLOW'S SPARROW *Ammodramus henslowii*

Very rare visitor and summer resident. Endangered Species in New Jersey. Stone (1937) called Henslow's Sparrow a "common summer resident" of the Cape May Peninsula at that time, and even at mid-century they were still uncommon and local breeding birds throughout New Jersey (Fables 1955, Bull 1964). Since then, they have declined drastically both here and throughout eastern North America, the steepest decline of any grassland species (Herkert et al. 2002, Sauer et al. 2008). There have been only three confirmed breeding records in the state since 1972, one at Lakehurst in 1994 (where individuals have been seen on several occasions since then) and two at Duke Farms, Somerset County, in 2006 and 2008. Henslow's Sparrow was added to the Review List in 1996, and there have been fifteen accepted records since then. The few fall migrants have been recorded between mid-October and mid-November.

Review Species

Records since 1996

LE CONTE'S SPARROW *Ammodramus leconteii*

Very rare. There has been a total of twenty-nine accepted records of Le Conte's Sparrow in New Jersey, starting with one at Tuckerton, 26 September–2 October 1976. Seventeen of them are from the coast, but there are four records for Bergen County as well. Twenty-one of the Le Conte's Sparrows have been found between 26 September and 16 November, and seven were discovered between 17 December and 17 February, three of the latter remaining until late March and one to 5 April. The latest spring bird was one photographed at Cape May, 21 April 1992. Le Conte's Sparrows have been recorded on five CBCs. (*See photo page 152.*)

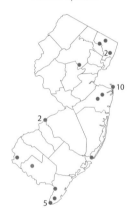

Review Species

NELSON'S SPARROW *Ammodramus nelsoni*

Status poorly known. Probably a fairly common fall migrant, scarce winter resident, uncommon spring migrant. Considered conspecific with the next species until 1995, birders paid relatively little attention to the different forms until recently, and we are still learning about its status in New Jersey. There are three subspecies of this shy and secretive denizen of fresh and saltwater marshes, all of which occur in the state (Sibley 1997), but the Atlantic coastal form, *subvirgatus*, appears to be the most common. The Interior forms, *nelsoni* and *alterus*, are scarce to uncommon—but largely overlooked—at freshwater sites inland, but all forms are found in coastal marshes. The birds arrive in October and early November, most continuing farther

south, but small numbers are found in early winter along the coast, although they decline later in the season as the weather gets harsher. Little is known about the spring migration, but there are records for Nelson's Sparrow as late as mid-May (Sibley 1997), and it is probably a scarce, but regular, migrant in mid- to late May.

SALTMARSH SPARROW *Ammodramus caudacutus*

Fairly common fall and uncommon spring migrant, uncommon and local summer resident, scarce to uncommon early winter resident, diminishing in numbers after December. Saltmarsh Sparrows, formerly considered conspecific with Nelson's Sparrow, nest in the salt marshes of Raritan Bay, the Atlantic coast from Ocean to Cape May counties, and the Delaware Bayshore of Cape May and Cumberland counties. Stone (1908) considered them abundant throughout their range in New Jersey, but widespread ditching, draining, and filling of the marshes during the twentieth century have reduced their numbers. Migrants from farther north augment the local populations during October and early November, and most Saltmarsh Sparrows leave the state for warmer climes. An average of fifteen has been found on CBCs in recent years (but note the sixty-three on the 1 January 2010 Cape May CBC), and small numbers can be found in the Bayshore marshes all winter. Little is known about their spring migration, but local nesting birds probably return in late April or early May (Walsh et al. 1999).

SEASIDE SPARROW *Ammodramus maritimus*

Common but local summer resident, fairly common spring and fall migrant, scarce to uncommon winter resident. Seaside Sparrows are locally common breeding birds in the salt and brackish marshes of Raritan Bay, the Atlantic coast, and Delaware Bayshore. Their numbers declined substantially during the twentieth century due to the ditching and draining of much of the marshland (Stone 1937, Bull 1964), but they seem to be more tolerant of habitat alteration than Saltmarsh Sparrow. Local breeding birds arrive on territory in mid- to late April, when they are readily detected by the persistent singing from exposed perches. The departure of breeding birds in the fall is poorly documented, but Seaside Sparrows are much less common in winter. An average of only twelve has been recorded on CBCs in recent years, but the birds' secrecy and the inaccessibility of most of the habitat make winter numbers very uncertain. Like other marsh sparrows, they are less regular in winter after December.

FOX SPARROW *Passerella iliaca*

Fairly common fall and uncommon spring migrant, uncommon winter resident. The first Fox Sparrows arrive from the North in mid- to late October, but the main flights come during November, when they are found throughout the state in numbers that may vary widely from year to year. They winter over much of the state, except the extreme northwest, but are much more common in southern New Jersey than in the north. CBC totals have averaged about 450 in recent years. In spring, most northbound Fox Sparrows pass through in mid-March to early April, with only a few remaining into mid-April.

One of our largest sparrows, Fox Sparrow breeds in the far north, and arrives for the winter in late fall and departs in early spring. It is more common in winter in the southern counties and regularly visits bird feeders, especially in snowy weather. *Photograph by Kevin Karlson.*

SONG SPARROW *Melospiza melodia*

Common and nearly ubiquitous resident and migrant. Song Sparrows are among the most common breeding birds in New Jersey, nesting throughout the state except for parts of the Pine Barrens. In fall, they migrate from September into December, but passage birds are difficult to separate from local nesters. Peak numbers are encountered

from October to mid-November, including a high count of 2,000+ at Sandy Hook, 23 October 1989, but Song Sparrows are common wintering birds as well. Statewide CBC totals average about 6,000, with every region well represented. The northbound movement can be detected by early March, with peak movement later in the month.

The common and familiar Song Sparrow is a year-round resident in New Jersey, with the breeding population augmented by migrants and winter residents at other times of the year. Its cheerful song in early spring can be heard almost anywhere, from urban parks and suburban yards to farm fields and woodland edges. *Photograph by Kevin Karlson.*

LINCOLN'S SPARROW *Melospiza lincolnii*

Uncommon fall and scarce spring migrant, casual in winter. Southbound Lincoln's Sparrows may appear as early as mid-September, but the main passage is from early to mid-October, with small numbers continuing into November. The birds are more common inland than along the coast and, although usually found in ones and twos, may occasionally be numerous, such as twenty-five at Lyons, Somerset County, 2 October 1994. Lincoln's Sparrows are increasingly encountered in early winter, and one to three are found on CBCs every year, but there are only a few records for midwinter. They are much less common in spring than in fall, with most reports coming from mid- to late May, when they are often detected by their song.

SWAMP SPARROW *Melospiza georgiana*

Common fall and uncommon spring migrant, fairly common summer resident, fairly common winter resident. Swamp Sparrows nest in both freshwater and saltwater wetlands in New Jersey and can be found throughout the state wherever suitable habitat is available. They are most common in the northern part of the state, parts of the Pine Barrens, and the Delaware Bayshore, the latter home to a distinct subspecies known as the "Coastal Plain" Swamp Sparrow. Fall migration begins in late September and continues through November, with occasional large flights from late October to mid-November, such as the estimated 5,000 at Sandy Hook, 23 October 1989. In winter, Swamp Sparrows are more common in the southern half of the state than in the north, and CBC totals average about 700 individuals. Spring migration begins in late March, with a peak from mid-April to early May (Walsh et al. 1999).

WHITE-THROATED SPARROW *Zonotrichia albicollis*

Very common winter resident, common spring and very common to abundant fall migrant, rare and very local summer resident. In fall, migrant White-throated Sparrows begin to arrive in late September, with peak numbers from mid-October to November in flights that can be spectacular, such as the estimated 100,000+ at Sandy Hook, 23 October 1989. They are one of the most common winter songbirds in New Jersey and are familiar visitors to bird feeders throughout the state. CBC totals have averaged about 20,000 in recent years, having increased significantly since the 1970s (~7.4 birds/party hour vs. ~4.0 birds/party hour). They begin to depart in early April, with occasional large flights in late April and migration continuing into mid-May. White-throated Sparrows are one of our rarest breeding songbirds, probably not nesting in every year, and found only at higher elevations in the Highlands and Kittatinny Mountains. Occasional nonbreeders may show up in summer in odd places like Cape May, Cumberland County, and even the Hackensack Meadowlands.

White-throated Sparrow is a common and familiar visitor to thickets and feeding stations from late fall to early spring. It can be abundant in migration but leaves the state in summer, only rarely nesting in the northwestern counties. White-throated is a member of the genus *Zonotrichia*, which sing their songs throughout the year. *Photograph by Kevin Karlson.*

HARRIS'S SPARROW *Zonotrichia querula*

Review Species

This large sparrow is a very rare vagrant from its normal mid-continent range. There are seventeen accepted records from diverse places around the state. Following the first occurrence in 1935, there was a thirty-one-year gap before the next appearance in 1966. Between 2000 and 2010 there have been four records, three in Monmouth County and one in Hunterdon County. All but three of New Jersey's Harris's Sparrows have appeared in the northern half of the state, and the majority, as is the case in neighboring states, have been inland. Most records have been in late fall and winter, but there are three from spring.

Our largest sparrow, Harris's Sparrow breeds in north-central Canada and winters primarily in the central and southern Great Plains. It has strayed to New Jersey on eighteen occasions, mainly from late fall through winter, although there are a couple of spring records as well. This adult in nonbreeding plumage spent a week at Big Brook Park, Monmouth County, 10–17 November 2002. *Photograph by Chris Davidson.*

WHITE-CROWNED SPARROW *Zonotrichia leucophrys*

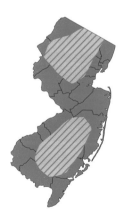

Uncommon fall migrant and local winter resident, scarce spring migrant. White-crowned Sparrows are most common in New Jersey during fall migration, mainly mid- to late October, but numbers fluctuate considerably from year to year. Usually only a few are encountered at any one site, but the 23 October 1989 flight that brought huge numbers of passerines to Sandy Hook included an estimated 500 to 700 White-crowned Sparrows. The first documented occurrence of wintering in New Jersey was during 1953–1954 (Fables 1955), but they are now uncommon, but regular, winter residents in parts of the state, especially the southwestern counties. CBC totals average about 300. The spring movement is inconspicuous, beginning in late April and running through May. The pale-lored White-crowned Sparrow of the subspecies *gambelli*, nesting in Canada west of Hudson Bay and in northern Alaska, was added to the Review List in 1996 and has been documented ten times, mostly in fall and early winter.

GOLDEN-CROWNED SPARROW *Zonotrichia atricapilla*

Casual. There are six accepted records of this western sparrow, including one that visited a backyard in Boonton for three consecutive winters in the 1970s. The remaining five are from scattered parts of the state, including two in Cape May County. Cape May produced the first state record in 1962, whereas the most recent was a bird present for four days near Thompson Park, Colts Neck, Monmouth County, in January 2006.

Review Species

Golden-crowned Sparrow is a large sparrow that breeds in Alaska and far western Canada and winters in the Pacific Coast states. Nevertheless, it has occurred as a vagrant in many of the northeastern states and provinces, including six times in New Jersey. This first-winter bird was at Cold Spring, Cape May County, 1 January–29 February 1998. *Photograph by Kevin Karlson.*

DARK-EYED JUNCO *Junco hyemalis*

Very common winter resident, common spring and fall migrant, rare and very local summer resident. Migrant Dark-eyed Juncos begin to arrive in fall in mid- to late September, but most come south from mid-October into early Decem-

ber and large numbers remain for the winter. They are, along with White-throated Sparrows, the two most common winter visitors to bird feeders throughout the state. CBC totals have averaged about 18,000 in recent decades, and the "Snowbird" is a welcome sight on a frigid January morning. Dark-eyed Juncos begin moving north in late February, with peak flights from late March to mid-April, and they are rare after early May. They were first confirmed nesting in New Jersey in Passaic County in 1972 and are rare breeders at high elevations in the Highlands and Kittatinny Mountains. "Oregon" Juncos from western North America are reported in the state almost every year, but a fair number are misidentified young female Slate-coloreds. Oregon Junco was added to the Review List in 1996, and there have been eleven accepted records through 2009.

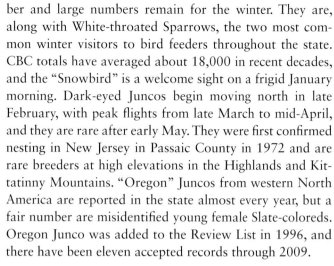

The Dark-eyed Junco, or "Snowbird," is one of our most common and familiar winter residents, arriving in late fall and departing in early spring. It is a rare breeder in northwestern New Jersey. The male is black and white, but the female, shown here, is also attractive in her more subdued slate gray or brownish gray and white; both sexes show the pink bill and white outer tail feathers. *Photograph by Kevin Karlson.*

LAPLAND LONGSPUR *Calcarius lapponicus*

Rare to scarce fall migrant and winter resident, very rare spring migrant. The occurrence of Lapland Longspurs in New Jersey is erratic and unpredictable. A few are seen each fall from October to December, most often along the coast in the company of Horned Larks or Snow Buntings. CBC totals have averaged about three for the past twenty-five years, but in five of those years there were none. In addition to the coast, there are several inland areas that regularly prove attractive to the longspurs (see map). Numbers have declined substantially since the 1970s and early 1980s, when flocks of up to 21 were encountered. In spring, a few are seen in passage, and wintering birds have de-

parted by mid-March in recent years, although there are records for April and even a few in May. A remarkably late bird was at Cape May, 11 June 1993 (Sibley 1997).

SMITH'S LONGSPUR *Calcarius pictus*

Review Species

Accidental. There are two records of this bird of the prairies, one each in spring and fall. A male in breeding plumage discovered at Cape May in April 1991 lingered for five days and was seen by many. The bird found at Island Beach in October 1995, apparently in immature plumage, obliged by staying around for an entire week.

19–23 APR 1991, CAPE MAY, CAPE MAY CO. (RNJB 17[3]:64; NJPF)
18–24 OCT 1995, ISLAND BEACH ST. PARK, OCEAN CO. (RNJB
    22[1]:21; NJPF)

Smith's Longspur breeds on the tundra in northern Canada and Alaska and winters in the south-central U.S. It has occurred just twice in New Jersey, an adult male in spring 1991 and this juvenile at Island Beach, Ocean County, 18–24 October 1995. *Photograph by Kevin Karlson.*

CHESTNUT-COLLARED LONGSPUR *Calcarius ornatus*

Review Species

Accidental. There are just two records of this attractive species of the prairie states, both males, at opposite ends of the coast and during opposite seasons. The first was a one-day June 1980 visitor to Cape May Point, while the second was discovered at Sandy Hook in mid-January 1984 and spent several weeks during a spell of bitterly cold weather.

18 JUN 1980, CAPE MAY POINT, CAPE MAY CO. (RNJB 6[4]:74; NJPF)
14 JAN–MID-FEB 1984, SANDY HOOK, MONMOUTH CO. (RNJB
    10[2]:43)

SNOW BUNTING *Plectrophenax nivalis*

Fairly common fall and uncommon spring migrant, fairly common winter resident. Unpredictable and nomadic, the first Snow Buntings usually arrive in New Jersey at the end of October, with peak flights from mid-November to early December. They may occur inland, especially in the northern part of the state, as well as along the entire coast. CBC totals have averaged about 425 in recent years, but these numbers are highly variable and probably not a reliable indicator of abundance because of the species' nomadic behavior. Numbers of both migrants and wintering birds appear to have declined during the past few decades, perhaps in response to a warming climate or the reduction in the farming practice of spreading manure on fields in winter. Wintering and spring passage birds are seen in late February and early March, but all have departed by the end of March.

Family Cardinalidae: Cardinals and Allies

SUMMER TANAGER *Piranga rubra*

Uncommon and local summer resident, scarce spring and fall migrant, accidental in winter. Summer Tanagers disappeared as breeding birds from southern New Jersey during the latter part of the nineteenth century, and the first modern nesting record was in Cumberland County in 1955 (Kunkle et al. 1959). The next confirmed nesting was at Dividing Creek, Cumberland County, in 1975, but from that foothold they gradually spread to colonize much of the southern parts of the Coastal Plain and Pine Barrens, albeit in small numbers. Summer Tanagers arrive on their breeding grounds in late April and early May, and spring overshoots are annual in scattered sites north of their normal range. This led to isolated nesting records in Hunterdon and Essex Counties during the Atlas period. Most breeding birds have departed by early September, but a few birds have been seen as late as late October, and one spent the winters of 1984–1985 and 1985–1986 in Medford, Burlington County. There are at least two other January records.

SCARLET TANAGER *Piranga olivacea*

Fairly common to common and widespread summer resident, fairly common spring and fall migrant. Scarlet Tanagers are most common as breeding birds in the northern

third of New Jersey, but they are widely distributed and fairly common in the Pine Barrens and Coastal Plain as well. During the Atlas, they were largely absent from the heavily urbanized areas of the northeast and the lower Delaware Valley, as well as from the barrier islands. They arrive on the breeding grounds beginning around the first of May, with migrants passing through to mid-month. Fall migration occurs mainly during September, with a peak in mid-month, and they are very rare after mid-October. There are no documented winter records of Scarlet Tanager in New Jersey.

Scarlet Tanager is a widespread and fairly common breeding bird in the state from May to September. The stunning male, in scarlet and black, can be surprisingly difficult to spot as he sings high up in an oak or maple, but the female, in her greenish-yellow plumage, is even less conspicuous. *Photograph by Kevin Karlson.*

WESTERN TANAGER *Piranga ludoviciana*

Review Species

Very rare visitor. There have been more than sixty reports of Western Tanager in New Jersey and thirty-eight accepted records. The first state record was at Island Beach, 10 March 1938, but most occurrences are from late September to January, with most of the winter birds present at feeders and some of them remaining into the spring. There are just two cases of spring migrants (11–18 April to 16–17 May), and a most unusual singing male at Kinnelon, Morris County, 5–22 June 1977. Identification of adult males is straightforward, but immature birds and females need careful documentation because of potential confusion with female orioles or female and young Scarlet Tanagers, some of which have faint wing bars.

Western Tanager is a widespread species of western North America that is closely related to Scarlet Tanager. It is one of the most frequently occurring western vagrants in the East—mostly in fall and winter—and has been found in New Jersey on almost forty occasions. This adult male was an unusual spring visitor to a Plainfield, Union County, feeder, 11–18 April 2009. *Photograph by William J. Boyle, Jr.*

NORTHERN CARDINAL *Cardinalis cardinalis*

Northern Cardinal is a common and nearly ubiquitous permanent resident of New Jersey, but it was not always so. At the turn of the twentieth century, Stone (1908) reported that cardinals were absent from the northern part of the state, while Griscom (1923) considered them very local, perhaps augmented by escaped caged birds, as the species was commonly kept in captivity in the nineteenth and early

One of everybody's favorite birds, the Northern Cardinal is a relatively recent settler in the northern part of the state but is now found throughout. It manages to survive snow storms, when it flocks to feeders. The male is unmistakable, but the female, with red bill and mix of brown and red tones, is also very attractive. *Photograph by Kevin Karlson.*

twentieth centuries. A dramatic increase in the cardinal population in northern New Jersey was noted by Fables (1955) and Bull (1964), and Boyle (1986) predicted that the species "would be hard to miss in a day's birding anywhere" in the state.

ROSE-BREASTED GROSBEAK *Pheucticus ludovicianus*

Fairly common and widespread summer resident in the northern half of the state, fairly common spring and fall migrant, very rare in winter. Rose-breasted Grosbeaks may arrive in spring beginning in late April, but peak numbers pass through in early to mid-May, when their cheerful, warbling song can be heard throughout the state. They appear somewhat regularly at this season at feeders. Rose-breasted Grosbeaks nest sparingly in western Burlington County, but are common and widely distributed breeders in deciduous woodlands in northern New Jersey, except in parts of the urbanized northeast. Fall migration begins in late August, with highest numbers in mid- to late September, and very few seen after mid-October. Rose-breasted Grosbeaks have been recorded on seven CBCs, but only three since 1981, and there are several midwinter reports of birds at feeders. Late fall and winter birds should be identified with care, as the following species is actually more likely at those seasons.

Like the Scarlet Tanager, the colorful male Rose-breasted Grosbeak can be hard to find as it sings its warbling song high in a deciduous tree. The female, who also sings, wears a very different plumage, brown above, and white with heavy streaking below. This male shows the retained brownish primaries of the immature plumage, indicating he is a yearling. *Photograph by Lloyd Spitalnik..*

Review Species

BLACK-HEADED GROSBEAK *Pheucticus melanocephalus*

This close relative of our familiar Rose-breasted Grosbeak is a very rare visitor from the western United States. There have been about forty reports of this species, of which twenty-five have been accepted; several others are most likely correct but were inadequately documented. Unlike most western vagrants, which typically appear in the fall, most of the Black-headed Grosbeaks have appeared between December and February. The first state record occurred in 1954, and the next sixteen were reported between then and 1979. Since 1979, there have been only eight additional records, including just two during the first decade of the twenty-first century.

BLUE GROSBEAK *Passerina caerulea*

Blue Grosbeak, an uncommon and local summer resident, is a relatively recent addition to the list of regular breeding birds in New Jersey. The first modern nesting was in Cumberland County in 1952, but the species expanded rapidly during the next few decades to reach its present limit in southern Hunterdon, Somerset, and Middlesex counties. The range expansion is continuing, however, and may soon reach Warren County. It is most common in the counties bordering Delaware Bay and is largely absent from the heart of the Pine Barrens. Blue Grosbeaks arrive beginning in late April and most depart by the end of September, though one or two linger into November almost annually at Cape May.

INDIGO BUNTING *Passerina cyanea*

Common and widespread summer resident, common spring and fall migrant, casual into early winter. Indigo Buntings have clearly increased their presence in New Jersey since the mid-twentieth century. Fables (1955) reported that breeders were found mainly from Monmouth County north, and were scarce or absent from the Pine Barrens, the southwestern counties, and the Cape May Peninsula. Today they are uncommon in the Pine Barrens, but common everywhere else. Spring migrants first appear during the last half of April, while the southbound migration peaks in late September, but the local population is so high that it is difficult to distinguish migrants from residents (Walsh et al.

1999). A few individuals are noted regularly into early No-vember, and Indigo Buntings were found on five CBCs be-tween 1978 and 2009. There is one midwinter record from Verona, Essex County, in January 1957 (Bull 1964).

PAINTED BUNTING *Passerina ciris*

Review Species

Very rare but increasingly recorded visitor from the South. Since the first occurrence of Painted Bunting in New Jersey in May 1958, there have been thirty-five accepted records of this species, roughly equally divided between males and fe-males. Surprisingly, almost half of the birds have appeared in winter and another eight in May, the remainder from Sep-tember to early December. Many of the early records were questioned because of the possibility of escaped cage birds, but the frequency of occurrence, twenty-seven individuals from 1993 to 2009, and the seasonal pattern leave little doubt that most of them are of wild provenance.

Like other buntings in the genus *Passerina*, male and female Painted Buntings dif-fer markedly in appearance. This southern and southwestern species has ap-peared in New Jersey with increasing frequency in recent decades, with more than twenty records since 1990, about half of them in the winter. This beautiful male spent more than five months at an Erma, Cape May County, feeder and was photographed here on 3 January 2005. The bird on the right, photographed at Island Beach, Ocean County, 7 December 2007, resembles the female, but the darker green on the head and back, plus the hint of lime green developing on the mantle suggest that it is a young male. *Photographs by Richard Crossley (left) and Alex Tongas (right).*

DICKCISSEL *Spiza americana*

Scarce fall and rare spring migrant, rare and very local summer resident, very rare winter resident. The vast major-ity of records of Dickcissel in any given year come from Cape May during fall migration, any time from late August to early November, but especially in mid-October. Most of these and other coastal birds in fall are calling fly-overs. They have been recorded on CBCs in nineteen years since 1973, with a high of six in 1996, but only a few have overwintered, mainly at feeders with House Sparrows. Dickcissels are rarely encountered in spring migration, but in most years, one or a few pairs take advantage of available habitat somewhere in the state and attempt to nest. The majority of these nestings end in failure due to early mowing or harvesting of fields, but a few have succeeded when mowing has been delayed (Walsh et al. 1999).

Family Icteridae: Blackbirds

BOBOLINK *Dolichonyx oryzivorus*

Fairly common spring and common fall migrant, especially along the coast, uncommon and local summer resident. Bobolinks benefited from the clearing of forests in colonial times, but have declined severely in New Jersey and other eastern states since the mid-1800s for a variety of reasons (Walsh et al. 1999). In recent decades, the early mowing of hay fields, as well as the continuing loss of these fields to development, has limited their breeding opportunities. Hopefully, efforts to preserve grasslands will benefit this species. In spring, male Bobolinks arrive beginning in early May, a week before the females, and migrants continue to pass through to the end of May. Southbound birds can be seen at nonbreeding sites as early as late June, but the main flights occur from mid-August to mid-September and can be impressive along the coast. Diminishing numbers trickle through in October, and a few have lingered into December. Bobolinks were recorded on five CBCs from 1972 to 1996, but there have been none since.

Male Bobolink resembles the female for most of the year, but is strikingly different in its black-and-white breeding plumage with a buffy nape. This species undertakes one of the longest migrations of any American passerine, wintering in southern South America. *Photograph by Kevin Karlson.*

RED-WINGED BLACKBIRD *Agelaius phoeniceus*

Very common and nearly ubiquitous summer resident, common spring and fall migrant, fairly common winter resident. Red-winged Blackbirds are one of the most abundant species in North America and can be found nesting almost anywhere in New Jersey. They prefer wetlands of any type, but will settle for pastures and weedy fields. Post-breeding flocks begin to gather in late summer, and large movements of migrants, sometimes in concentrations of tens or even hundreds of thousands, occur in October and November. Red-winged Blackbirds largely retreat from the northern part of the state, especially in snowy winters, but spectacular foraging flocks and roosts of mixed species of blackbird often occur in the southwestern counties. CBC numbers have averaged about 50,000 in recent years, but have ranged from 19,000 in 2007 to 567,000 in 1998. Male Red-winged Blackbirds move north in mid- to late February and begin to claim territories before the females arrive a few weeks later.

EASTERN MEADOWLARK *Sturnella magna*

Uncommon, local, and declining summer resident, uncommon spring and fairly common fall migrant, uncommon winter resident. Like other grassland species, Eastern Meadowlarks have declined as breeding birds in New Jersey during the past century due to loss of habitat. They continue to nest in the farmlands of the Kittatinny Valley and Hunterdon and Salem counties, but are rapidly disappearing from the central part of the state. Some movement away from breeding areas occurs in August, but the main migration is in mid- to late October. Although they formerly wintered in the northwestern part of the state, wintering birds are now concentrated in the southern tier of counties, where most of the CBC average of about 360 individuals are found. Spring migration is mainly in the second half of March.

WESTERN MEADOWLARK *Sturnella neglecta*

Accidental. The first state record of Western Meadowlark was a bird found singing in South Plainfield, Middlesex County, 28 April 1940 (Hunn 1941). From 1951 to 1965, there were records of six additional individuals, all but

one of which stayed for multiple days, including one that spent the entire summer (unmated) at Columbus, Burlington County. The only occurrence in recent years was of a bird recorded singing at Colt's Neck, Monmouth County, 26 May 1997. Arrival in New Jersey of this western species coincided with a rapid eastward expansion of its breeding range during the early 1900s, reaching Michigan, southwestern Ontario, and western Ohio in the 1930s (Cadman et al. 1987, Peterjohn and Rice 1991), although it has retreated in recent decades. In addition to New Jersey, New York and Massachusetts had their first records in the 1940s, and the species has bred at least twice in New York.

YELLOW-HEADED BLACKBIRD
Xanthocephalus xanthocephalus

Rare migrant and winter resident. Prior to 1955, there were only three records of Yellow-headed Blackbirds in New Jersey (Fables 1955), but their numbers increased during the second half of the twentieth century as their breeding range expanded eastward (Twedt and Crawford 1995), and several are recorded in the state every year. Fall records are mainly of single birds in flocks of Red-winged Blackbirds during August and September, most often along the coast. In winter, one or two are usually associated with large blackbird flocks in Salem County, although the frequency of occurrences has declined since about 2000, perhaps because the eastward expansion has stalled or even reversed a bit. Yellow-headed Blackbirds have been recorded on eleven CBCs in seven different years, but only once since 1991. There were numerous April reports in the 1980s and 1990s, but none after March in recent years.

RUSTY BLACKBIRD *Euphagus carolinus*

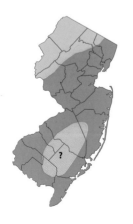

Uncommon to locally fairly common migrant and winter resident. Although Rusty Blackbird populations have suffered a drastic decline over the past several decades (Greenberg et al. 2010), they continue to be uncommon to fairly common migrants in the wooded swamps of New Jersey. The first southbound birds arrive in early October, with the main passage from mid-October to mid-November. Numbers of wintering birds vary from year to year depending on the severity of the season, and recent CBC totals have ranged from a low of 80 in 2003 to a high of 2,214 in 2006. Many birds move farther south in January, but begin to return in late February, with peak migration from mid-March to mid-April. Only a few remain by the beginning of May.

Rusty Blackbird is named for its winter dress, with the male all black and the female mostly gray in breeding plumage. Both sexes show varying amounts of rusty tones in non-breeding plumage, the female more so than the male. This female was photographed in New York in November 2006. Rusty Blackbirds prefer bogs and wooded swamps and are not usually found with other blackbirds. Their numbers have declined precipitously in recent decades for reasons not yet understood. *Photograph by Lloyd Spitalnik.*

BREWER'S BLACKBIRD *Euphagus cyanocephalus*

Review Species

Very rare visitor. There have been several dozen reports of Brewer's Blackbird in New Jersey, dating from 1955. However, the historical review committee (Halliwell et al. 2000) could not find satisfactory documentation for most of them, and only fifteen records have been accepted. Most of these reports involve small flocks of one to nine individuals, with several of them returning for two or three years, including one large contingent that numbered up to fifty birds at Fort Elfsborg, Salem County. All but three of the records are from Cape Island or western Salem County, and all are from late fall into early spring. Brewer's Blackbirds are particularly fond of livestock pens, especially those with horses.

COMMON GRACKLE *Quiscalus quiscula*

Common to abundant summer resident throughout the state, abundant migrant both spring and fall, and variably uncommon to locally abundant winter resident. Common Grackle has long been a widely distributed breeding bird in New Jersey (Stone 1908, Boyle 1986), but the reversion of

much farmland to second-growth woodland and the fragmentation of forests caused by suburban sprawl appear to have provided ideal conditions for the proliferation of the species. Migratory flocks can contain staggering numbers of birds (tens or even hundreds of thousands); winter numbers are highly variable, but can include huge feeding flocks and roosts in farmland in the southern counties and along the Delaware River.

BOAT-TAILED GRACKLE *Quiscalus major*

Fairly common summer resident, uncommon spring and fall migrant (although true migrants are somewhat difficult to detect), uncommon winter resident. There were only four records of Boat-tailed Grackles in New Jersey prior to 1952, when three small colonies were found in Cumberland County (Fables 1955). By 1982 they had expanded to the entire Delaware Bayshore and the Atlantic coast north to Sandy Hook, more recently to Raritan Bay in Middlesex County (Walsh et al. 1999). Boat-tailed Grackles are never found far from salt water and are largely resident, although there is a modest migration along the coast from mid-September to mid-November. CBC totals average about 1,500, up from 500 in the 1970s, and any variation is probably related to weather conditions during the counts. Returning birds in March and April combine with wintering locals to announce the season with their raucous calls.

BROWN-HEADED COWBIRD *Molothrus ater*

Common and nearly ubiquitous summer resident, common spring and fall migrant, uncommon to common winter resident. Brown-headed Cowbirds nest throughout New Jersey and parasitize a wide variety of songbirds. Their fall movements are largely timed with those of other blackbirds and are especially noticeable from late October to mid-November. In winter, most cowbirds leave the state or stay in the southern counties, but CBC numbers vary wildly, from a high of 208,000 in 1992 to just 2,844 the following year. Large numbers may be found in mixed-species flocks of foraging and roosting blackbirds during the late fall and winter. Spring-migrant Brown-headed Cowbirds begin to return to northern New Jersey in late March or early April.

ORCHARD ORIOLE *Icterus spurius*

Fairly common and widespread summer resident, uncommon spring and fall migrant. Orchard Orioles have long been common breeding birds in southern New Jersey, but their abundance in the northern part of the state fluctuated during the twentieth century. At present, they seem to be near an all-time high in both numbers and area covered. They arrive in late April and early May, but because relatively few breed to the north of New Jersey, they are not common in passage. Southbound Orchard Orioles are among the earliest of migrant passerines, the "fall" flight beginning in mid-July and essentially being complete by the end of August. The latest recent record is from mid-September.

BULLOCK'S ORIOLE *Icterus bullockii*

Accidental. There are several dozen old reports of Bullock's Oriole in New Jersey, but most were of immatures or females in late fall and winter—many at feeders—at a time when the difficulty of distinguishing Bullock's and dull-plumaged Baltimore Orioles was not fully appreciated. The two orioles were considered conspecific by the AOU from 1983 to 1995, and the Bullock's was deleted from the State List in 1996 because of the lack of any fully documented record. Fortunately, reports of two well-photographed females and most recently an adult male have been accepted. The April record is particularly unusual in the East.

Review Species

DEC 2000–MAR 2001, BLAWENBURG, SOMERSET CO. (NJBRC 2002-028; NJPF)

26–27 APR 2004, ISLAND BEACH SP, OCEAN CO. (NJBRC 2005-015; NJPF)

27 NOV–2 DEC 2007, CAPE MAY, CAPE MAY CO. (NJBRC 2008-069; NJPF)

Bullock's Oriole is the western counterpart of Baltimore Oriole and a very rare vagrant to the East. Females and immatures of the two species can be very tricky to tell apart, but adult males are much easier. There have been only three accepted records of Bullock's for New Jersey, including this male at Cape May, 27 November–2 December 2007. *Photograph by Michael O'Brien.*

BALTIMORE ORIOLE *Icterus glabula*

Fairly common to common and widespread summer resident, common spring and fall migrant, very rare winter resident. Baltimore Orioles have long been common breeders in northern New Jersey, but were largely absent from the Pine Barrens and southern counties in the early twentieth century (Stone 1908, Fables 1955). They have since expanded their range to include almost the entire state, although they are still less common in the Pine Barrens than elsewhere. The first spring migrants arrive in late April with the main passage in early and mid-May. Fall migration begins in mid-August and is almost complete by late September. Numerous stragglers remain through October or early November and even into December, when they are recorded almost every year on CBCs, with a recent average of seven per year and a high of twenty in 2001. A few of these survive the winter at feeding stations offering fruit. (*See photo page 152.*)

Family Fringillidae: Finches and Allies

Review Species

BRAMBLING *Fringilla montifringilla*

Accidental. There are two records of this Eurasian finch, both believed to be wild birds. The first was present at Stanton, Hunterdon County, for three days in December 1958. It was collected and the specimen is now in the Field Museum of Natural History in Chicago (#309430). This was the first record for North America. Another Brambling visited a feeder in Branchville for three days in April 1965. Since 1958, there have been one or more records for most of the northeastern states and several eastern Canadian provinces.

15–17 DEC 1958, STANTON, HUNTERDON CO. (AFN 13[3]:280)
20–22 APR 1965, BRANCHVILLE, SUSSEX CO. (AFN 19[4]:457)

Review Species

PINE GROSBEAK *Pinicola enucleator*

Very rare migrant and winter resident. Pine Grosbeaks staged major irruptions into New Jersey eight times during the twentieth century. The last one was in 1981–1982, although there was a minor influx in 1985–1986. There were just three reports during the 1990s, all involving seven birds or less. Pine Grosbeak was added to the Review List in 2006, and there was just one record in the 2006–2010

Records since 2006

time period. When flight years occur, the birds usually arrive in December or January and depart by mid-March.

24 DEC 2007, ISLAND BEACH SP, OCEAN CO. (NJBRC 2008-092; NJPF)

PURPLE FINCH *Carpodacus purpurea*

Uncommon to fairly common fall and uncommon spring
migrant, uncommon to fairly common winter resident, uncommon and local summer resident. Purple Finches expanded their breeding range in New Jersey during the
twentieth century, but are still confined almost exclusively
to coniferous or mixed woodlands at higher elevations in
the Kittatinny Mountains and the Highlands. Fall migrants
may arrive in early September, but peak numbers, which
vary widely from year to year, occur anytime from mid-
October to late November. A big fall flight does not guar-
antee high winter numbers, which are also erratic, as shown
by CBC totals that have recently been as low as 26 in 2006
and as high as 629 in 2007. Northbound Purple Finches
may be encountered anytime from late March to mid-May,
but they are usually less numerous than in the fall. There
appears to have been an overall decline in numbers during
the new century.

HOUSE FINCH *Carpodacus mexicanus*

Common and nearly ubiquitous resident. House Finches,
native to western North America, were introduced into
Long Island, NY, in the early 1940s, reached New Jersey by
1949, colonized all of the state by 1973, and spread across
most of the eastern states during the next few decades.
They can be found throughout the state, usually near human habitation, except for some places in the heart of the
Pine Barrens. Populations peaked during the 1980s and
early 1990s, but declined abruptly in the mid-1990s with
the spread of an incapacitating bacterial conjunctivitis.
CBC totals dropped from an average of about 18,000 from
1985 to 1994 to 7,500 from 1999 to 2008.

RED CROSSBILL *Loxia curvirostra*

Rare and unpredictable migrant and winter visitor, very
rare summer resident. Red Crossbills are an irruptive and
nomadic species that occasionally stage major invasions
into New Jersey. In most years, there are only a few reported in fall or winter, but in the big flights that occur at

irregular intervals, often a decade or more apart, sizeable flocks numbering in the hundreds may arrive in November. Sometimes these flocks dissipate and only a few remain for the winter, while in other years good numbers are recorded throughout the season, mainly in the northern counties and along the coast. CBC totals vary widely, with a maximum of 682 in 1975, but Red Crossbills were missed completely in six of the ten years from 2000 to 2009, with a high of only 11 birds in 2007. Following a winter invasion, some may linger into May and even early June. There have been three confirmed nestings, all from the Pine Barrens, in 1941, 1956, and 1963.

Red Crossbill is a nomadic and unpredictable species that occasionally stages irruptive invasions, usually in late fall and winter, into New Jersey. The unique crossed bill, which it shares with its congener White-winged Crossbill, facilitates extracting seeds from pine and other conifer cones. Pictured here are an adult male, female, and subadult male. *Photograph by Karl Lukens.*

WHITE-WINGED CROSSBILL *Loxia leucoptera*

Very rare migrant and winter visitor. White-winged Crossbills are infrequent, irruptive visitors to New Jersey. Major invasions (more than 500 birds) occurred just four times in the twentieth century, the last in 1981–1982, but there was a minor irruption in 1997–1998 and a major one in 2008–2009. In flight years, some birds may arrive as early as late October or early November, as happened in 1981 and 1997, or they may not appear until January, as happened in 2008. Most records are from the northern and inland parts of the state, but some incursions have reached all the way to the southernmost counties. White-winged Crossbills usually depart in March, but there are a few reports as late as May or even early June following invasion years.

COMMON REDPOLL *Acanthis flammea*

Rare to uncommon migrant and winter resident. Common Redpolls are irruptive migrants from the north, whose winter numbers in New Jersey may range from only a few to many hundreds or thousands. During moderate or major invasion years, they may begin to show up in November and may occur anywhere in the state, although much more commonly in the northern counties. CBC totals vary widely, recently from zero in 2006 to 320 in 2007 (record 924 in 1997), but some incursions don't occur until later in the winter, often after a major snowfall. Common Redpolls usually depart by the end of March, but may remain rarely into early April. There have been no recent invasions on the scale of several in the mid-twentieth century (Walsh et al. 1999).

HOARY REDPOLL *Acanthis hornemannii*

Review Species

Casual winter visitor. There have been more than twenty reports of Hoary Redpoll in New Jersey, but only four have been accepted by the NJBRC. Many of the other reports are probably correct, but given the difficulty of separating the two redpoll species in the field, a photograph and detailed description are preferred for acceptance (Walsh et al. 1999).

1 APR 1960, WEST ENGLEWOOD, BERGEN CO. (UMMZ #155142)
11–16 FEB 1978, PLAINFIELD, UNION CO. (RNJB 4:23; NJPF)
18 JAN–26 MAR 1994, ROCKAWAY, MORRIS CO. (RNJB 20:33; NJPF)
27 DEC 2007, LYNDHURST, BERGEN CO. (NJBRC 2008-114; NJPF)

PINE SISKIN *Spinus pinus*

Rare to common migrant and winter resident, rare summer resident. Pine Siskins are an irruptive species whose movements are presumably tied to food availability. In some years very few are seen in fall, while in others there are major influxes of birds, often in late October or November. Following a big fall flight, siskins will sometimes overwinter in large numbers, but sometimes they continue farther south. As a result, recent CBC totals vary widely from as few as 6 in 2002 to as many as 549 in 2008 (record 4,642 in 1977). Even after a major invasion, the spring migration in March and April is much less noticeable than the fall flight. Pine Siskins have nested in New Jersey as far south as Middlesex County on at least a dozen occasions, always following a big winter incursion, as in 2009 when there were multiple reports of nesting and juvenile birds.

AMERICAN GOLDFINCH *Spinus tristis*

Common and nearly ubiquitous resident and migrant. New Jersey's state bird, the American Goldfinch, is a familiar feature of feeding stations and weedy fields throughout the state. It is one of the latest breeding songbirds, often not nesting until August or even September. Goldfinches are present year-round, but they are also common migrants, especially in late autumn along the coast. An estimated 9,000 were at Cape May, 17 November 2008, but flocks of 500 to 1,000 are more typical. CBC totals average about 5,000, and, although there is substantial year to year variation, their numbers have remained fairly consistent for several decades. Spring migration is less noticeable than that in fall, but runs from late March to May.

EVENING GROSBEAK *Coccothraustes vespertinus*

Rare migrant and winter resident. Evening Grosbeaks spread east across the continent during the late nineteenth and early twentieth centuries and had become common late fall migrants and winter residents in New Jersey by the 1950s. The largest incursion was in January 1950, when there were 3,000 birds in Bergen County alone, but there were two nesting records in 1962 following a major flight. CBC totals reached their peak in 1977 and 1981 at more than 2,000, but both numbers and frequency of occurrence have declined markedly since the mid-1980s. The last sizeable flight occurred in 1998, and the species has been seen on only four CBCs since then, involving a total of only 9 birds. Oddly, Evening Grosbeaks actually increased as breeding birds in New York and northern New England from 1980 to 2005 (Young 2008).

HOUSE SPARROW *Passer domesticus*

Common to abundant permanent resident throughout the state, wherever there is human habitation. Native to Eurasia, House Sparrows were introduced into the United

States in the mid-nineteenth century and spread rapidly, colonizing most of North America. In New Jersey, they are most common in urban areas and are missing only from parts of the Pine Barrens, where there are large, unbroken tracts of forest, and from some of the wilder parts of the northwestern counties (Walsh et al. 1999). Unlike some other regions, CBC data indicated that House Sparrow populations have remained fairly constant in recent decades, except for a brief dip around the turn of the twenty-first century.

APPENDIX A

Exotics and Species of Uncertain Provenance or Status

Trumpeter Swan *Cygnus buccinator*
A few Trumpeter Swans have begun appearing in New Jersey annually since 2005, usually on lakes or suburban ponds. Some are known by neck collars or wing tags to have originated from the successful reintroduction program in Ontario, but most have no collars and could come from other reintroduction efforts. The species has recently spread into northern and western New York, where it is successfully breeding. As the eastern population grows and becomes fully established, Trumpeter Swan will likely become a regular visitor to the state and will be added to the State List. An apparently introduced pair nested successfully in Morris County in 2010.

Harris's Hawk *Parabuteo unicinctus*
This southwestern species has occurred in New Jersey on several occasions, but is commonly used in falconry and kept in zoos, so determining the provenance is problematic. An individual that flew by the Montclair Hawk Watch on 10 November 1995 wore no jesses or bands and might have been of wild provenance.

White-tailed Hawk *Buteo albicaudatus*
An adult White-tailed Hawk appeared at Great Swamp NWR, 25–26 April 2006, just one day after a three-day visit by one in Hadley, MA, and one day before one was seen in Truro, MA, suggesting a wandering bird. However, although it is not known to be kept by falconers, it is generally a sedentary, nonmigratory species, with no eastern records beyond coastal Louisiana, and seems an unlikely candidate for vagrancy to the Northeast. Nevertheless, wild provenance cannot be ruled out.

Crested Caracara *Caracara cheriway*
This species has occurred twice in New Jersey. A bird in Colonia, Middlesex County, March– June 1976, was tame and surely an escapee. The second was seen flying around Sandy Hook, 5 May 2007, and might have been of wild provenance. There have been numerous extralimital reports of caracaras since the mid-1990s, primarily in the

West and Midwest, including two from Massachusetts. The Massachusetts Avian Records Committee has added Crested Caracara to that state's list based on 1999 and 2007 occurrences, the latter just nine days after the Sandy Hook appearance. The NJBRC has elected to retain the species on the Uncertain Provenance List pending further evidence of vagrancy.

Black-billed Magpie *Pica hudsonia*
There have been more than a dozen records of Black-billed Magpie in New Jersey, dating back to 1933. Most of them are known to have escaped from captivity, but the provenance of the rest cannot be established. Six of the occurrences were in the 1950s, but there have been only three since 1966 and none since 1998. Magpies were often kept as pets in the past (one in Bridgewater in 1988 could be hand fed), and without a new pattern of vagrancy, the species is best relegated to the Uncertain Provenance List.

Eurasian Siskin *Spinus spinus*
Two records from Essex County in 1983, probably the same bird. Almost certainly an escapee.

European Goldfinch *Carduelis carduelis*
Introduced in northeastern New Jersey during the nineteenth century, but extirpated by 1915. All records since then are presumed to be escaped cage birds.

APPENDIX B

Not Accepted Species

The following are species that have either appeared in earlier versions of the State List or have been cited in various publications as occurring or possibly occurring in New Jersey, but which the NJBRC does not currently accept.

Yellow-billed Loon *Gavia adamsii*
Black-browed Albatross *Thalassarche melanophris*
Masked Duck *Oxyura dominica*
European Sparrowhawk *Accipiter nisus*
Ferruginous Hawk *Buteo regalis*
Eurasian Hobby *Falco subbuteo*
Whooping Crane *Grus americana*
European Golden-Plover *Pluvialis apricaria*
Black Oystercatcher *Haematopus bachmani*
Long-toed Stint *Calidris subminuta*
Great Snipe *Gallinago media*
Mew Gull *Larus canus*
Smooth-billed Ani *Crotophaga ani*
Great Gray Owl *Strix nebulosa*
Western Wood-Pewee *Contopus sordidulus*
Hammond's Flycatcher *Empidonax hammondii*
Brown-crested Flycatcher *Myiarchus tyrannulus*
Great Kiskadee *Pitangus sulphuratus*
Gray Jay *Perisoreus canadensis*
Sprague's Pipit *Anthus spragueii*
Brewer's Sparrow *Spizella breweri*

APPENDIX C

List of NJBRC Review Species

Black-bellied
  Whistling-Duck
Fulvous Whistling-Duck
Brant[1]
Barnacle Goose
Cinnamon Teal
Garganey
Tufted Duck
Barrow's Goldeneye
Pacific Loon
Eared Grebe
Western Grebe
Yellow-nosed Albatross
Black-capped Petrel
Buller's Shearwater
White-faced Storm-Petrel
Leach's Storm-Petrel
Band-rumped Storm-Petrel
White-tailed Tropicbird
Red-billed Tropicbird
Masked Booby
Brown Booby
Anhinga
Magnificent Frigatebird
Great Blue Heron[2]
Western Reef-Heron
Reddish Egret
White Ibis
White-faced Ibis
Roseate Spoonbill
Wood Stork
Swallow-tailed Kite
White-tailed Kite
Swainson's Hawk
Eurasian Kestrel
Gyrfalcon

Yellow Rail
Corn Crake
Purple Gallinule
Northern Lapwing
Pacific Golden-Plover
Lesser Sand-Plover
Wilson's Plover
Spotted Redshank
Eskimo Curlew
Whimbrel[3]
Long-billed Curlew
Black-tailed Godwit
Bar-tailed Godwit
Red-necked Stint
Little Stint
Sharp-tailed Sandpiper
Curlew Sandpiper
Eurasian Woodcock
Franklin's Gull
Black-tailed Gull
California Gull
Thayer's Gull
Sabine's Gull
Ross's Gull
Ivory Gull
Brown Noddy
Sooty Tern
Bridled Tern
Large-billed Tern
White-winged Tern
Whiskered Tern
Arctic Tern
Great Skua
South Polar Skua
Common Murre
Thick-billed Murre

[1] Forms other than "Atlantic" Brant.
[2] "Great White" Heron.
[3] "Eurasian."

Black Guillemot
Long-billed Murrelet
Band-tailed Pigeon
Eurasian Collared-Dove
White-winged Dove
Common Ground-Dove
Groove-billed Ani
Northern Hawk Owl
Boreal Owl
Lesser Nighthawk
Green Violet-ear
Black-chinned
   Hummingbird
Calliope Hummingbird
Rufous Hummingbird
Allen's Hummingbird
Red-cockaded Woodpecker
American Three-toed
   Woodpecker
Black-backed Woodpecker
Pacific-slope/Cordilleran
   Flycatcher
Say's Phoebe
Vermilion Flycatcher
Ash-throated Flycatcher
Sulphur-bellied/Streaked
   Flycatcher
Gray Kingbird
Scissor-tailed Flycatcher
Fork-tailed Flycatcher
Loggerhead Shrike
Bell's Vireo
Cassin's Vireo
Brown-chested Martin
Violet-green Swallow
Boreal Chickadee
Brown-headed Nuthatch
Rock Wren

Bewick's Wren
Northern Wheatear
Mountain Bluebird
Townsend's Solitaire
Varied Thrush
Sage Thrasher
Bohemian Waxwing
Virginia's Warbler
Yellow-rumped Warbler[4]
Black-throated Gray
   Warbler
Townsend's Warbler
Swainson's Warbler
MacGillivray's Warbler
Green-tailed Towhee
Spotted Towhee
Cassin's Sparrow
Bachman's Sparrow
Black-throated Sparrow
Lark Bunting
Henslow's Sparrow
Le Conte's Sparrow
Harris's Sparrow
White-crowned Sparrow[5]
Golden-crowned Sparrow
Dark-eyed Junco[6]
Smith's Longspur
Chestnut-collared
   Longspur
Western Tanager
Black-headed Grosbeak
Painted Bunting
Western Meadowlark
Brewer's Blackbird
Bullock's Oriole
Brambling
Pine Grosbeak
Hoary Redpoll

[4] "Audubon's" Warbler.
[5] "Gambel's" White-crowned Sparrow.
[6] Forms other than "Slate-colored" Junco.

APPENDIX D

Identification Information for Captions
by Kevin Karlson

Snow and Ross's Geese *(page 18)*

Greater Snow Goose (right) is noticeably larger in size, but also has a longer, bulkier body; longer, thicker neck; larger, deeper head; and longer, heavier bill with prominent, dark "grin patch." Ross's has a rounder body and head shape and shorter, more triangular bill. A reliable plumage feature for separating Ross's from Snow Goose is the shape of the feathering at the base of the bill. In Ross's Goose, the feathering is straight and vertical from the bottom of the bill base to the top, while Snow Goose shows a curved border to the bill base feathering. A supporting feature not always noticeable in field conditions is a bluish cast to the bill base on Ross's Goose, but not present on Snow Goose. Ross's Goose also lacks a sizable dark "grin patch" but, contrary to some popular opinion, can show a small one.

Common and King Eiders *(page 30)*

Comparison photo and flight photo of King Eider: Common Eider has a larger head and bill than King Eider and more exposed bare bill extending up onto the forehead. Common's longer bill also slopes noticeably to a rising forecrown, which gives it a different head shape impression than King Eider with its shallower crown. Because of these bill and head shape differences, Common's bill appears to be angled toward the water, while King seems to hold its bill more horizontal. This different profile is valuable when trying to identify these species in rough sea conditions. Common Eider also has a more elongated body compared to King's more compact appearance. This stockier body structure is evident in the flight photo, as are the distinctive white underwing patches and characteristic head and bill shape and color on this young male.

Pacific Golden-Plover *(page 143)*

Pacific Golden-Plover was formerly considered conspecific with American Golden-Plover, but was split into its own species in the late 1900s. A combination of structural features, plumage patterns, and molt strategy are important for separating this bird from the very similar American Golden Plover. This individual is in the early stage of its second life year, which can be determined by the worn, retained juvenile tertials and wing coverts. This molt strategy differs from American Golden-Plover, which replaces flight feathers, tertials, and wing coverts in its first winter of life. This different molt pattern is often helpful when identifying problematic birds.

Pacific Goldens tend to be more "chesty" and front heavy in body structure than American Goldens, with a more upright posture when relaxed. They also typically have longer legs (resulting in a slightly more lanky appearance), shorter wings, larger heads, and longer, heavier bills than American Goldens—all of which structural impressions are shown in this bird. Because of these different structural features, Pacific Golden-Plover's overall posture and shape more closely resembles Black-bellied than American Golden-Plover, and this bird is no exception. A few helpful plumage features include the bolder, more prominent feather fringes and notches on the upperpart breeding feathers, and the wider supercilium past the eye that creates a narrower brownish feather pattern on the nape.

Lesser Nighthawk *(page 161)*
This photo shows the first record of this species for NJ. Although this bird appears grayer overall than most Lesser Nighthawks, this is a result of the bird sitting in deep shade, with warm tones of natural light not present. Presence of the white wing patch past the longest tertial feather and the outer primary being shorter than the next inner primary are solid ID field marks for this species. Wingtips that are more rounded than Common Nighthawk are also visible in this photo.

Immature female Black-chinned & Ruby-throated Hummingbird *(page 165)*
Although nearly identical in size and shape to Ruby-throated Hummingbird, Black-chinned averages shorter billed and longer tailed in comparison. This female, however, shows a longer bill than males and more closely resembles Ruby-throated in length. Wingtips fall short of the tail in adult male Black-chinned, but about the same length as immature females.

Immature Black-chinned Hummingbirds have duller,

more brownish-green upperparts and crown compared to Ruby-throateds' greener upperparts and crown. Black-chinneds also show duller, dusky underparts and a brownish cheek compared to Ruby-throateds' whitish underparts and contrasting blackish cheeks. A helpful feature for separating these two species is the shape of the primaries. Black-chinneds have broader, more rounded primaries versus narrower, more pointed primaries in Ruby-throateds. This feature is obvious when viewed in direct comparison.

BIBLIOGRAPHY

Ainley, D., D. Nettleship, H. Carter, and A. Storey. 2002. Common Murre (*Uria aalge*). In *The Birds of North America Online*, ed. A. Poole. Ithaca, NY: Cornell Lab of Ornithology. http://bna.birds.cornell.edu/bna/species/666.

Altman, B., and R. Sallabanks. 2000. Olive-sided Flycatcher (*Contopus cooperi*). In *The Birds of North America Online*. http://bna.birds.cornell.edu/bna/species/502.

American Ornithologists' Union. 1998. *Check-list of North American Birds*. 7th ed. Washington, DC: American Ornithologists' Union.

Arnett, J. H. 1953. European Lapwing in Delaware and New Jersey. *Cassinia* 40:33–34.

Armistead, G., and J. Feenstra. 2007. A First Record of a *Myiodynastes* Flycatcher in New Jersey. *New Jersey Birds* 33(4): 71–74.

Arterburn, J., and J. Grzybowski. 2003. Hybridization between Glossy and White-faced Ibises. *North American Birds* 57(1):136–39.

Audubon, J. J. 1843. Pied Duck. *The Birds of North America from Drawings Made in the United States and Their Territories*. 6:329–31. Philadelphia: J. J. Audubon.

Austin, J., and M. Miller. 1995. Northern Pintail (*Anas acuta*). In *The Birds of North America Online*. http://bna.birds.cornell.edu/bna/species/163.

Bacinski, P. 1980. North Central Jersey Highlands: Breeding Bird Survey 1979. *Urner Field Observer* 17:26–33.

———. 1990. Region No. 5. *Records of New Jersey Birds* 16(3): 50.

Baltz, M., and S. Latta. 1998. Cape May Warbler (*Dendroica tigrina*). In *The Birds of North America Online*. http://bna.birds.cornell.edu/bna/species/332.

Bardon, K., and P. Lehman. 1998. First Documented Record of Thayer's Gull in New Jersey. *Records of New Jersey Birds* 24(1):2–4.

Barnes, S. 2006. New Jersey's First Green Violet-ear. *New Jersey Birds* 32(4):77.

———2009. New Jersey's First Record of Long-billed Murrelet. *New Jersey Birds* 35(1):2–3.

Beach Nesting Birds 2002. Summary Table of New Jersey Least Tern Population and Nesting Success. New Jersey Division of Fish and Wildlife. http://www.state.nj.us/dep/fgw/ensp/bnb02.htm.

Beason, R. 1995. Horned Lark (*Eremophila alpestris*). In *The Birds of North America Online*. http://bna.birds.cornell.edu/bna/species/195.

Bechard, M., and T. Swem. 2002. Rough-legged Hawk (*Buteo lagopus*). In *The Birds of North America Online*. http://bna.birds.cornell.edu/bna/species/641.

Bent, A. C. 1925. *Life Histories of North American Wild Fowl*. Washington, DC: United States National Museum Bulletin, no. 130.

Benzinger, J. 1987. Northern Saw-whet Owls in North Jersey Highlands. *Records of New Jersey Birds* 3(1):2.

Benzinger, J., and J. Van de Venter. 1995. Whip-poor-wills at Picatinny Arsenal. *Records of New Jersey Birds* 20(4):86–88.

Bevier, L., A. Poole, and W. Moskoff. 2005. Veery (*Catharus fuscescens*). In *The Birds of North America Online*. http://bna.birds.cornell.edu/bna/species/142.

Bildstein, K., and K. Meyer. 2000. Sharp-shinned Hawk (*Accipiter striatus*). In *The Birds of North America Online*. http://bna.birds.cornell.edu/bna/species/482.

Bolgiano, N. 2004. Cause Effect: Changes in the Boreal Bird Irruptions in Eastern North America Relative to the 1970s Spruce Budworm Infestation. *American Birds* 58:26–33.

Bosakowski, T., R. Kane, and D. Smith. 1989a. Status and Management of Long-eared Owl. *Records of New Jersey Birds* 15(3):42–45.

———. 1989b. Decline of the Long-eared Owl in New Jersey. *Wilson Bulletin* 101:241–245. http://elibrary.unm.edu/sora/Wilson/v101n03/p0481-p0485.pdf.

Boyle, W. J., Jr. 1986. *A Guide to Bird Finding in New Jersey*. 1st ed.. New Brunswick, NJ: Rutgers University Press.

———. 2002. *A Guide to Bird Finding in New Jersey*. 2nd ed.. New Brunswick, NJ: Rutgers University Press.

Boyle, W. J., Jr. and L. Larson. 2009. "Old Crooked Toe" and the Grus Cranes of Southern New Jersey. *New Jersey Birds Online* 35(2): 20–25. http://www.njaudubon.org/Research/PDF/NJBSpring09.

Brady, A. 1992. Major Offshore Nocturnal Migration of Blackpoll Warblers, Herons, and Shorebirds. *Cassinia* 64:28–29.

Brooks, E. W. 1998. Bewick's Wren (*Thryomanes bewickii*). In *Bull's Birds of New York State*, ed. E. Levine, pp. 418–19. Ithaca, NY: Comstock Publishing Associates.

Brooks, S. C. 1927. Hawk Owl at New Brunswick, N. J. *Auk* 44:215–52. http://elibrary.unm.edu/sora/Auk/v044n02/p0251-p0252.pdf.

Buckley, P.A., and S. S. Mitra. 2003. Williamson's Sapsucker, Cordilleran Flycatcher, and Other Long-Distance Vagrants at a Long Island, New York, Stopover Site. *North American Birds* 57(3):292–304.

Bull, J. 1964. *Birds of the New York Area*. New York: Harper & Row.

Burger, J., J. Jones, and M. Gochfeld. 1985. Caspian Terns Nesting in New Jersey. *Records of New Jersey Birds* 10(4):74–76.

Burger, J., F. Lesser, and M. Gochfeld. 1993. Brown Pelicans Attempt Nesting in New Jersey. *Records of New Jersey Birds* 18(4):78–79.

Burgiel, J., J. Danzenbaker, S. Forte, and J. Meritt. 1999. Reddish Egret—A First New Jersey Record. *Records of New Jersey Birds* 25(3):64–66.

Cade, T., and E. Atkinson. 2002. Northern Shrike (*Lanius excubitor*). In *The Birds of North America Online*. http://bna .birds.cornell.edu/bna/species/671.

Cadman, M., P. Eagles, and F. Helleiner, eds. 1987. *Atlas of the Breeding Birds of Ontario*. Waterloo, ON: Univ. of Waterloo Press.

Cavitt, J., and C. Haas. 2000. Brown Thrasher (*Toxostoma rufum*). In *The Birds of North America Online*. http://bna .birds.cornell.edu/bna/species/557.

Ciaranca, M., C. Allin, and G. Jones. 1997. Mute Swan (*Cygnus olor*). In *The Birds of North America Online*. http://bna .birds.cornell.edu/bna/species/273.

Cimprich, D., F. Moore, and M. Guilfoyle. 2000. Red-eyed Vireo (*Vireo olivaceus*). In *The Birds of North America Online*. http://bna.birds.cornell.edu/bna/species/527.

Cink, C., and C. Collins. 2002. Chimney Swift (*Chaetura pelagica*). In *The Birds of North America Online*. http://bna .birds.cornell.edu/bna/species/646.

Clark, K. 2004. Thirty Years of Osprey Recovery in New Jersey: 1973 to 2003. *New Jersey Birds* 30(1):2–6.

———. 2009. *The 2009 Osprey Project in New Jersey*. New Jersey Department of Environmental Protection, Division of Fish and Wildlife. http://www.state.nj.us/dep/fgw/ensp/pdf/ osprey09.pdf.

Clark, W. S. 1974. Second Record of the Kestrel (*Falco tinnunculus*) for North America. *Auk* 9(1):172.

Confer, J. 1992. Golden-winged Warbler (*Vermivora chrysoptera*). In *The Birds of North America Online*. http://bna.birds .cornell.edu/bna/species/020.

Conway, C. 1999. Canada Warbler (*Wilsonia canadensis*). In *The Birds of North America Online*. http://bna.birds.cornell .edu/bna/species/421.

Crossley, R. 1997. Black-chinned Hummingbird (*Archilochus alexandri*) First New Jersey Record. *Records of New Jersey Birds* 23 (3):53–54.

———. 1999. Whiskered Tern in Cape May—Again! *Records of New Jersey Birds*, 25(3):67–68.

———. 2003. New Jersey's First Pacific Golden-Plover. *New Jersey Birds* 28(3):57–60.

———. 2006. New Jersey's First Brown-headed Nuthatch. *New Jersey Birds* 32(4):78–80.

Cruickshank, A. D. 1942. *Birds Around New York City*. New York: American Museum of Natural History.

Dalton, R. 2003. *Physiographic Provinces of New Jersey*. New Jersey Geological Survey Information Circular. http://www.njgeology.org/enviroed/infocirc/provinces.pdf.

Dasey, W. 1999. N. Saw-whet Owls Breed in Palmyra. *Records of New Jersey Birds* 25(1):2–3.

Duffy, K., and P. Kerlinger. 1992. Autumn Owl Migration at Cape May Point, New Jersey. *Wilson Bulletin* 104:312–20. http://elibrary.unm.edu/sora/Wilson/v104n02/p0312-p0320.pdf.

Dunning, J. B. 2006. Bachman's Sparrow (*Aimophila aestivalis*). In *The Birds of North America Online*. http://bna.birds.cornell.edu/bna/species/038.

Dykstra, C., J. Hays, and S. Crocoll. 2008. Red-shouldered Hawk (*Buteo lineatus*). In *The Birds of North America Online*. http://bna.birds.cornell.edu/bna/species/107.

Eaton, W. F. 1936. *A List of the Birds of Essex County and of Hudson County, New Jersey*. New York: Proceedings of the Linnaean Society, no. 47.

Eddleman, W., R. Flores, and M. Legare. 1994. Black Rail (*Laterallus jamaicensis*). In *The Birds of North America Online*. http://bna.birds.cornell.edu/bna/species/123.

Ellison, W. G. 1992. Blue-gray Gnatcatcher (*Polioptila caerulea*). In *The Birds of Noth American Online*. http://bna.birds.cornell.edu/bna/species/023.

Fables, D. A., Jr. 1955. *Annotated List of New Jersey's Birds*. Newark, NJ: Urner Ornithological Club.

Fahey, P. 1979. Spotted Redshank at Brigantine. *NJ Audubon Supplement* 5(1):3.

Fazio, V., III, and R. Wiltraut. 2009. Eastern Highlands and Upper Ohio River Valley. *North American Birds* 63:75–81.

Fialkovich, M., and P. Hess. 2003. First Confirmed Record of Sharp-tailed Sandpiper (*Calidris acuminata*) in New Jersey. *New Jersey Birds* 29(3):59–61.

Fingerhood, E. D. 1992. Bewick's Wren (*Thyromanes bewickii*). In *Atlas of Breeding Birds in Pennsylvania*, ed. D. W. Brauning, pp. 435–36. Pittsburgh: University of Pittsburgh Press.

Finnegan, S. 2001. First Yellow-nosed Albatross (*Thalassarche chlororhynchos*) for New Jersey. *Records of New Jersey Birds* 27(3):58–62.

Frederick, P. C. 1997. Tricolored Heron (*Egretta tricolor*). In *The Birds of North America Online*. http://bna.birds.cornell.edu/bna/species/306.

Freiday, D. 1986. Ivory Gull at Liberty State Park. *Records of New Jersey Birds* 12(2):20.

Frier, J. 1982. Osprey (Pandion haliaetus). In *New Jersey's Endangered and Threatened Plants and Animals*, ed. W. J. Chromartie, pp. 196–98. Pomona, NJ: Center for Environmental Research, Stockton State College.

Fritz, M. 2008. New Jersey's First Royal Tern Nesting Colony. *New Jersey Birds* 34(2):22–25.

Galli, J. 1982. Great Blue Heron (*Ardea Herodias*). In *New Jersey's Endangered and Threatened Plants and Animals*, pp. 184–86.

Galli, J., and J. Penkala. 1978. White-faced Ibis in New Jersey. *NJ Audubon Research Unit Supplement* 4(1):36.

Galli, J., and R. Kane. 1981. 1979 Colonial Waterbird Populations in New Jersey. *Records of New Jersey Birds* 7(3):36–43.

Gamble, L., and T. Bergin. 1996. Western Kingbird (*Tyrannus verticalis*). In *The Birds of North America Online*. http://bna.birds.cornell.edu/bna/species/227.

Giraud, J. P. 1844. *The Birds of Long Island*. New York: Wiley and Putnam; retrieved from Open Library: http://openlibrary.org/b/OL23281753M/birds-of-Long-Island.

Giudice, J., and J. Ratti. 2001. Ring-necked Pheasant (*Phasianus colchicus*). In *The Birds of North America Online*. http://bna.birds.cornell.edu/bna/species/572.

Gochfeld, M., and J. Burger. 1994. Black Skimmer (*Rynchops niger*). In *The Birds of North America Online*. http://bna.birds.cornell.edu/bna/species/108.

Gochfeld, M., J. Burger, and F. Lesser. 1989. First Royal Tern Nest in New Jersey. *Records of New Jersey Birds* 14(4):66.

Gochfeld, M., J. Burger and I. Nisbet. 1998. Roseate Tern (*Sterna dougallii*). In *The Birds of North America Online*. http://bna.birds.cornell.edu/bna/species/370.

Goguen, C., and D. Curson. 2002. Cassin's Vireo (*Vireo cassinii*). In *The Birds of North America Online*. http://bna.birds.cornell.edu/bna/species/615.

Greenberg, R., et al. 2010. International Rusty Blackbird Technical Working Group. Migratory Bird Center, Smithsonian National Zoological Park. http://nationalzoo.si.edu/ConservationAndScience/MigratoryBirds/Research/Rusty_Black bird/twg.cfm.

Griscom, L. 1923. *Birds of the New York City Region*. New York: The American Museum of Natural History, no. 9.

Grubb, Jr., T. Pravosudov, and V. Pravosudov. 2008. White-breasted Nuthatch (*Sitta carolinensis*). In *The Birds of North America Online*. http://bna.birds.cornell.edu/bna/species/054.

Guris, P. 2007. New Jersey's Pelagic Boundaries. *New Jersey Birds* 33(1):2–3.

Guzy, M., and G. Ritchison. 1999. Common Yellowthroat (*Geo-

thlypis trichas). In *The Birds of North America Online.* http://bna.birds.cornell.edu/bna/species/448.

Haggerty, T., and E. Morton. 1995. Carolina Wren (*Thryothorus ludovicianus*). In *The Birds of North America Online.* http://bna.birds.cornell.edu/bna/species/188.

Halliwell, T., R. Kane, L. Larson, and P. Lehman. 2000. The Historical Report of the New Jersey Bird Records Committee. *Records of New Jersey Birds* 26(1):13–44.

Hamel, P. 2000. Cerulean Warbler (*Dendroica cerulea*). In *The Birds of North America Online.* http://bna.birds.cornell.edu/bna/species/511.

Hanisek, G. 1986. Summer Field Notes 1976 (Region 1). *Records of New Jersey Birds* 2(11)5–6.

———. 1981. First New Jersey Black Vulture Nesting. *Records of New Jersey Birds* 7(2):34–35.

Hanson, J. 2008. Cave Swallows in New Jersey: Removed from the Review List. *New Jersey Birds* 34(3):50.

———. 2010. List of Accepted Records of Birds in New Jersey. New Jersey Bird Records Committee. http://www.njbrc.net/documents.ARL.pdf.

Harrington, B. A. 2001. Red Knot (*Calidris canutus*). In *The Birds of North America Online.* http://bna.birds.cornell.edu/bna/species/563.

Hatch, J., and D. Weseloh. 1999. Double-crested Cormorant (*Phalacrocorax auritus*). In *The Birds of North America Online.* http://bna.birds.cornell.edu/bna/species/441.

Hayes, J. 1984. American White Pelicans in New Jersey. *Records of New Jersey Birds* 10(3):46.

Heath, S., E. Dunn, and D. Agro. 2009. Black Tern (*Chlidonias niger*). In *The Birds of North America Online.* http://bna.birds.cornell.edu/bna/species/147.

Herkert, J., D. Kroodsma, and J. Gibbs. 2001. Sedge Wren (*Cistothorus platensis*). In *The Birds of North America Online.* http://bna.birds.cornell.edu/bna/species/582.

Herkert, J., P. Vickery, and D. Kroodsma. 2002. Henslow's Sparrow (*Ammodramus henslowii*). In *The Birds of North America Online.* http://bna.birds.cornell.edu/bna/species/672.

Hohman, W., and R. Eberhardt. 1998. Ring-necked Duck (*Aythya collaris*). In *The Birds of North America Online.* http://bna.birds.cornell.edu/bna/species/329.

Holt, P. 1997. Mongolian Plover in New Jersey. *Records of New Jersey Birds* 22(4):84–87.

Howell, S.N.G. 2002. *Hummingbirds of North America: The Photographic Guide.* San Diego: Academic Press.

Hughes, J. M. 1999. Yellow-billed Cuckoo (*Coccyzus americanus*). In *The Birds of North America Online.* http://bna.birds.cornell.edu/bna/species/418.

————. 2001. Black-billed Cuckoo (*Coccyzus erythrophthalmus*). In *The Birds of North America Online*. http://bna.birds .cornell.edu/bna/species/587.

Hunn, J. 1941. Western Meadowlark in New Jersey. *Auk* 58:265. http://elibrary.unm.edu/sora/Auk/v058n02/p0265-p0265 .pdf.

Iverson, E., and R. Kane. 1975. Eskimo Curlew Specimen for New Jersey. *Records of New Jersey Birds*, 1(7):2.

Jackson, J., and H. Ouellet. 2002. Downy Woodpecker (*Picoides pubescens*). In *The Birds of North America Online*. http:// bna.birds.cornell.edu/bna/species/613.

Jackson, J., H. Ouellet, and B. Jackson. 2002. Hairy Woodpecker (*Picoides villosus*). In *The Birds of North America Online*. http://bna.birds.cornell.edu/bna/species/702.

Jehl, J. 1960. Bell's Vireo in New Jersey. *Wilson Bulletin* 72:404. http://elibrary.unm.edu/sora/Wilson/v072n04/p0404 -p0404.pdf.

Johnston, R. F. 1992. Rock Pigeon (*Columba livia*). In *The Birds of North America Online*. http://bna.birds.cornell.edu/bna/ species/013.

Jones, S., and J. Cornely. 2002. Vesper Sparrow (*Pooecetes gramineus*). In *The Birds of North America Online*. http://bna .birds.cornell.edu/bna/species/624.

Kane, R. 1996. Northern Shrike Invasion. *Records of New Jersey Birds* 22(2):30–31.

Kane, R., and D. Roche. 1975. New Jersey's First Franklin's Gull. *Records of New Jersey Birds* 1(4):2.

Kane, R., P. A. Buckley, and J. Golub. 1989. Large-billed Tern in New Jersey: North America's First Confirmed Occurrence. *American Birds* 43(5):1275–76.

Karlson, K. 1998. First Record of MacGillivray's Warbler in New Jersey. *Records of New Jersey Birds* 24(3):69–71.

————. 2003. New Jersey's First Vermilion Flycatcher. *New Jersey Birds* 29(3):56–58.

Kaufman, K. 1996. *Lives of North American Birds*. Boston: Houghton Mifflin.

Kerlinger, P., and C. Sutton. 1989. Black Rail in New Jersey. *Records of New Jersey Birds* 15(2):22–26.

Kisiel, C. 2008. Results of the 2008 Wading Bird Aerial Survey in the Coastal Marshes of New Jersey. Paper presented at the annual meeting of the New York–New Jersey Harbor Herons Meeting, Lyndhurst, NJ.

Knapton, R. 1994. Clay-colored Sparrow (*Spizella pallida*). In *The Birds of North America Online*. http://bna.birds.cornell.edu/bna/species/120.

Knopf, F., and R. Evans. 2004. American White Pelican (*Pelecanus erythrorhynchos*). In *The Birds of North America Online*. http://bna.birds.cornell.edu/bna/species/057.

Komar, N., S. Langevin, S. Hinten, H. Nemeth, E. Edwards, D. Hettler, B. Davis, R. Bowen, and M. Bunning. 2003. Experimental Infection of North American Birds with the New York 1999 Strain of West Nile virus. *Emerging Infectious Diseases* 9:311–22. http://www.cdc.gov/ncidod/EID/vol10 no4/pdfs/Vol10No4.pdf.

Kunkle, D. (Chairman), and the State List Committee. 1959. *First Supplement to the Annotated List of New Jersey Birds.* Newark, NJ: Urner Ornithological Club.

Leck, C. F. 1984. *The Status and Distribution of New Jersey's Birds.* New Brunswick, NJ: Rutgers University Press.

Lehman, P. A. 1997. First Record of Calliope Hummingbird in New Jersey. *Records of New Jersey Birds* 23(3):54–57.

———. 1998a. Brown-chested Martin in Cape May! First New Jersey and Second Documented North American Record. *Records of New Jersey Birds* 24(3):66–69.

———. 1998b. A Eurasian Collared-Dove at Cape May: First Sighting in New Jersey. *Records of New Jersey Birds* 24(1): 5–6.

———. 1998c. Skuas off New Jersey. *Records of New Jersey Birds* 23(5):78, 80.

Limpert, R., and S. Earnst. 1994. Tundra Swan (*Cygnus columbianus*). In *The Birds of North America Online.* http://bna .birds.cornell.edu/bna/species/089.

Longcore, J., D. McAuley, G. Hepp, and J. Rhymer. 2000. American Black Duck (*Anas rubripes*). In *The Birds of North America Online.* http://bna.birds.cornell.edu/bna/species/481.

Loos, G., and P. Kerlinger. 1993. Road Mortality of Saw-whet and Screech-Owls on the Cape May Peninsula. *J. Raptor Res.* 27:210–13. http://elibrary.unm.edu/sora/jrr/v027n04/p00 210-p00213.pdf.

Lowther, P., A. Poole, J. Gibbs, S. Melvin, and F. Reid. 2009. American Bittern (*Botaurus lentiginosus*). In *The Birds of North America Online.* http://bna.birds.cornell.edu/bna/ species/018.

Mack, D., and W. Yong. 2000. Swainson's Thrush (*Catharus ustulatus*). In *The Birds of North America Online.* http://bna .birds.cornell.edu/bna/species/540.

Marks, J., D. Evans, and D. Holt. 1994. Long-eared Owl (*Asio otus*). In *The Birds of North America Online.* http://bna .birds.cornell.edu/bna/species/133.

Marti, C., A. Poole, and L. Bevier. 2005. Barn Owl (*Tyto alba*). In *The Birds of North America Online.* http://bna.birds .cornell.edu/bna/species/001.

McCaskie, G., and M. Patten. 1994. Status of the Fork-tailed Flycatcher (*Tyrannus savanna*) in the United State and Canada. *Western Birds* 25(3):113–27.

McGowan, K. J. 2008. American Crow (*Corvus brachyrynchos*). In *The Second Atlas of Breeding Birds in New York State,* ed. K. J. McGowan and K. Corwin, pp. 382–83.Ithaca, NY: Cornell University Press.

———. 2008. Merlin (*Falco columbarius*). In *The Second Atlas of Breeding Birds in New York State*, pp. 208–209.

Medler, M. D. 2008. Common Nighthawk (*Cordeiles minor*). In *The Second Atlas of Breeding Birds in New York State*, pp. 306–7.

Melvin, S., and J. Gibbs. 1996. Sora (*Porzana carolina*). In *The Birds of North America Online*. http://bna.birds.cornell.edu/bna/species/250.

Mid-Winter Waterfowl Survey. Laurel, MD: Division of Migratory Bird Management, U.S. Fish and Wildlife Service. http://migbirdapps/fws/gov.

Minerals Management Service, U.S. Department of the Interior. 2008. Mid-Atlantic Planning Area. https://www.gomr.mms.gov/homepg/offshore/atlocs/atl_mid_well.pdf.

Mitra, S. S. 2008. Chuck-will's-widow (*Caprimulgus carolinensis*). In *The Second Atlas of Breeding Birds in New York State*, pp. 308–9.

Mlodinow, S., and K. Karlson. 1999. Anis in the United States and Canada. *North American Birds* 53(3)237–45.

Morse, D., and A. Poole. 2005. Black-throated Green Warbler (*Dendroica virens*). In *The Birds of North America Online*. http://bna.birds.cornell.edu/bna/species/055.

Morton, E. S. 1998. Pairing in Mallards and American Black Ducks: A New View on Population Decline in American Black Ducks. *Anim. Cons.* 1:239–44.

Moscatello, B., and J. Ambrozy. 2001. First Record of Black-bellied Whistling Duck (*Dendrocygna autumnalis*) in New Jersey. *Records of New Jersey Birds* 27(3):56–57.

Murphy, M. 1996. Eastern Kingbird (*Tyrannus tyrannus*). In *The Birds of North America Online*. http://bna.birds.cornell.edu/bna/species/253.

Murphy, R., and W. Vogt. 1933. The Dovekie Influx of 1932. *Auk* 50:325–349. http://elibrary.unm.edu/sora/Auk/v050n03/p0325-p0349.pdf.

Murray, B. G., Jr. 1989. A critical review of the transoceanic migration of the Blackpoll Warbler. *Auk* 106:8–17.

New Jersey Division of Fish and Wildlife. Colonial Waterbird Survey 1985–2007. Unpublished data.

New Jersey Division of Fish and Wildlife. New Jersey's Endangered and Threatened Wildlife, *Pied-billed Grebe*. http://www.state.nj.us/dep/fgw/ensp/pdf/end-thrtened/pbgrebe.pdf.

Nichols, J. T. 1935. The Dovekie Incursion of 1932. *Auk* 52: 448–49. http://elibrary.unm.edu/sora/Auk/v052n04/p0448-p0449.pdf.

Nixon, G., and F. Lesser. 2000. First Red-necked Stint in New Jersey. *Records of New Jersey Birds* 26(3):101–2.

Nye, P. E. 2008. American Kestrel (*Falco sparverius*). In *The*

Second Atlas of Breeding Birds in New York State, pp. 206–7.

Obercian, E. 2000. November 6–7, 1999, Flight at Cape May Point. *Records of New Jersey Birds* 26(2):85–86.

O'Brien, M., and M. Gustafson. 2002. First Record of Allen's Hummingbird (*Selasphorus sasin*) in New Jersey. *Records of New Jersey Birds* 28(3):55–57.

O'Brien, M., and T. Tarlach. 1998. First Record of Garganey in New Jersey. *Records of New Jersey Birds* 24 (2):35, 55.

Parsons, K., A. Maccarone, and J. Brzorad. 1991. First Breeding Record of Double-crested Cormorant (*Phalacrocorax auritus*) in New Jersey. *Records of New Jersey Birds* 17(3):51–52.

Peterjohn, B., and D. Rice. 1991. *The Ohio Breeding Bird Atlas.* Columbus: The Ohio Department of Natural Resources.

Petersen, W., B. Nikula, and D. Holt. 1986. First Record of Brown-chested Martin for North America. *American Birds* 40(2): 192–93.

Phillips, A. 1986. *Hirundinidae to Mimidae; Certhidae.* Part 1 of *The Known Birds of North and Middle America.* Denver: Privately published.

Pochek, A., and T. Halliwell. 2000. White-tailed Kite: New to New Jersey. *Records of New Jersey Birds* 26(1):2–3.

Reed, A., D. Ward, D. Derksen, and J. Sedinger. 1998. Brant (*Branta bernicla*). In *The Birds of North America Online.* http://bna.birds.cornell.edu/bna/species/337.

Remsen, J. 2001. True Winter Range of the Veery (*Catharus fuscescens*). *Auk* 118:838–48. http://elibrary.unm.edu/sora/Auk/v118n04/p00838-p00848.pdf.

Richardson, M., and D. Brauning. 1995. Chestnut-sided Warbler (*Dendroica pensylvanica*). In *The Birds of North America Online.* http://bna.birds.cornell.edu/bna/species/190.

Rimmer, C., K. McFarland, W. Ellison, and J. Goetz. 2001. Bicknell's Thrush (*Catharus bicknelli*). In *The Birds of North America Online.* http://bna.birds.cornell.edu/bna/species/592.

Robertson, R., B. Stutchbury, and R. Cohen. 1992. Tree Swallow (*Tachycineta bicolor*). In *The Birds of North America Online.* http://bna.birds.cornell.edu/bna/species/011.

Robinson, T., R. Sargent, and M. Sargent. 1996. Ruby-throated Hummingbird (*Archilochus colubris*). In *The Birds of North America Online.* http://bna.birds.cornell.edu/bna/species.

Rohwer, F., W. Johnson, and E. Loos. 2002. Blue-winged Teal (*Anas discors*). *The Birds of North America Online.* http://bna.birds.cornell.edu/bna/species/625.

Romagosa, C. M. 2002. Eurasian Collared-Dove (*Streptopelia decaocto*). In *The Birds of North America Online.* http://bna.birds.cornell.edu/bna/species/630.

Sauer, J., J. Hines, and J. Fallon. 2008. *The North American*

Breeding Bird Survey, Results and Analysis 1966–2007. Version 5.15.2008. Laurel, MD: USGS Patuxent Wildlife Research Center. http://www.mbr-pwrc.usgs.gov/bbs/bbs .html.

Shaffer, S., Y. Tremblay, H. Weimerskirch, D. Scott, D. Thompson, P. Sagar, H. Moller, G. Taylor, D. Foley, B. Block, and D. Costa. 2006. Migratory Shearwaters Integrate Oceanic Resources across the Pacific Ocean in an Endless Summer, *Proc. Nat'l. Acad. Sci.* 103:12700–802; published online before print 14 August 2006, doi:10.1073/pnas.06037 15103.

Shriner, C. A. 1897. *The Birds of New Jersey.* Fish and Game Commission of New Jersey.

Sibley, D. A. 1994. Identification of Chickadees in New Jersey: A Tool for the Breeding Bird Atlas. *Records of New Jersey Birds* 20(1):13–15.

———. 1997. *The Birds of Cape May.* Bernardsville, NJ: New Jersey Audubon Society.

Smith, C. 2008. Clay-colored Sparrow (*Spizella pallida*). In *The Second Atlas of Breeding Birds in New York State,* pp. 548–49.

Smith, L., and K. Clark. 2009. *New Jersey Bald Eagle Project, 2009.* New Jersey Department of Environmental Protection, Division of Fish and Wildlife. http://www.state.nj.us/ dep/fgw/ensp/pdf/eglrpt09.pdf.

Spears, L., M. Lewis, M. Myers, and R. Pyle. 1988. The recent occurrence of Garganey in North America and the Hawaiian Island. *American Birds* 42(3):385–92.

Speiser, R., and T. Bosakowski. 1984. History, Status and Management of Goshawk Nesting in New Jersey. *Records of New Jersey Birds* 10(2):29–33.

Stedman, S. J. 2000. Horned Grebe (*Podiceps auritus*). In *The Birds of North America Online.* http://bna.birds.cornell .edu/bna/species/505.

Stewart, P. 1982. Migration of Blue Jays in Eastern North America. *North American Bird Bander* 7(3):107–12. http:// elibrary.unm.edu/sora/NABB/v007n03/p0107-p0112.pdf.

Stewart, R., and C. Robbins. 1958. *Birds of Maryland and The District of Columbia.* Washington, DC: U.S. Department of the Interior.

Stone, W. 1908. *The Birds of New Jersey, Their Nests and Eggs. Report of the New Jersey State Museum.* Trenton, NJ: The John L. Murphy Publishing Co.

———. 1937. *Bird Studies at Old Cape May,* vols. 1 and 2. Philadelphia: The Delaware Valley Ornithological Club at the Academy of Natural Sciences of Philadelphia.

Sullivan, B. 2002. Black-tailed Gull (*Larus crassirostris*) in New Jersey. *Records of New Jersey Birds* 28(1):2–5.

Sutton, C., and P. Sutton. 1986. Breeding Birds of Bear Swamp,

Cumberland County, 1981–1985. *Records of New Jersey Birds* 12(2):21–24.

Sutton, P. 1996. Road Mortality of N. Saw-whet Owls in Southern New Jersey, Winter 1995–96. *Records of New Jersey Birds* 22(2):31–32.

Swanson, D., J. Ingold, and G. Wallace. 2008. Ruby-crowned Kinglet (*Regulus calendula*). In *The Birds of North America Online*. http://bna.birds.cornell.edu/bna/species/119.

Tarof, S., and J. Briskie. 2008. Least Flycatcher (*Empidonax minimus*). In *The Birds of North America Online*. http://bna .birds.cornell.edu/bna/species/099.

Telfair, R. C., II. 2006. Cattle Egret (*Bubulcus ibis*). In *The Birds of North America Online*. http://bna.birds.cornell.edu/bna/ species/113.

Turnbull, W. P. 1869. *The Birds of East Pennsylvania and New Jersey*. Philadelphia: H. Grambo & Co. http://openlibrary .org/b/OL23281739M/birds_of_east_Pennsylvania_and_ New_Jersey.

Twedt, D., and R. Crawford. 1995. Yellow-headed Blackbird (*Xanthocephalus xanthocephalus*). In *The Birds of North America Online*. http://bna.birds.cornell.edu/bna/species/ 192.

Underdown, C. E. 1930. Black Guillemot (*Cepphus grylle*) at Cape May, NJ. *Auk* 47:242. http://elibrary.unm.edu/sora/ Auk/v047n02/p0242-p0242.pdf.

Van Horn, M., and T. Donovan. 1994. Ovenbird (*Seiurus aurocapilla*). In *The Birds of North America Online*. http://bna. birds.cornell.edu/bna/species/088.

Veit, R., and P. Guris. 2008. Recent Increases in Alcid Abundance in the New York Bight and New England Waters. *New Jersey Birds* 34(4):83–87.

Veit, R., and W. Petersen. 1993. *Birds of Massachusetts*. Lincoln, MA: Massachusetts Audubon Society.

Verbeek, N., and P. Hendricks. 1994. American Pipit (*Anthus rubescens*). In *The Birds of North America Online*. http://bna. birds.cornell.edu/bna/species/095.

Vickery, P. 1996. Grasshopper Sparrow (*Ammodramus savannarum*). In *The Birds of North America Online*. http://bna .birds.cornell.edu/bna/species/239.

Walsh, J., V. Elia, R. Kane, and T. Halliwell. 1999. *Birds of New Jersey*. Bernardsville, NJ: New Jersey Audubon Society.

Wander, W. 1986. *Biological Resources*, vol. 2 of *New Jersey Turnpike 1985–1990 Widening Technical Study*, p. 91; cited in Walsh, J., et al. 1999.

Warkentin, I., N. Sodhi, R. Espie, A. Poole, L. Oliphant, and P. James. 2005. Merlin (*Falco columbarius*). In *The Birds of North America Online*. http://bna.birds.cornell.edu/bna/ species/044.

Wenzelburger, G. 2004. New Jersey's First Masked Booby. *New Jersey Birds* 29(4):81–82.

Wiebe, K., and W. Moore. 2008. Northern Flicker (*Colaptes auratus*). In *The Birds of North America Online*. http://bna.birds.cornell.edu/bna/species/166a.

White, C., N. Clum, T. Cade, and W. Hunt. 2002. Peregrine Falcon (*Falco peregrinus*). In *The Birds of North America Online*. http://bna.birds.cornell.edu/bna/species/660.

Whitehead, D., and T. Taylor. 2002. Acadian Flycatcher (*Empidonax virescens*). In *The Birds of North America Online*. http://bna.birds.cornell.edu/bna/species/614.

Williams, J. 1996. Bay-breasted Warbler (*Dendroica castanea*). In *The Birds of North America Online*. http://bna.birds.cornell.edu/bna/species/206.

Witmer, M., D. Mountjoy, and L. Elliot. 1997. Cedar Waxwing (*Bombycilla cedrorum*). In *The Birds of North America Online*. http://bna.birds.cornell.edu/bna/species/309.

Wolfarth, F. 1973. Field Notes (Region 1). *New Jersey Nature News* 28:156–59.

Woodin, M., and T. Michot. 2002. Redhead (*Aythya americana*). In *The Birds of North America Online*. http://bna.birds.cornell.edu/bna/species/695.

Yosef, R. 1996. Loggerhead Shrike (*Lanius ludovicianus*). In *The Birds of North America Online*. http://bna.birds.cornell.edu/bna/species/231.

Young, M. A. 2008. Evening Grosbeak (*Coccothraustes vespertinus*). In *The Second Atlas of Breeding Birds in New York State*, pp. 620–21.

Zimpfer, N., W. Rhodes, E. Silverman, G. Zimmerman, and M. Koneff. 2009. Trends in Duck Breeding Populations, 1955–2009. *Administrative Report—July 1, 2009.* Laurel, MD: Division of Migratory Bird Management, U.S. Fish and Wildlife Service.

INDEX